FootprintAfrica

Cape Town
& Garden Route

Lizzie Williams

Cape Peninsula

Introducing the region

Cape Town

About the region

Winelands

Garden Route

Practicalities

Contents

About the author

Acknowledgements

Thanks to the following friends in the tourism industry in Cape Town including, Leanne Guild of Africa Travel Co, Wendy Gore from Overseas Adventure Travel/Grand Circle, Barbra and Barry Futter from Adventure Works, Chris Mears from Acacia Africa and Darren Humphrys and Kate Hassall from Compass Odyssey. Mostly for testing out restaurants with me. Thanks also to Darren for his photographs. Thanks to the staff at Cape Town's two tourist offices, the staff at the V&A Waterfront information centre, and Hanlie Kotzefrom Wines of South Africa for the wine information. Gratitude goes out to the various regional tourism offices, bureaus and associations that cover just about every *dorp* (village) in South Africa and do a fine job of promoting South Africa. Acknowledgements for resources and information must also go to the Green Point Stadium Visitor Centre, Kahshiefa Ryklief from the Table Mountain Aerial Cableway, the Cape Town City Partnership, the 2010 Central City Partners Forum, Iziko Museums, South Africa National Parks and South African Tourism. Readers of the South Africa Handbook who write in with recommendations and useful suggestions include Julien Pradelles, Emma Wright, David and Lauren Gardner, Lucy Davenport, Craig and Charlotte Mckenna, Polly and Jeff Wright, Pete Stocken, Laura Swanepool, Jack Davenport, Lucy and George Perry and David Plett. Finally thanks to all at Footprint for putting it altogether including Felicity Laughton, Alan Murphy, Kassia Gawronski and Angus Dawson.

Originally from London, **Lizzie Williams** has worked and lived in Africa for 14 years. Starting out on trips across the continent as a tour leader on overland trucks, she has sat with a gorilla, slept amongst elephants, fed a giraffe and swum with a hippo and is now something of an expert on border crossings and African beer. For Footprint she is author of the South Africa, Namibia, Kenya and Tanzania handbooks; she has written the only country guide to Nigeria and the first city guide to Johannesburg for Bradt; is author of the AA Key Guide to South Africa, AA Spiral Guide to South Africa and Africa Overland, a glossy look at the overland route from Nairobi to Cape Town; has written Frommer's Cape Town Day to Day; is co-author of the DK Eyewitness to Kenya; and has contributed to Turkey and Egypt for Rough Guides. She had written various online African destination guides for leading websites in the UK and US, including Frommer's, British Airways and worldtravelguide.net. When not on the road, Lizzie lives in Cape Town.

Sleeping price codes
RRRR over US$200 per night for a double room in high season.
RRR US$100-200
RR US$50-100
R under US$50

Eating & drinking price codes
RRR over US$30 per person for a 2-course meal with a drink, including service and cover charge
RR US$20-30
R under US$20

About the book

The guide is divided into four sections: Introducing the region; About the region; Around the city/region and Practicalities.

Introducing the region comprises: **At a glance**, which explains how the region fits together by giving the reader a snapshot of what to look out for and what makes this region distinct from other parts of the country; **Best of Cape Town, Winelands & Garden Route** (top 20 highlights); **A year in Cape Town, Winelands & Garden Route**, which is a month-by-month guide to pros and cons of visiting at certain times of year; and **Cape Town, Winelands & Garden Route on screen & page**, which is a list of suggested books and films. **About the region** comprises: **History; Architecture in the Cape;**

The Beautiful Game, which is an introduction to the 2010 FIFA World Cup South Africa™; **Nature & environment** (an overview of the landscape and wildlife); **Festivals & events; Sleeping** (an overview of accommodation options); **Eating & drinking** (an overview of the region's cuisine, as well as advice on eating out); **Entertainment** (an overview of the region's cultural credentials, explaining what entertainment is on offer); **Shopping** (what are the region's specialities and recommendations for the best buys); and **Activities & tours. Around the region** is then broken down into four areas, each with its own chapter. Here you'll find all the main sights and at the end of each chapter is a listings section with all the best sleeping, eating & drinking, entertainment, shopping and activities & tours options plus a brief overview of public transport.

Picture credits

Lizzie Williams 15, 78, 99.

Darren Humphrys 11, 16, 56, 62, 79, 90, 91, 123, 125, 129, 138, 274, 276.

Shutterstock pages 1, 21, 55, 112, 194: PhotoSky4 com; pages 2, 6: Craig T; pages 3, 268: Olly; page 10: Stuartapsey; pages 12, 17, 144: David Peta; pages 12, 82: Dhoxax; page 13: Albert Mendelewski; page 17: Juergen Schonnop; page 18: Karel Gallas; page 19: Theunis Jacobus Botha; pages 20, 132, 153, 155, 156: Neil Bradfield; page 28: David Ryznar; pages 29, 154: Squareplum; page 30: Melissa Schalke; page 32: Zbynek Burival; page 34: Eco images; page 37: Darrenp; page 44: Merryl McNaughton; page 46: Paulsly; pages 47, 71, 233: Four Oaks; page 47: Fiona Ayerst; page 58: Elzbieta Sekowska; page 66: Simone Janssen; pages 85, 92, 238: Abraham Badenhorst; page 93: Vatikaki; page 146: Francois Loubser; page 173: ShutterVision; pages 177, 189, 198, 243, 246: Sean Nel; page 218: Steve Noakes; pages 219, 240: Christopher Salerno; page 225: Will Davies; page 237: Mark Atkins; pages 239, 266: Peter Betts; pages 242, 247: Louie Schoeman; page 245: Vistoria Field; pages 249, 277: Senai aksoy; page 251: Nathan Chor.

Hemis.Fr pages 2, 26, 64, 65, 76, 84, 89, 101, 104, 109, 115, 143, 148, 157, 170, 181, 183, 202: Ludovic Maisant; pages 2, 9, 68, 74, 106, 107, 136: Bertrand Rieger; page 15: Bruno Perousse; pages 139, 141, 145: David Garry: pg 139, 141, 145.

Tips Images pages 2, 9 174: Chad Ehlers; pages 3, 9, 35, 39, 216: Chris Sattlberger; page 23: Mond'Image; pages 33, 86; Guido Alberto Rossi; page 40: Imagestate; pages 61, 275: Photononstop; pages 96, 106, 149, 159: Arco Digital Images.

Alamy page 42: Jaco Wolmarans; page 50: B.O'Kane.

Istock pages 67, 69, 110, 151, 176: RapidEye; pages 77, 97, 147: Neil Bradfield; page 152: AwieBadenhorst; page 171: David Garry; page 188: carole castelli; page 179: Dale B Halbur; page 191: Pjmalsbury; page 192: Elena Ta; page 195: Tom Charnock; page 196: Fotomedia; page 222: Hougaardmalan; page 223: Capephotoshop; page 228: Mensovw; page 231: Wayne Photography; page 232: Aklucas; page 234: Stray cat; page 259: Casarsa.

Miscellaneous page 25: Radom House; page 52: Constantia Uitsig Spa; page 43: 2010 FIFA South African World Cup™; pages 53, 116: Daddy Long legs; page 54: La Fontaine Guest House; page 56: Steenberg Hotel Catharina's restaurant; page 59: Aubergine Restaurant; page 72: Garden Route Game Lodge; page 72: Kagga Kamma Private Game Reserve; page 73: Plettenberg Bay Game reserve; page 94: Gary Hirson/Table Mountain Aerial Cableway; page 120: Aubergine; page 130: Africa Music Store; page 160: Hout Bay Manor; pages 161, 165: Chapman's Peak Hotel; page 185: Eikendal; page 186: Simonsig; page 187: Vergelegen Estate; page 200: Rhebokskloof; page 203: Spier Hotel; page 205: La Cabrière Country House; page 206: La Fontaine Guest House; page 210: Le Quartier Français; page 214: Saxenburg; page 229, 252: Botlierskop Private Game reserve; page 257: Hunters Country House.

Alamy (Arco Images GmbH) Front cover.
Alamy (Eric Nathan) Back cover.
Getty Images (Fran Lemmens) Back cover.

Contents

Atlantic Seaboard beach.

Introducing the region

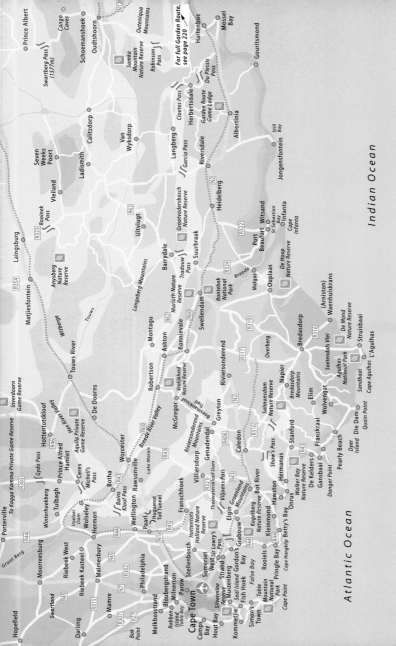

For full Garden Route, see page 220

N

20 km
20 miles

Indian Ocean

Atlantic Ocean

Prince Albert
Cango Caves
Swartberg Pass (1577m)
Schoemanshoek
Oudtshoorn
Outeniqua Mountains
Mossel Bay
Hartenbos
Gouritsmond
Samka Mountain Nature Reserve
Robinson Pass
Du Plessis Pass
Garden Route Game Lodge
Herbertsdale
Albertinia
Still Bay
Cloetes Pass
Calitzdorp
Van Wyksdorp
Langberg
Garcia Pass
Riversdale
Jongensfontein
Seven Weeks Poort
Ladismith
Vlieland
Rooinek Pass
Laingsburg
Matjiesfontein
R354
Anysberg Nature Reserve
Witberge
Witteberg
Touws River
R62
Uitvlugt
Langeberg Mountains
Barrydale
Marloth Nature Reserve
Tradouw Pass
Suurbraak
R322
Port Beaufort
Witsand
St Sebastian Bay
Cape Infanta
Infanta
De Hoop Nature Reserve
Grootvadersbosch Nature Reserve
R323
Heidelberg
N2
R60
Bonnievale
Ashton
Montagu
Robertson
McGregor
Vrolijkheid Nature Reserve
Boesmanskloof Trail
R62
R324
Malgas
Breede
Ouplaas
Bontebok National Park
Swellendam
Rivlersonderend
Napier
Overberg
Bredasdorp
R319
R317
Waenhuiskrans
(Arniston)
De Mond Nature Reserve
Struisbaai
L'Agulhas
Cape Agulhas
Soetendals Vlei
R316
Agulhas National Park
Bredasdorp Mountains
Elim
Wolvengat
Sandbaai
Die Dam
Quoin Point
Salmonsdam Nature Reserve
Riviersonderend Mountains
Greyton
Genadendal
Villiersdorp
Theewaterskloof Dam
R406
N2
Caledon
Shaw's Pass
Stanford
Franskraal
Pearly Beach
Dyer Island
Danger Point
Gansbaai
De Kelders
R43
Walker Bay Nature Reserve
Hermanus
Onrus
Stanford
Bot River
Kleinmond
Kogelberg Nature Reserve
Betty's Bay
Hawston
Cape Hangklip
Pringle Bay
Rooiels
Grabouw
Elgin
Groenland Mountain
Viljoen's Pass
R321
Franschhoek
Hottentots Holland Nature Reserve
Sir Lowry's Pass
Gordon's Bay
Strand
Somerset West
Helderberg
R44
Stellenbosch
Paarl
N1
Wellington
Rawsonville
Worcester
De Doorns
R43
Breede River Valley
R60
Lake Marais
Huguenot Toll Tunnel
R45
Bains Kloof Pass
Wolseley
Hermon
Mamre
Botha
Ceres
Michell's Pass
Tulbagh
Winterhoekberg
Gydo Pass
Prince Alfred Hamlet
R46
Aquila Private Game Reserve
Witteberg
Hex River Valley
Inverdoorn Game Reserve
To Kagga Kamma Private Game Reserve
R303
Hottentots-Holland
Porterville
Moorreesburg
Riebeek West
Riebeek Kasteel
Malmesbury
R45
Darling
Swartland
R315
R307
R27
Philadelphia
Hopefield
Bok Point
Saldanha
Vredenburg
Paternoster
R44
Groot Berg
Melkbosstrand
Bloubergstrand
Milnerton
Paarow
R302
Table Mountain National Park
Cape Town
Table Bay
Robben Island
Camps Bay
Hout Bay
Kommetjie
Fish Hoek
Silvermine Reserve
Muizenberg
Seal Island
False Bay
Simon's Town
Cape Point

Heidelberg
Garden Route Game Lodge

Introduction

South Africa's 'Mother City', dominated by Table Mountain and surrounded by the wild Atlantic, has unquestionably one of the most beautiful city backdrops in the world and is an instantly likeable and captivating city. Despite being a considerable urban hub, its surroundings are surprisingly untamed, characterized by a mountainous spine stretching between two seaboards along the Cape Peninsula edged by rugged coast and dramatic beaches.

Central Cape Town with its grandiose colonial buildings, Victorian suburbs, beautiful public gardens and clutch of modern skyscrapers, lies in the steep-sided bowl created by Table Mountain, while the Atlantic Seaboard with its promenade and dense crop of holiday flats and the popular V&A Waterfront development hug the coast. Further out on False Bay are the Cape Flats, their sprawling townships a lasting testimony of the Apartheid era. Beyond, in the beautiful Winelands region, the old towns of Stellenbosch, Franschhoek and Paarl nestle in a range of low mountains and scenic valleys covered by the historic wine estates which have been cultivating grapes for some 300 years.

Just a few hours' drive away to the east, the Garden Route is a 200-km stretch of rugged coast backed by mountains, and few visitors to Cape Town miss it. The area is undeniably beautiful, with long stretches of sand, nature reserves, leafy forests and tourist-friendly seaside towns.

Few places in the world can offer mountain hiking, lazing on a beach, tasting world-class wines and drinking beer in a township shebeen all in one day. Put simply, it is a city worth crossing the world for.

At a glance
A whistle-stop tour of Cape Town, Winelands & Garden Route

Described by Sir Francis Drake as "the fairest Cape in all the circumference of the earth" the tip of South Africa's Western Cape has attracted seafarers since the 16th century and is today classed as one of the world's top tourist destinations. Few can deny the region's beauty; magnificent Table Mountain dominates the sleek and cosmopolitan city with its pockets of quaint historical buildings, while the Cape Peninsula features dramatic beaches and ocean vistas. The Winelands has scenic Cape Dutch gabled wine estates surrounded by vines, and the Garden Route is a verdant strip of forests and coastline backed by the sun-baked mountains of the interior.

Table Mountain from Bloubergstrand.

Cape Town

To get the best idea of Cape Town's layout, head to the top of Table Mountain. From its summit, the city stretches below in a horseshoe formed by the mountains: Table Mountain is in the centre, with Devil's Peak to the east and Lion's Head and Signal Hill to the west. Straight ahead lies the City Bowl, the central business district backed by leafy suburbs. This is also the site of Cape Town's historical heart and where all the major museums, historical buildings and sights are. Further down is the Victoria & Alfred Waterfront, a slick development of shopping malls and restaurants, and following the coast around to the west, you come to the modern

The lowdown

Money matters
In first-rate luxury hotels, expect to pay in excess of R4000 for a double per night, but if staying in simple B&Bs and guesthouses, budget R500-1000. A dorm in a backpackers will cost little more than R100. Budget R250-400 per day for car hire, but if you don't want to drive, day tours in and around Cape Town cost in the region of R350 for a half-day tour and R600 for a full day. The three most popular are tours of the Cape Peninsula, the Winelands and the townships. Longer five- to seven-day tours of the Garden Route start from around R4500 per person (see page 227). A two-course evening meal with wine in a reasonable restaurant costs around R150 per person, the bill is more likely to be nearer R600 for two in a gourmet restaurant.

Opening hours & holidays
Most tourist attractions are open seven days a week. The Table Mountain Aerial Cableway is closed in July for two weeks for annual maintenance. Many of the wine estates in the Winelands are closed on Sundays. Shops are open Monday to Friday 0900-1700, Saturday 0900-1300, but the large malls are open all day, every day. Formal restaurants open for lunch and dinner, while more informal restaurants are open all day from breakfast. December and January are the long South African school holidays when the entire coast is popular with domestic holidaymakers. While the beaches and restaurants get busy and you'll have to book well ahead for accommodation, this is the best time of year in terms of weather.

Discounted tickets
The cableway (see page 93) offers good value family-of-four tickets and a number of other sights offer substantial discounts for children. Kids under 16 go free in the Iziko museums.

Tourist information
Cape Town Tourism (The Pinnacle, corner of Burg and Castle streets, T021-487 6800, tourismcapetown.co.za, Mon-Fri 0800-1900, Sat 0830-1400, Sun 0900-1300, closes 1 hr earlier in winter – Apr-Sep), the official city tourist office, can help with bookings and tours throughout the Western Cape. There are 18 other branches/desks throughout the Cape, the most useful of which is at the Victoria & Alfred Waterfront (T021-4054500, daily 0900-2100).

Tip...
The Robben Island ferry and Table Mountain Aerial Cableway are weather dependent; always phone or check their websites on the day to see if they are running.

Robben Island ferry embarking from the V&A Waterfront.

Introducing the region

residential districts of Green Point and Sea Point. In the opposite direction the southern suburbs stretch west and south, dipping from the mountain's slopes, and here, under a blanket of trees, are Cape Town's largest mansions as well as beautiful Kirstenbosch Botanical Gardens. Cape Town's population is the most cosmopolitan in the country, with a mix of cultures, ethnicities and religions that drive the very pulse of the city. The mishmash of people, including white descendants of Dutch and British settlers, a black African population and the distinctive 'Cape Coloured' community, results in a vibrant cultural scene.

Cape Peninsula

The stunning coast road winds its way through the Atlantic Seaboard on the western side of the peninsula through exclusive Clifton, Camps Bay and Llandudno. These have some of Cape Town's most sought-after properties and whitewashed modern mansions with their brilliantly blue swimming pools climb up the hillsides, while the pristine beaches are popular with the beautiful people. Further south the road winds its way above the rocky shoreline and below the magnificent Twelve Apostles, the spine of mountains from the back of Table Mountain, before dropping into Hout Bay and the back end of the Constantia Valley. It then continues south down to Cape Point and the Cape of Good Hope at the southern tip of the peninsula, and then up again through the quaint fishing settlements on

the False Bay coast on the eastern side. As well as fine ocean and mountain views, there are a number of attractions to stop for including the boat trip from Hout Bay to see the seals on Duiker Island, the spectacularly scenic Chapman's Peak Drive, climbing to the lighthouse at Cape Point, and the penguins at Boulders Beach. There are also ample places to stop for lunch in a scenic location.

Winelands

After Cape Town was established as a refreshment stop for passing ships, there was a need for additional land to be brought under cultivation,

Left: Upmarket suburb of Camps Bay.
Above: The climb to the lighthouse at Cape Point.
Opposite page: Vineyards in the Franschhoek Valley.

and the Winelands is South Africa's oldest and most beautiful wine-producing area. Wine was produced to fight off scurvy among the sailors and it kept better than water on long voyages. The vines are planted in a fertile series of valleys quite unlike the rest of the Western Cape. It is the Cape's biggest attraction after Cape Town, and its appeal is simple: it offers the chance to sample several hundred different wines in a historical and wonderfully scenic setting. This was the first region after Cape Town to be settled, and the towns of Stellenbosch, Paarl and Franschhoek are some of the oldest in South Africa. Today, their streets are lined with beautiful Cape Dutch and Georgian houses, although the real architectural gems are the manor houses on the wine estates. While the wine industry flourished during the 18th and 19th centuries, the farmers built grand homesteads with cool wine cellars next to their vines. Most of these have been lovingly restored and today can be visited as part of a Winelands tour – many have even been converted into gourmet restaurants or luxury hotels.

Garden Route
Officially the route runs from Heidelberg in the west to the Tsitsikamma National Park in the east, though the most popular stretch is the coast from Mossel Bay to Storms River in Tsitsikamma National Park. The region is separated from the interior by the Tsitsikamma and Outeniqua mountain ranges. In contrast to the dry and treeless area of the Karoo on the interior side of the mountains, rain falls all year round on the Garden Route, and the ocean-facing mountain slopes are covered with luxuriant forests. It is this dramatic change in landscape, which occurs over a distance of no more than 20 km, which prompted people to refer to the area as the Garden Route. The larger towns, such as Plettenberg Bay and Knysna, are highly developed tourist resorts, while other areas offer untouched wilderness and wonderful hikes. The beaches are stunning, providing a mix of peaceful seaside villages and livelier surfer spots, and there are various attractions hugging the N2 to distract the motorist. Finally, the Garden Route is coming into its own as an adventure destination and there are numerous activities on offer from bungee jumping to mountain biking.

Best of Cape Town, Winelands & Garden Route

Top 20 things to see & do

❶ Company's Garden

Originally a vegetable garden for the Dutch East India Company, this ornamental garden provides a pleasant green lung in the middle of Cape Town and is home to a number of museums, galleries, libraries and the ornate parliament buildings on and around Government Avenue. There are ever-present views of Table Mountain and you may spot a grey squirrel. Page 85.

❷ District Six Museum

Once Cape Town's most vibrant suburb, which was home to a largely coloured community and also attracted bohemian whites, the Apartheid government razed District Six to the ground in 1966 and forcibly removed its residents to the Cape Flats. This powerful museum tells the story of the Group Areas Act that resolutely split communities apart. Page 88.

❸ Castle of Good Hope

Built in 1666 by the Dutch East India Company to defend the Cape from rival European powers, the imposing castle is South Africa's oldest building. It now houses several museums and you can admire the fortifications from the courtyard's crunchy gravel and manicured lawns and watch the ceremonial changing of the guard at noon. Page 89.

❹ Long Street

Cape Town's quirkiest and most Bohemian street is home to some fine examples of Victorian architecture with lattice balconies and pointed turrets. It's well known for its raucous nightlife, off-beat boutiques, second-hand bookshops, antique shops and arty hotels. Greenmarket Square, a short stroll away, is best known for its large curio market. Page 92.

❺ Table Mountain

The dizzying ride to the top of Table Mountain on the Aerial Cableway is a must on a visit to Cape Town; the more athletic can walk up. From the top are staggering views of the city at the foot of the mountain, and on a clear day Robben Island and the fertile valleys in the Winelands. Page 93.

❻ Bo-Kaap

The working-class district was developed in the late 1770s by freed slaves who were originally imported by the Dutch East India Company from Malaysia, Indonesia and other parts of Asia. Their descendants are today's residents, the Cape Malays. A museum tells their story and the boxy artisan houses are painted in a range of photogenic pastel colours. Page 97.

❼ Victoria & Alfred Waterfront

Cape Town's original Victorian harbour was completely restored in the early 1990s into a lively district packed with restaurants, bars and shops. Original buildings stand shoulder to shoulder with mock-Victorian shopping malls, museums and cinemas, all crowding along a waterside walkway with Table Mountain towering beyond. Page 100.

❽ Two Oceans Aquarium

The Victoria and Alfred's flagship attraction celebrates the Cape's rich and varied marine life and is home to over 3000 sea creatures. Highlights include the giant kelp tank and the predator tank,

7 View of Table Mountain from the Victoria & Alfred Waterfront.
6 Boxy artisans' houses in Bo-Kaap.

where you can watch a ragged tooth shark glide by seemingly centimetres away and children will love the touch pool. Page 106.

Robben Island

Robben Island is best known for its notorious prison that held many of the ANC's most prominent members, including Nelson Mandela and Walter Sisulu, during their many years of incarceration by the Apartheid government. Now a UNESCO World Heritage Site, the former prison buildings have been turned into a fascinating museum. Page 106.

Kirstenbosch National Botanical Garden

South Africa's oldest and most exquisite botanical garden lies in a magnificent position on the eastern slopes of Table Mountain and displays more than 7000 indigenous specimens. The formally laid out gardens are a delight to walk around and there are many paths up to the fynbos natural vegetation on the mountain. Page 112.

Atlantic Seaboard beaches

Cape Town's swankiest suburbs not only have the most expensive real estate in South Africa, but the city's best beaches. Clifton Beaches 1-4 are sandy and sheltered by giant boulders, Camps Bay Beach is a beautiful swathe of powder-fine white sand pounded by cobalt-coloured waves, while Llandudno Beach is famous for its good surfing and as an excellent vantage point to watch the sun set. Page 142.

Table Mountain National Park

Formerly the Cape of Good Hope Nature Reserve, Cape Point and the Cape of Good Hope now fall within the jurisdiction of the Table Mountain National Park. It's a dramatically wild place of towering cliffs, empty beaches and ocean vistas, and you can climb to the lighthouse at Cape Point. Page 148.

Groot Constantia

Originally home to Cape Governor Simon van der Stel between 1699 and 1712, this superbly restored wine estate has a magnificent manor house decorated with period furniture, plus a museum depicting the history of wine-making in the Constantia Valley, good restaurants and a wine-tasting centre, all set in rolling vineyards. Page 151.

10 Kirstenbosch National Botanical Garden.

14 African penguins on Boulders Beach.

20 Tsitsikamma National Park.

⑭ Simon's Town & Boulders Beach

A historic port and naval base, Simon's Town has an interesting line of museums and Victorian architecture, but the real reason to come here is to visit Boulders Beach penguin colony. From just two breeding pairs in 1985, the colony has flourished to 3000 and you can watch them waddling, grooming and frolicking in the waves. Page 157.

⑮ Stellenbosch

Surrounded by the more than 130 wine estates of the Stellenbosch Wine Route, the second oldest town in South Africa after Cape Town has streets lined with Cape Dutch, Georgian, Regency and Victorian architecture and magnificent old oak trees. The museums take a look at early settler life. Page 180.

⑯ Spier

One of the Winelands most popular estates for visitors, with some attractive whitewashed gabled farm buildings set in manicured gardens, a pleasant park for picnicking along the river, a comprehensive wine-tasting centre and additional attractions and activities for children such as pony rides and the cheetah and the birds of prey centres. Page 185.

⑰ Franschhoek

This historic overgrown village was originally settled by French Huguenots in the 17th century, but today it's famous as a culinary destination. The main street is lined with gourmet restaurants and the beautiful wine estates in the surrounding valley offer superb food and some of the region's finest wines. Page 190.

⑱ Wilderness National Park

This incorporates a large wetland eco-system of several rivers and four lakes and a 28-km-long expanse of broad beach with sand dunes. It's popular for walking and canoeing, and the forests are full of birds and wild flowers in spring, including South Africa's national flower, the protea. Page 238.

⑲ Knysna

A summer playground for the wealthy, this attractive seaside town lies on a scenic series of wetlands in the heart of the Garden Route. The lagoon can be explored by boat to see the famous Heads, where the ocean crashes through a dramatic rock formation and the surrounding forests can be explored on foot or by mountain bike. Page 240.

⑳ Tsitsikamma National Park

This is a beautiful 80-km stretch of forest-filled coastline, which is popular for hiking and birdwatching and has incredible views of the ocean where dolphins ride the pounding waves. The dense canopy of giant trees provides shady and peaceful walks and there's the opportunity to spot rare birds like the Knysna lourie. Page 250.

Month by month

A year in Cape Town, Winelands & Garden Route

January & February

January in Cape Town and around is the middle of the long dry summer when daytime temperatures seldom dip below 26°C and often rise to the early 30s. There is an average of 11 hours of sunshine during the day and in the evening long sunsets over the ocean, when the sun sets as late as 2100. The Table Mountain Aerial Cableway has special offers of two for the price of one after 1900 to go up and watch the sunset. January and February are however the season for a southeasterly wind, which many Capetonians refer to as the 'Cape Doctor' as it blows the pollution off the city. It can

Spring blooms in Kirstenbosch.

get fairly strong and is irritating, so if you're heading to the beach consider Clifton or the False Bay beaches which are the most sheltered. January is the second month of the long summer school holidays when the Western Cape gets busy with families from Gauteng and other cities in the interior. Accommodation needs to be booked well in advance, and it's a good idea to make

reservations at restaurants. It gets busy, so expect crowded beaches and queues at the Aerial Cableway and Two Oceans Aquarium. The Robben Island excursion needs to be booked weeks, or even months, in advance. January and February (and December) are when the long summer entertainment events occur, including the open-air concerts at Kirstenbosch (page 51), and Shakespeare

Clifton Beach.

at the Maynardville Open-Air Theatre (page 63). At the end of January, the J&B Met (page 48) is the principal event on Cape Town's summer social calendar – a celebrity-studded event at Kenilworth Race Course when the clothes and the bling are just as important as the racing – and tickets need to be booked well in advance. The rugby season starts with the Super 14s in mid-February and finishes in mid-May.

International Jazz Festival (page 49) in early April, and the Old Mutual Two Oceans Marathon (page 49) on the Easter weekend, all attract thousands of South Africans, so accommodation again needs to be booked well in advance. The Cape Town Opera (page 127) season starts in April and runs through to October. The vineyards in the Winelands look their best in the autumn when the vines turn an array of gold and brown colours.

March & April

As autumn arrives, temperatures drop a little to the low 20s and towards the end of April there are some rainy days. Easter is another long holiday for domestic tourism when Cape Town and the Garden Route are busy, and it is usually the time of the year for a last beach holiday. 27 April is another public holiday and many South Africans take the days off between then and the next public holiday on 1 May as a long weekend, so this is another popular local holiday period. The Pick 'n' Pay Cape Argus Cycle Tour (page 48), the Cape Town

May & June

Heading towards winter, temperatures drop to the late teens and it starts to get cool at night. May through to August is the rainy season in the Western Cape and on average there are only six hours of sunshine per day. The shortest day is 21 June when the sun sets as early as 1800. It is during this time that you should go straight to the top of Table Mountain as soon as it's clear as it may be covered with cloud by the afternoon and for several days to come (the cableway closes in bad weather). The Cape Town International Conference

Centre (CTICC) is busy with events including the Good Food and Wine Show (page 49) at the end of May and the Cape Town International Book Fair (page 50) in mid-June. June is when southern right whales begin to migrate to the coast.

July & August

July is the coolest month and it receives the most rainfall. Temperatures rarely top 15°C on a sunny day and fall to around 7°C at night when you may have to ask for an extra blanket (central heating is a rarity in South Africa). The high mountain peaks around the Winelands are covered in snow and occasionally the top of Table Mountain gets a light dusting. The Table Mountain Aerial Cableway (tablemountain.net) closes for annual maintenance for two weeks in winter (check the website for exact dates). Festivals in winter include the Knysna Oyster Festival (page 50), at the beginning of July, which has sporting events, gala dinners, live entertainment and of course oysters, and the Bastille Festival in Franschhoek (page 50), on the second weekend in July, which celebrates all things Francophile including food and wine and French movies. Also in the cinema, the annual Encounters: South African International Film Festival (page 50) holds court at the Nu-Metro cinema at the Victoria and Alfred Waterfront for two weeks in July, which offers some winter night entertainment. The CTICC hosts Cape Town Fashion Week (page 50) in early August when designers from across Africa get heads turning to the catwalk. The Stellenbosch Wine Festival (page 50) is at the beginning of August, which includes plenty of food and drink, live entertainment and wine-tasting of over 500 wines. On Sunday mornings in July and August, Kirstenbosch holds chamber music concerts accompanied by a buffet breakfast in the tea room. In rugby, South Africa goes head to head with Australia and New Zealand in the Tri-Nations during July and August and the local Currie Cup takes place between July and October. The winter months are the best for surfing as the swells are at their optimum, but the ocean (as always) is very cold.

September & October

The worst of the cold snaps and rain are over, daytime temperatures recover to a moderate average of 20°C and days get longer with an average eight hours of sunshine. The Cape Town International Comedy Festival (page 51) takes place at various venues throughout the city in September and attracts top international comedians. The Out in Africa South African Gay and Lesbian Film Festival (page 51) is also in September at various venues and showcases films from around the world. This is the best time of year for spotting whales off the coast as they calve in the sheltered bays and on the Garden Route you can take whale-watching trips by boat. It's also the best time to see spring flowers and is a good time to visit Kirstenbosch.

November & December

Days are long, warm and sunny with pleasant temperatures of about 25°C and these are the driest months with only an average of three days per month of rain. This is the best time for outdoor activities without the wind, which comes in the late summer. December however, like January, is when Cape Town and the coast get horribly crowded with domestic tourists and you will need to book everything well in advance. Nevertheless this is the best time to visit the beach and the region does have a holiday atmosphere. The long outdoor entertainment arts programmes (see January) begin and, in particular, Capetonians pounce on the programme for Kirstenbosh, as a summer must-do is to picnic in the gardens while enjoying a Sunday afternoon concert. The Cape Times/Discovery Big Walk (page 51) happens on the second Sunday in November and attracts some 25,000 people on eight different walks of varying lengths around the city. It's the city's biggest family day out.

Right: Walking through Cape Town's parks.
Opposite page: Winter day in Cape Town.

Screen & page

Cape Town, Winelands & Garden Route in film & literature

Films

Mandela & De Klerk
Joseph Sargent, 1997
As the name suggests, this covers Mandela's historic release from prison and the subsequent negotiations between the two men who broke down Apartheid. Sidney Poitier and Michael Caine play the two formidable characters.

In My Country
John Boorman, 2004
This was shot entirely in Cape Town and is based on the memoirs of Antjie Krog, *Country of my Skull*, who was a journalist covering the Truth and Reconciliation Commission. It covers the testimonies of Apartheid victims through the eyes of a South African journalist (played by Juliette Binoche) and an American journalist (Samuel L Jackson).

u-Carmen e-Khayelitsha
Mark Dornford-May, 2005
This film starring Pauline Malefane, a critically acclaimed Khayelitsha-born choral singer in the title role, puts Carmen as a factory worker and her lover a policeman. The passionate story takes place in the township of Khayelitsha on the Cape Flats and is sung in isiXhosa.

Goodbye Bafana
Billie August, 2007
This tells the story of a racist prison warder (Joseph Fiennes), when his outlook is softened after his relationship with Nelson Mandela (Dennis Haysbert), whom he guarded on Robben Island for 20 years.

More Than Just a Game
Junaid Ahmed, 2007
Told through the eyes of five former prisoners, this tells the true story about the formation of the Makana Football Association on Robben Island in the 1960s. As much about football, it's a story that shows how hard life was in the prison.

Hansie
Regardt van den Bergh, 2008
An account of the life of former South African cricket captain Hansie Cronje, who was banned from cricket in 2000 over a match-fixing scandal with Indian bookmakers and then died in a plane crash near George in 2002.

Invictus
Clint Eastwood, 2009
Filmed in Cape Town and Johannesburg this is about when South Africa won the 2005 Rugby World Cup. When Nelson Mandela (Morgan

Freeman) embraced captain François Pienaar (Matt Damon) wearing a Springbok green and gold jersey, it was a moment that melted the hearts of all South Africans. Previously rugby had been an enclave for whites.

White Wedding
Ken Follet, 2009

Locally made and entertaining rom-com about a groom from Johannesburg who goes to Durban to pick up his best man and then they go on a road trip to Cape Town for his wedding. They get lost along the way in the Eastern Cape with good comic consequences.

Books

Fiction
An Instant in the Wind
André Brink, 1975

A historical novel set in 1749 about the Cape's first settlers, this beautifully written love story between a white woman and a slave was shortlisted for the 1976 Booker Prize.

Film locations of box-office hits

Film-makers for movies and commercials are attracted to Cape Town because of South Africa's highly acclaimed film crews, good infrastructure and good weather. In *Lord of War* (2005) starring Nicholas Cage as a global arms dealer, various locations in Cape Town appeared in 57 scenes as places in the Middle East, Afghanistan, Bolivia and Sierra Leone. *Ask the Dust* (2007) starring Colin Farrell and Salma Hayek is a love story set in 1930s Los Angeles but was filmed in Cape Town, mostly on a set constructed on a playing field. In the beach scene, before sunset, the ocean is on the left, and the shadows are stretching towards the camera. This cannot happen in Los Angeles, where the ocean is in the west and sun is in the south. The southern Californian feel was again recreated in *Flashbacks of a Fool* (2008) starring Daniel Craig in a story about a Hollywood actor who reflects on his over-excessive life after the death of a friend. Among many locations used for filming was the Ambassador Hotel and Salt (page 164) restaurant in Bantry Bay. Much of *Blood Diamond* (2006) starring Leonardo DiCaprio about diamond smuggling in Sierra Leone was filmed in South Africa and features shots of Cape Town International Airport.

Robben Island, the location for films *Goodbye Bafana* and *More Than Just a Game*.

Birds of Prey
Wilbur Smith, 1997
This book and the subsequent books in the Courtney series follow the arrival of the Courtney family at the Cape in the 1600s and their epic adventures around Africa.

Disgrace
J M Coetzee, 1999
Penned by South Africa's best-known novelist who won the Nobel Prize for Literature in 2003, this is a powerful story about a disgraced lecturer at Cape Town University who has to start a new life after seducing a student.

The Pickup
Nadine Gordimer, 2002
Written by South Africa's other Nobel Prize for Literature winner (in 1991), this is an intense love story between a privileged white girl and an illegal Arab immigrant who she meets at a garage in Cape Town where he fixes cars. She goes on to follow him to his own North African country.

Heart of a Hunter
Deon Meyer, 2003
This is an action-packed post-Apartheid thriller involving a kidnapping and South African intelligence agencies. Meyer is a well-regarded South African crime novelist who is often compared to John le Carré. Most of his books, including *Blood River (2009)* and *Devil's Peak (2007)*, are set in Cape Town.

Playing in the Light
Zoe Wicomb, 2006
In 1990s Cape Town, a single Afrikaans woman who runs a travel agency, for the first time employs and befriends a black woman. With her help she goes through a journey of her own past to discover that her grandmother was coloured.

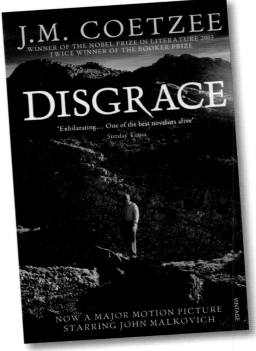

J.M. COETZEE
WINNER OF THE NOBEL PRIZE IN LITERATURE 2003
TWICE WINNER OF THE BOOKER PRIZE

DISGRACE

'Exhilarating... One of the best novelists alive'
Sunday Times

NOW A MAJOR MOTION PICTURE
STARRING JOHN MALKOVICH

VINTAGE

Star of the Morning
Pamela Jooste, 2008
A moving story about two Cape Coloured sisters in Apartheid South Africa who are orphaned and have to deal with life growing up in an orphanage and confront the barriers that Apartheid enforced on the poor. Jooste's other novels are also about the Cape Coloured community.

Mixed Blood
Roger Smith, 2009
A racy crime-thriller involving an American ex-bank robber hiding out in a wealthy suburb in Cape Town, where he is confronted by gangs from the Cape Flats and a crooked Afrikaner policeman.

Non-fiction
Long Walk to Freedom
Nelson Mandela, 1995
Mandela's epic autobiography and a fascinating insight into the struggle, much of which he wrote secretly on Robben Island. There are more than 130 books published on Nelson Mandela.

No Future Without Forgiveness
Desmond Tutu, 2000
Former Anglican Archbishop of Cape Town, tireless anti-Apartheid activist, and winner of the Nobel Peace Prize in 1984, this is his remarkable account of the wrenching findings of the Truth and Reconciliation Commission, which he chaired from 1995 to 1998.

Best Walks on the Cape Peninsula
Mike Lundy, 2006
A great book for hikers from strenuous ascents of Table Mountain to gentle strolls on Noordhoek beach, with detailed trails, notes on nature, advice on mountain safety and weather conditions, and maps.

The Making of Modern South Africa:
Conquest, Apartheid, Democracy
Nigel Worden, 2007
Frequently updated, this is probably the best account of South Africa's modern history. Written engagingly, it is a penetrative analysis of the forces that have shaped South Africa.

Diamonds, Gold and War: The British, the
Boers and the Making of South Africa
Martin Meredith, 2008
A comprehensive look at the wealth that built South Africa and an expert analysis on how the diamond and gold rushes laid the foundation for Apartheid. He brings the characters of Rhodes, Kruger and the like to life.

Gangs, Politics and Dignity in Cape Town
Steffen Jensen, 2008
A look at gang life in the townships on the Cape Flats and the relationship between the people and the police, but also touches on how people living in the townships maintain their dignity in the face of danger and hardship.

Cape Town
Gerald Hoberman, 2009
Hoberman is one of Cape Town's best-loved photographers and his aerial shots are particularly striking; he spends a lot of time flying over Cape Town by helicopter. This is a fine pictorial souvenir of the city, and in Cape Town look out for his postcards.

Table Mountain to Cape Point
Carrie Hampton, 2009
A comprehensive coffee-table book on Cape Town with evocative photographs and includes anecdotes from people who live around the Cape Peninsula.

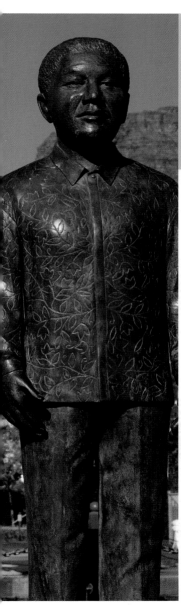

Contents

About the region

Statues of Nelson Mandela and President De Klerk
in Nobel Square, Victoria & Alfred Waterfront.

History

The arrival of the colonists

First people

The first evidence of human inhabitants in the Cape has been dated back to nearly 30,000 years ago. Rock art found in the area was created by nomadic San people (also known as Bushmen), a hunter-gatherer group which roamed across much of Southern Africa. Some San groups survive today, mostly in Namibia and Botswana. The original San were replaced about 2000 years ago by Khoi groups, a semi-nomadic people who settled in the Cape with herds of sheep and cattle. When the Dutch arrived, they were thought to number about 100,000 but many died in smallpox epidemics brought by the Europeans and the rest intermingled with slaves or were driven into the interior.

First landing

The first ship to round the Cape was captained by Bartholomeu Dias who named it Cabo de Bõa Esperança or the Cape of Good Hope. António de Saldanha, a Portuguese admiral who lost his way going east, was the first to land in Table Bay in 1503. He and his party went ashore in search of drinking water. They followed a stream to the base of Table Mountain and then proceeded to climb to the top. From here Saldanha was able to get a clear view of the surrounding coastline. On his return, he found the rest of his crew unsuccessfully trying to barter with local indigenous Khoi for livestock. The trade quickly developed into a row which ended in

Above: Cape of Good Hope.
Opposite page: The French Huguenot Monument in Franschhoek.

bloodshed. There was another battle between the Portuguese and the Khoi in March 1510. On this occasion the Khoi had struck back after children and cattle were stolen by the sailors. Seventy-five Portuguese were killed, including Dom Francisco de Almeida, who had just finished five years as the first Portuguese Viceroy to India. Few Portuguese ships landed in Table Bay after this.

The Dutch & the VOC

By the end of the 16th century British and Dutch mariners had caught up with the Portuguese and they quickly came to appreciate the importance of the Cape as a base for restocking ships with drinking water and fresh supplies as they made their long journeys to the East. The first moves to settle in the Cape were made by the Dutch, and on 6 April 1652 Jan van Riebeeck landed in Table Bay. His ships carried wood for building and some small cannons, and the first building to be erected was a small fort (where Grand Parade in the centre of Cape Town is today). Van Riebeeck was in charge of the supply station that belonged to the Dutch East India Company (Vereenigde Oost-Indische Compagnie or VOC). After the fort was built, gardens for fruit and vegetables were laid out and pastures for cattle acquired. Surprisingly, the early settlers were forbidden from enslaving the Khoi; instead, slaves were imported by the VOC from Indonesia and Malaysia. These slaves were the origin of the Cape Malay community.

In 1662 Jan van Riebeeck was transferred to India. Because of rivalries in Europe, the VOC was worried about enemy ships visiting the Cape, so work started on a new stone fort in 1666. Over the next 13 years several governors came and went. One of the most energetic, Simon van der Stel, arrived in 1679 and for the next 20 years he devoted his energies to creating a new Holland in southern Africa. He paid particular attention to the growth and development of Cape Town and the surrounding farmlands. The Company's Garden was replanted, nursery plots were created and new experimental plants were collected from around the world. North of the gardens he built a large

hospital and a lodge to house VOC slaves. New streets were laid out which were straight and wide with plenty of shade. New buildings in the town were covered in white limewash, producing a smart and prosperous appearance. In 1685, in appreciation for his work, he was granted an estate by the VOC, which he named Constantia. During his life he used the estate as an experimental agricultural farm and to grow oak trees which were then planted throughout the Cape.

One of his more significant contributions was the founding of the settlement at Stellenbosch. He directed the design and construction of many of the town's public buildings, and then introduced a number of the crops to be grown on the new farms. For many years he experimented with vines in an effort to produce wines as good as those in Europe. He was particularly pleased when in 1688 French Huguenot refugees arrived in the Cape. He saw to it that they were all settled on excellent farmlands in what came to be known as Franschhoek ('French corner'), the upper valley of the Berg River. In 1693 he had the foresight to appoint the town's first engineer to tackle problems of a clean water supply, and the removal of rubbish. Van der Stel died in June 1712 at Constantia. By then, the population of the colony was around 5700, of which about half were slaves. The next governor, Hendrik Swellengrebel, built Swellendam in 1713 and was responsible for erecting the first Cape Dutch churches in the Cape.

About the region

Arrival of the British

The next period of Cape Town's history was closely related to events in Europe, particularly the French Revolution. When the French invaded Holland, the British decided to seize the Cape to stop it from falling into French hands. After the Battle of Muizenberg in 1795, Britain took over the Cape from the representatives of the VOC, which was by then bankrupt. In the Treaty of Amiens (1803) the Cape was restored to the Batavian Republic of the Netherlands. In 1806 the British took control again at the resumption of the Anglo-French wars.

The first concern for the British for managing the colony was the persistent and inconclusive fighting along the colony's eastern frontier with the Xhosa. Some Xhosa groups had taken advantage of the instability in the colony to re-establish themselves to the west of the Fish River. The British decided that the only way to stop the persistent battles was to push the Xhosa back across the Fish River and establish a secure and clear frontier. What was needed was a group of permanent settlers on new farms, and in 1820 the British parliament released £50,000 to transport 5000 settlers from Britain to occupy this area. These became known as the 1820 Settlers and formed the nucleus of the subsequent British settler community. However, while the British authorities had intended that they should become farmers and hence occupy the disputed territory, most of the settlers were from urban artisan backgrounds and few had the skills or inclination necessary to

Dutch Reformed Church, Graaff-Reinet.

become successful cultivators in the difficult and unfamiliar environment of the Eastern Cape. Most of them quickly gravitated towards small towns, like Grahamstown and Graaff-Reinet, where they used their previous experience to become traders or skilled artisans.

It soon became apparent that the British attempts to create a permanent border between the Xhosa and settlers had failed and cattle raiding backwards and forwards across the border continued. The Xhosa tried on numerous occasions to reclaim their land, occupied now by the settlers, but these attempts always failed, despite many initial successes. The Frontier Wars between Xhosa and the settlers continued for the next half century with Xhosa independence and land occupation being progressively eroded until their remaining areas (which became known as Transkei), were eventually incorporated into the Cape Colony.

Abolishment of slavery
The other fundamental change that British rule brought about was the ending of the slave trade and then the total banning of slavery. The peripheral role of South Africa in the British colonial empire and the dispersed nature of its slave population meant that it was seldom considered in debates about slavery, which instead concentrated on the massive slave plantations of the West Indies. Nevertheless, when the British Parliament eventually decided to call an end to the institution that many felt was both inhumane and, more importantly, not beneficial to the empire's

economy, it was also banned in South Africa. In 1834 slaves throughout the British Empire were officially emancipated, though they were to remain with their owners as apprentices until 1838. In Cape Town the official emancipation happened on 1 December 1834 in Greenmarket Square, when 59,000 slaves were freed. In 1840 when Cape Town reached a population of about 20,000 it was declared a municipality, and again about half were former slaves or Khoi servants.

The Great Trek
Many of the original Dutch settlers were extremely unhappy about the emancipation of slaves, as now they were not only losing a large proportion of their 'property' (slaves) but were also being prevented from making sure they had a captive (cheap) labour supply. Though they were offered compensation at one third of the value of their slaves this had to be claimed in London. Many slave owners, therefore, sold their compensation rights to agents at usually about one fifth of the slave's value.

A number of Dutch settlers decided that they would set out with their families and servants in search of new land beyond the British colonial boundaries. Between 1835 and 1840 around 5000 people left the Cape Colony and headed east in a movement that later became known as the Great Trek. They became known as Voortrekkers (later when they settled, Boers, meaning farmers) and their experiences beyond the colonial frontiers became fertile ground for 20th-century Afrikaner nationalism. One thing not often celebrated in the national myths that grew up around the Great Trek is that accompanying the treks were a large number of Khoi servants and a small number of freed slaves still economically and socially bound to their masters. The Voortrekkers were by no means a unified movement, but over time, two separate republics were established: the Orange Free State and the Transvaal. By the 1850s, the British recognized these two states' sovereignty over most of the South African highveld to the east of the Orange River.

Cape Town's slave history

The museum at the Slave Lodge (see page 87) evocatively tells the story of slavery in the Cape and is housed in the former slaves' accommodation. Behind is Church Square (see page 88) where slaves used to be auctioned. The Slave Church Museum (see page 92) was used for religious instruction of slaves. Greenmarket Square (see page 90) is where slaves were freed in 1834, and Bo-Kaap (see page 97) is where many of the freed slaves settled in a working-class district.

The war years, diamonds & gold

European expansion

After leaving the Cape, one of the groups of Voortrekkers turned south and crossed the Drakensberg Mountains in search of a site for a new republic with access to the sea. In so doing they entered into the Zulu kingdom's domain. The Zulu king did not trust these new arrivals and the Zulu killed the Voortrekkers' leader when he came to negotiate a deal to be given land. A few months later, in the Battle of Blood River, the Voortrekkers extracted a terrible revenge and carved out a space for themselves south of the Tugela River. Their plans for a new republic with access to the sea however were scuppered, when the British annexed a site that became Durban and created the new colony of Natal in 1843.

Mineral revolution

Economically the Cape and Natal colonies both remained very much a backwater of the British Empire. Nevertheless, wool exports from the Karoo and wine from the Western Cape created some commercial interest, and a port was built in Cape Town to export commodities. The first truckload of construction rocks was tipped by Prince Alfred, the 16-year-old son of Queen Victoria, on 17 September 1860. The Alfred Basin was completed in 1870 and a dry dock was added in 1881.

But then South Africa's economy changed dramatically. In 1867 alluvial diamonds were discovered near the confluence of the Harts and Vaal rivers. A diamond rush began and by 1872 20,000 prospectors had converged on the site that soon revealed itself as the world's richest diamond pipe, and Kimberley grew into the world's diamond capital. At first there were numerous small individual mines but these soon became concentrated into the hands of one or two companies who bought up small claims. Eventually total control of the mines rested in the hands of Cecil Rhodes' De Beers Consolidated Mines.

In 1886 the next mineral discovery in South Africa was gold on the Witwatersrand in the

Above: Rough octahedral diamond crystal.
Opposite page: Diamond mines, Koffifontein, Kimberley.

Transvaal Republic. Miners from across the world rushed to the new reef, but just as at Kimberley, mine ownership was quickly consolidated into a few hands. The main town on the Rand, Johannesburg, grew rapidly from nothing to about 75,000 white residents and many more Africans by the turn of the 20th century.

These mineral discoveries fundamentally altered South African society. It was at the mines that many of the features that dominated life in 20th-century South Africa first came into existence; the pass laws, the migrant labour system, the compounds and the colour bar. The deep-level diggings and the complicated process of extraction from poor gold ores meant that production expenses were high and, as the gold price was fixed internationally, the one way mining companies could ensure high profits was to hold down or reduce labour costs; thus Africans were employed en masse on minimum wages.

Anglo-Boer War

When diamonds were discovered at Kimberley it was not quite clear who had sovereignty over the area, with a Tswana chiefdom, the Orange Free State, the Transvaal Republic and the Griquas all claiming the area. After a process of arbitration under the British, it was decided that the Griqua's claim was strongest, but the British immediately offered the Griqua leader substantial compensation if he agreed that the territory should be administered by the

British and the area was soon incorporated into the Cape Colony. Not surprisingly, the Boer republics were annoyed by this sleight of hand, but there was little they could do about it.

The Witwatersrand, on the other hand, was clearly within the Transvaal Republic. But the British were, not surprisingly, keen to control the world's largest supply of gold and mounted a sustained and ultimately successful bid to gain control of the whole of South Africa. Sensing that Britain was about to invade the Transvaal, the Orange Free State decided to strike before the reinforcements arrived and on 11 October 1899 declared war on Britain in an attempt to preserve their independence. Deciding that attack was the best form of defence, they invaded both the Cape and Natal colonies, thus continuing the Anglo-Boer (or South African) War, which lasted until 1902.

At first the Boer Republics had great success and drove back the British forces and laid siege to Ladysmith, Kimberley and Mafikeng. However, the general uprising of Afrikaners in the Cape that they had hoped for never materialized, and with the arrival of huge numbers of troops from Britain their fortunes changed. In 1900 the British advanced and took Pretoria, and Paul Kruger, the president of the Transvaal Republic, escaped into exile via the Portuguese colony of Mozambique. The sheer hopelessness of their situation led to the Boers surrendering to the British under the Treaty of Vereeniging in April 1902, and many Boer soldiers returned to their farms. The Act of Union was passed by the British Parliament in 1909 and the Union of South Africa came into being in 1910. In order to maintain good relationships within the Union, the British asked an ex-Boer general, Louis Botha to form the first government.

It's a fact...

In 1902 there was a massive outbreak of bubonic plague among the African communities living in slums in Cape Town. This prompted authorities to move about 7000 black people out of the city to a new township, Ndabeni, on the Cape Flats – the city's first township. These were later moved to Langa in 1923.

The powerful Apartheid Museum in Johannesburg.

Apartheid

The rise of Afrikaner nationalism

The ravages of war and the development of mechanized agriculture meant that many poorer Afrikaner farmers were forced off their land. Afrikaner politicians were fearful that the Afrikaner identity would be lost, and pushed for a stronger sense of nationalism. Historical events, such as the Great Trek, were deliberately celebrated, the Afrikaans language encouraged, and economic policies were developed to help Afrikaner small businesses. Ideas began to be considered by a group of Afrikaner intellectuals who saw the total separation of the races as being the only way in which whites could maintain political power over South Africa. They began to argue that if Africans were allowed to take part in the white capitalist economy they could rightly expect to be given political rights, so the solution was to keep them in a totally separate political and economic sphere where they could exercise their own rights. In order to achieve this, there was a deepening of segregationist policies in the urban areas – designed to keep black and white apart. The first legislative framework to be put in place was the Native's Land Act in 1913, which prevented land ownership by non-whites, followed by the Native Urban Areas Act in 1923, which required all non-whites to carry passes. In 1936 the Representation of Natives Act denied Africans the vote. After the Second World War, the economic boom caused by the war led to massive African urban migration, and in Cape Town, Nyanga and Guguletu were built. The National Party (NP), led by DF Malan, was able to use this flow to stir up the white, especially Afrikaner, voters. In 1948, the NP won an election promising a new ideology of Apartheid.

Apartheid policy

The government set about a massive national campaign to remove all Africans from urban areas and legislation, such as the Group Areas Act of 1950, tightened previous segregation regulations. Africans living in vibrant communities, such as District Six in Cape Town, had their homes bulldozed and they were forcibly relocated to distant townships. Only those with passes could enter the city to work, and those without passes were returned to the reserves, later restyled as homelands. In the countryside, Africans who had retained access to land either as freeholders or tenant farmers, in areas that were labelled 'black spots', were also forcibly removed to the homelands. Segregation of all amenities – like transport, healthcare and education – was tightened and there became no areas of African life where the state did not intervene. Any opposition or refusal to cooperate was inevitably dealt with extremely harshly. Apartheid became in essence a way of ensuring a continual supply of cheap African labour whilst denying Africans any political rights.

African opposition

In 1912 a group of African leaders called for a national convention for all African political groups in the country. This gathering in Bloemfontein marked the formation of a more organized phase in African opposition to racist legislation and lead to the South African Native National Congress, later renamed the African National Congress (ANC). Despite the formation of a national opposition organization, early African protest tended to be extremely moderate, and many African leaders placed a special emphasis on education as a means to achieving political recognition. During the Second World War, however, there was an upswing of African protest culminating in a series of protest movements amongst squatters outside Johannesburg and a massive African mineworkers strike. After the war African protest entered a more radical phase as younger leaders came to the forefront. The 1950s saw an unprecedented display

Nelson Mandela

Nelson Rolihlahla Mandela was born in 1918 in the Eastern Cape, and moved to Johannesburg as a young man where he became a lawyer. He joined the ANC under the leadership of Walter Sisulu, Oliver Tambo and Albert Luthuli and rose through the ranks to become leader of the ANC's armed wing, Umkhonto we Sizwe, in 1961. Mandela described the move to armed struggle as a last resort; years of increasing repression and violence from the state convinced him that non-violent protest against Apartheid had not, and could not, achieve any progress. In 1962 he was arrested and the following year (along with other ANC leaders) was convicted of sabotage and began his 27 years of incarceration, mostly on Robben Island. Following his release from prison in 1990, and along with President FW De Klerk, he helped lead the transition towards multi-racial democracy in South Africa, for which the pair jointly won the Nobel Peace Prize in 1993. After the 1994 democratic elections he became president until 1999, when he stepped down in favour of Thabo Mbeki. Since then, he has been a respected elder statesman, and South African's refer to him as Madiba, an honorary title for elders in Mandela's clan.

of African political opposition to the white state and the ANC membership mushroomed. In 1955, in Johannesburg the ANC adopted the Freedom Charter, calling for equality for all, which today is the backbone of South Africa's constitution.

including Walter Sisulu and Govan Mbeki, were arrested (Mandela had been arrested the previous year), and after a lengthy trial, they were all sentenced for treason and began life imprisonment on Robben Island.

The struggle

Moves towards armed resistance

In 1960, the Sharpville Massacre in Gauteng – when police opened fire on a crowd with machine guns and shot dead 69 (mostly in the back) during a pass book demonstration – marked a turning point in African political opposition. As news of the killings spread around the country Africans rioted and refused to go to work. In Cape Town there was a series of huge marches from the townships into the city centre, but the leaders were arrested and the Cape Flats townships erupted into rioting. A nationwide state of emergency was declared and the police arrested thousands of political activists from across the country. Strikers were beaten and township food supplies cut off to force people back to work. The ANC and other groups were banned and many of their leaders thrown into prison under new security legislation that meant they could be held without being charged. Over the next few months the unprecedented harshness of the police action broke the back of the widespread resistance. It also convinced many anti-Apartheid activists that non-violent action meant nothing if it was met by police brutality.

Under the leadership of Nelson Mandela, the ANC established an organized armed wing, Umkhonto we Sizwe (Spear of the Nation), to carry out sabotage attacks on economic targets but not to threaten human lives. From 1961, the organization carried out a total of 200 attacks on targets such as post offices, government buildings, electricity sub-stations and railway lines. But the organization was effectively neutralized by the security forces in July 1963, when its headquarters at Lilliesleaf Farm in Rivonia (Johannesburg) was raided. The majority of the ANC's leadership,

Apartheid in Cape Town

Visit the District Six Museum (see page 88) for a history of forced relocations, go on a township tour (see page 133) to experience both the reality of segregation and the vibrancy of township life, and Robben Island (see page 106) for the life story of the world's most famous political prisoner.

The darkest days

With organized opposition smashed, and their leaders either in prison or exile, political opposition by Africans to the Apartheid state was muted in the 1960s, and morale was low. The 'separate development' policies of the nationalists began to be applied with more rigour and economic opportunities for Africans became even more constrained. The winds of change may have been sweeping across the rest of Africa but for most South Africans the 1960s represented the darkest days. The economic divide between white and black widened, and forced removals increased as the government set about dividing the country into clear white, Indian, coloured and black zones. The official policy was that all Africans should live

Entrance to Robben Island Prison.

About the region

within rural homelands if they didn't have jobs in the cities, and by the 1970s a process had begun of making these autonomous. The first homeland to take independence was Transkei in 1976 and over the next five years Ciskei, Bophuthatswana and Venda followed suit.

Soweto Uprising

South Africa entered a new era of opposition to Apartheid in the early 1970s, but this time not led by organized political groups but by the trade unions (from 1973 there was a sudden huge rise in strike activity) and students – a generation born into Apartheid. One single event upped the struggle once and for all. On 16 June 1976, in Johannesburg, a Soweto school pupils' committee organized a mass march to deliver their complaints to the local authroities about the use of the Afrikaans language as a medium in schools. This peaceful march was met with a violent response when police opened fire – on defenceless school children. At first the pupils fled but then many turned and started throwing stones at the police. They then went on a rampage throughout the township destroying every symbol of their oppression that they could get to.

Rioting erupted around the country when news of the Soweto Uprising spread. The government was hard pressed to stop the unrest spreading beyond the townships but in a nationwide clampdown they eventually managed to quieten some of the protests. Many of the school pupil leaders found themselves under arrest or harassed by the police, and some young people involved in the uprising escaped across the border and joined the ANC's armed wing in exile. The Soweto Uprising, as the incident soon became known, marked an important turning point: from 1976 and onwards into the late 1980s, there was constant and violent unrest across South Africa as people demanded an end to Apartheid rule. The ANC made use of this new climate of opposition to begin to reinfiltrate South Africa. In the late 1970s they began a new campaign of sabotage, but now there was less care to avoid civilian casualties and

the ANC released a statement saying they were at war with the Apartheid state and, whilst their attacks were aimed at Apartheid and economic targets, they could not promise that civilians would not be caught up in the struggle.

Democracy

Breakdown of Apartheid

Unrest and international sanctions were hitting the economy hard. The NP did the unthinkable and sat down to negotiate with the ANC. Firstly ANC members in exile, then ministers, and eventually president Botha himself, met with Mandela. They offered him his freedom if he repudiated the use of violence as a weapon in the fight against Apartheid. Mandela refused.

In 1989, FW De Klerk became president. In 1990 he unbanned the ANC and other political parties, released Mandela and other political leaders, and squashed all remaining Apartheid legislation. In Cape Town, half a million people heard Mandela's first speech as a free man at the Grand Parade. Peace talks between De Klerk and Mandela began to break down the last components of racist policies and to draw up a new constitution, which was passed by the Constitutional Assembly in May 1996; the 1994 elections being held under an interim version.

1994 Elections

The ANC won South Africa's first democratic elections in April 1994 by a huge 63% majority. Nelson Mandela was duly elected President with Thabo Mbeki from the ANC and FW De Klerk, from the NP, as his deputy presidents. Parliament sits in Cape Town and government ministries are in Pretoria. This geographical division dates from the Act of Union in 1910 as a way of balancing power between the two former British colonies and the two former Boer republics. After the elections, reports of atrocities during Apartheid came out of the hearings of the Truth and Reconciliation Commission (TRC) chaired by Desmond Tutu (see page 87). This was a court-like body which invited anyone who felt that they were a victim of Apartheid's violence to come forward and be heard. Perpetrators of violence could also give testimony and request amnesty from prosecution. In late 1998, the commission presented its final report; it categorically condemned both sides for committing human rights abuses.

Modern politics

In 1999 Nelson Mandela passed the mantle of power as president of the ANC to Thabo Mbeki. In the national elections the ANC won again (66.3%), despite a widespread feeling that they had still to deliver on promises they made when they first came to power in 1994; particularly on service delivery – housing and basic amenities – which remains a contentious issue to this day. Nevertheless, Mbeki became the second democratically elected (black) president. The elections saw some growth in support for the Democratic Party (DP), later to become the Democratic Alliance (DA) in 2000, which got 9.6% of the vote. The DP's line on crime and tough talk in Cape Town from its leader, Tony Leon, won it a substantial proportion of the white vote.

In April 2004 the ANC won again (69.7%), and the DA (9.6%) retained its position in parliament as the opposition. The DA's strength is in the Western Cape, and in 2006, the outspoken and much admired Helen Zille took over from Tony Leon as head of the party and was Mayor of Cape Town from 2006 to 2009; an accolade that won her the title of World Mayor of the Year in 2008 for her aggressive and successful policies across Cape Town.

A member of the ANC since 1959, and part of its armed struggle in the early years of resistance to Apartheid (which earned him a 10-year spell in prison on Robben Island), Jacob Zuma was elected deputy president to Mbeki in 1999 and again in 2004, so for two terms was groomed as Mbeki's successor. Despite being involved in a corruption trial, Zuma was elected president of the ANC in 2007. Just days after Zuma's trial, in September 2008, Mbeki announced his resignation after being recalled by the ANC's National Executive

Archibishop Desmond Tutu in 1994.

Committee. This followed a conclusion by a judge of possible political interference by Mbeki and others in Zuma's trial. He was replaced by 'caretaker' president Kgalema Motlanthe, who headed the state until the 2009 elections.

In 2009 the ANC, headed by Zuma, won with a 69.69% majority. The DA increased its position with 20 more seats in parliament and took 13.6% of the vote. In the Western Cape, however the DA beat the ANC and took 51.2% of the vote, which instated Zille as Premier of the Western Cape, and has put her in a powerful position as leader of the opposition. It's early days for the Zuma government, but like the previous post-1994 governments, the main focus is service providing; since the demise of Apartheid, South Africans have wanted to see their votes turned into houses, jobs, amenities, education and healthcare.

Architecture in the Cape

Known as Cape Dutch style, the first homes in the Cape were designed and built by the Dutch settlers in the 17th century and the original style dates to medieval Holland and to Huguenot France. As the fortunes of the Cape grew in the 1700s, these were expanded into fine country houses and wine estates. Cape Town itself has a pleasing mixture of Georgian, Victorian and art deco buildings; the most attractive are in Bo-Kaap and De Waterkant. There's also some smart modern architecture and, unusually, many new buildings have been built within the façades of older ones.

Cape Dutch

Whitewashed Cape Dutch homesteads are unique to the Western Cape, and they are unquestionably beautiful, especially when contrasted against a leafy vineyard. The settlers' first homes were mostly single storeyed with just three or four rooms, with rafters and clay and rubble walls. Peach pips were often compacted to make a floor, sea shells provided the basis for lime-mortar and wild reeds were used to thatch the roofs. But by the beginning of the 1700s, Cape Town had become a port of major significance in world trade, and was visited by foreign governors, European aristocrats, and members of the professional classes including

Manor House at Boschendal winery.

surveyors and architects. Additionally the Cape wine industry was growing into an extremely profitable enterprise, and the buildings of the Cape were fashioned to reflect this prosperity. The houses expanded, and wings were added to form H-shaped buildings. They were built very symmetrically with wide front doors and evenly spaced windows with shutters, were whitewashed and slate (quarried on Robben Island) was used on the floors. Their most distinctive feature was the gable: a decorative parapet wall that roughly follows the line of the roof. Other buildings were added to the homesteads like stables, coach houses, slaves' quarters and wine cellars. Some had a *jonkershuis*, a separate house for the eldest son of the family. The size of the rooms can be directly related to the temperate climate; large rooms were cooler, but also the Dutch settlers were unused to such large plots of land (compared to an increasingly cramped Europe), and made the most of the newly found space by building grand houses.

Cape Malay

This Georgian architecture can be found in the Bo-Kaap and De Waterkant suburbs of Cape Town, and has its roots in the early 19th century when the area developed as a working-class district for freed slaves. It was common practice for the streets to be called after local developers and merchants; hence Dixon, Hudson and similarly named streets. These are lined with small, squat, flat-roofed dwellings, mostly semi-detached and typically with a *stoep* raised above the street (and the mud and refuse at the time), which was a place where the family socialized and where tradesmen worked. Even today, brightly coloured carpets can be seen being beaten over the walls of the *stoeps*. Front doors are in the middle of the front façade, usually with two sash windows on each sides, and a decorative plaster cornice along the edge of the roof at the front. Not more than 6 m across, the depth of the houses is quite deceptive, and several rooms run back from the façade. Bo-Kaap is still home to the

Five of the best

Cape Dutch manor houses

❶ **Vergelegen** (see page 186), meaning 'remotely situated' in Dutch, was built by Cape Governor Willem van der Stel in 1700. It's a beautiful and opulent gabled house with yellowwood floors and fine antiques and is flanked by five huge 300-year-old camphor trees.

❷ **Libertas Parva** (see page 182) is an H-shaped homestead built by Lambertus Pick in 1773, and has the only remaining pre-1790 baroque central gable in Stellenbosch. It has two front doors, one of which opens into a passage; the other does not open – it was only installed to maintain symmetry.

❸ **Boschendal** (see page 192) was built in 1812 by the De Villiers family, and is an imposing H-shaped house, the front gable, with its wavy outline ending in urns, reflects both the baroque and neoclassical traditions, and some indoor walls have painted friezes.

❹ **Nederburg** (see page 200) is flanked by rolling lawns and giant old oak trees, and was completed in 1800 by the founder of Nederburg, Philippus Wolvaart. The elegant homestead with its fort-like walls, high ceilings and airy rooms is one of the most recognizable Cape Dutch buildings in the Western Cape.

❺ **Drostdy** (see page 223) is Swellendam's most impressive H-shaped house, which dates to 1747, though it was extended in 1825. It has yellowwood timber rafters and lime-wash floors, and today is furnished in antiques as a museum.

Cape Malay community, and in the 1960s it became fashionable to paint the houses in bright colours, which make them so photogenic today. In the 1990s, De Waterkant became a trendy place to live, and although still small, most of the houses are now luxury homes. This led to the Cape Quarter development in 2001, which was extended considerably in 2009; an upmarket mall of boutiques and restaurants, and many of the old façades have been included in the development.

The Beautiful Game

Like the other host cities, since it was announced that South Africa is to host the 2010 FIFA World Cup South Africa™, development across Cape Town has gone into overdrive. Back in 2004, when FIFA president Sepp Blatter opened the envelope in Zurich and announced that South Africa had won the bid to host the 2010 FIFA World Cup South Africa™, his words were barely audible above the roaring crowd, and a collective cheer rose above South Africa. Sitting next to Blatter, Nelson Mandela couldn't hold back the tears as he raised the FIFA World Cup™ Official Trophy. Since then

Young soccer player on Green Point Common.

South Africa has been in the throes of organizing the biggest sporting event on earth and the host cities are finalizing their preparations for the tournament, which will take place from 11 June to 11 July.

In Cape Town, Green Point Stadium has been built on the demolished old one, and has a capacity of 68,000. It will host five first-round matches, one second-round match, a quarter final and a semi-final. The infrastructure around the stadium includes a 60-ha park, playing fields and an 18-hole golf course, new roads, including the Granger Bay Boulevard which connects it to the V&A Waterfront, an impressive elevated roundabout with pedestrian access underneath, a fan walkway through De Waterkant, which will bring fans from the railway station and minibus taxi depot, and extensive landscaping. Around the city, fan parks are being established where fans without tickets can watch matches on giant TVs, the largest of which is at the Grand Parade. City residents will benefit from improved transport; hundreds of kilometres of dedicated bus lanes are being laid out as part of the Integrated Rapid Transit (IRT) system, and the airport and the railway station have been upgraded. Services like electricity will be improved, with the building of new sub-stations, and thousands of meters of fibre-optic cables have been laid to improve internet connectivity (essential to stream live matches for TV).

Sports tourism has attracted visitors to Cape Town before. Both the rugby (1995) and cricket (2003) world cups have been held here as well as local events like the Cape Argus Pick 'n Pay Cycle Tour, which is now the biggest timed cycling event in the world, attracting more than 40,000 domestic and international participants.

It's a fact...

2010 is the 19th FIFA World Cup™ and the first to be played on African soil. The final 32 teams will play 64 matches at 10 stadiums in nine host cities. South Africa's team Bafana Bafana ('the boys') automatically qualify, and in total Africa will have six teams competing.

Zakumi

The official mascot for the 2010 FIFA World Cup South Africa™ is Zakumi, a leopard with green hair. His name derives from combining ZA, the international abbreviation for South Africa, and 'kumi', a word that means 10 in several African languages. The story goes that he was born on Youth Day (which commemorates the 1976 Soweto Uprising) in 1994, the same year as the birth of South Africa's democracy, and represents those in South Africa born in a free and democratic society. He will turn 16 on 16 June, which is also South Africa's second first-round match in the tournament. He wears a gold and green football strip, the same colours as not only Bafana Bafana, but South Africa's Springbok rugby team and Protea cricket team. Zakumi's priority is to turn the 2010 FIFA World Cup South Africa™ into one unforgettable party and show the thousands of international guests the warmth and spirit of the African continent.

© 2007 FIFA TM

2010 FIFA WORLD CUP™ OFFICIAL MASCOT

Nature & environment

South Africa's physical geography is dominated by one feature: a massive escarpment that runs right around the subcontinent dividing a thin coastal strip from a huge inland plateau. In the Western Cape, this escarpment supports a jumble of beautiful mountain ranges known as the Cape Folded Mountains, a series of sedimentary sandstone peaks, such as the Cederberg, the Tsitsikamma, the Swartberg and the Hottentot-Hollands. The meeting of the two oceans – the Indian and Atlantic – occurs off the Western Cape, providing unique marine and coastal environments.

Cape Town

Thought to be about 400 million years old, Table Mountain, Devil's Peak and Lion's Head are eroded remnants of a series of rock beds that once covered the entire Cape Flats and joined the Hottentot-Holland Mountains, some 90 km east of Cape Town. The top of Table Mountain and the other mountains on the Cape Peninsula are formed by resilient pale grey quartzite or baked sandstone, which forms the sharp edges and steep cliffs. An estimated 2200 species of fynbos are found on the mountain alone, including South Africa's national flower, the protea. Patches of indigenous forest can be found in a few of the wetter ravines but not on the exposed face above the city, which is too dry. The most common animal on the mountain is the dassie or rock hyrax, a small rodent-type creature seen around the Upper Cableway Station. Mongooses, porcupines and snakes also occur but are rarely seen.

The Protea, South Africa's national flower.

Cape Peninsula

The Peninsula mountain chain stretches some 50 km from Table Mountain down to Cape Point. The most dramatic view is of the Twelve Apostles from the Atlantic Seaboard. Distinctive large grey boulders are found along the western coast and at Boulders Beach in False Bay. These were formed when molten rock pushed up from the earth's crust solidified as granite. The Cape of Good Hope section of Table Mountain National Park is home to several species of antelope, including bontebok and red hartebeest, as well as ostrich and mountain zebra. Southern right and Bryde's whales and dolphins can be spotted in False Bay. There are several large troops of chacma baboons, which can be seen both in the Table Mountain National Park and from roads on the southern Peninsula.

Winelands

The regions around Stellenbosch, Paarl, Franschhoek and Wellington are generally termed Boland ('up land' in Afrikaans), referring to the higher valleys away from the coast. The vines are planted on the floors of several of these valleys, surrounded by fynbos-covered sandstone mountains reaching peaks of up to 2000 m. These provide an important water catchment area for the region, and the fnybos prevents rainwater run-off and erosion and also serves as a filter, so the water in the mountain streams, which run into reservoirs, is clear and clean. They are also fed by snow in winter. Away from the coastal salty air and fierce winds, the Mediterranean climate and clayey soils provide an ideal environment for growing vines.

Tip...

The colours of the Wineland's appealing viticulture landscapes change with the seasons and the vines are at their leafiest in spring just before the harvest.

Garden Route

Hemmed in between the Outeniqua and Tsitsikamma mountains and the coast, the Garden Route runs between the Slang River near Heidelberg, eastwards to the Tsitsikamma Forest and Storms River. The mountains provide a watershed for a diverse variety of flora on the coast, ranging from fynbos and protea flowers, to lush wetlands and dense tropical forests. The rugged coastline of the Indian Ocean supports a succession of bays, cliffs and coves, and there are some impressive sandy beaches. The interior, including the ostrich farming region of the Little Karoo, can only be reached by a number of scenic passes, and the inland plateau of the Cape is dominated by Karoo types of vegetation of low-lying shrubs and succulents, though in good rainfall years grasses can also make an appearance.

Cape Floral Region

A distinctive feature of the Western Cape, particularly around Cape Town and the Cape Peninsula, is fynbos, which is derived from the Dutch word for fine-leaved plants. The environment contains thousands of species of shrubs, grasses, flowers and reeds that can thrive in acidic and nutrient-poor soil. The Cape Floral Region comprises eight protected areas of fynbos stretching from the Cape Peninsula to the Eastern Cape, and was the sixth of the world's separate floral kingdoms declared a UNESCO World Heritage Site in 2004. Kirstenbosch National Botanical Garden falls in the region, and is the world's first botanical garden to be awarded this status. The Cape Floral Region is both the smallest and the richest of the world's floral kingdoms with the highest known concentration of plant species per unit area. There are over 7700 different plant species within the fynbos biome and of these over 5000 are endemic to the Western Cape. The 470 sq km of the Cape Peninsula alone, is home to 2256 different plant species – more than the whole of the UK, an area 5000 times bigger.

The Big Seven

A large proportion of people who visit South Africa do so to see its spectacular wildlife. There are a number of game parks and reserves around the country. The most popular animals are the Big Five, a term originally coined by trophy hunters. These are rhino, elephant, leopard, lion and buffalo, but there are many other equally interesting animals and birds. Additionally, thanks to the rich marine environment, the ocean is home to whales and sharks. Collectively these are termed as the Big Seven.

Rhino

The white rhino has a square muzzle and the black rhino a long, hooked upper lip and this is what distinguishes it rather than colour. Males are usually solitary, and females are seen in small groups with their calves. A white rhino mother walks behind, guiding her calf with her horn, while a black rhino mother walks in front of her offspring. Many of the Western Cape's private reserves are now home to white rhino, and the first calf born in the Cape for over 100 years was at Aquila (see page 72) in 2005.

White rhino in Pilansberg.

Elephant

Male elephants reach an average height of 3 m at the shoulder, making them the largest land mammal in the world. Female elephants live in sociable herds led by a matriarch, while male elephants are usually solitary. They use their tusks for debarking trees and digging, and their trunks for eating, drinking and bathing. Again elephants can be seen in the private reserves; you can interact with and ride elephants at the Knysna Elephant Park (see page 243), and there's possibly an elusive herd in the Knysna Forest (see page 242).

Leopard

One of many spotted cats, a leopard has rosettes rather than simple spots and is larger and less lanky than a cheetah. Primarily a nocturnal creature, it spends much of the day resting and sleeping in the branches of trees. There used to be leopard in the Cape's high mountains but few remain, though there is a population in the Cederberg Mountains and on Kagga Kamma Private Game Reserve (see page 73) but they are rarely seen.

Lion

The largest of the big cats in Africa and also the most common, lions live in sociable prides of up to

Tip...

Also look out for cheetah, crocodile, giraffe, hippo, black wildebeest, Burchell's and mountain zebra, springbok, gemsbok, steenbok, kudu, caracal (lynx), blesbok, bontebok, bat eared fox, ostrich, klipspringer, duiker, baboon, black backed jackal, eland and red hartebeest, and in the ocean, heavy-sided and bottlenose dolphin, African penguin, Bryde's, humpback and killer whale, and Cape fur seal.

around 30 animals and the females do most of the hunting. They are present on most of the Western Cape's private reserves and, as they are often not disturbed by the presence of humans, it's possible to get quite close to them.

Buffalo
Generally found on open plains but also at home in dense forest, they are fairly common in most African national parks but, like the elephant, they need a large area to roam in. They are grazers, live in herds and like to wallow in shallow water. Again, they are present in most of the Western Cape's private reserves.

Southern right whale
At 14-18 m long, this huge whale spends southern hemisphere summer months in the cold polar waters close to Antarctica, and then migrates north in winter for breeding in warmer waters off the coast of South Africa and South America. They can be seen off the coast from July to October, and the best vantage place is Hermanus (see page 188).

Great white shark
Reaching lengths of more than 6 m, weighing up to 2240 kg, and with serrated teeth, this is the world's largest predatory fish. They are present along the entire coast with especially large populations in False Bay and Shark Alley at Gansbaai, where they feed on seals. At the latter you can go shark cage diving (see page 135).

Above: African elephants on the move.
Right: Great white shark at Gansbaai.

Five of the best

South African Big Five destinations

❶ **Kruger** is the king of South African parks, and one of the best game-viewing areas in Africa. Covering an area the size of Israel, it certainly fulfils most visitors' expectations of seeing magnificent herds of game roaming across acacia-studded savannahs.

❷ **Addo**, easily visited at the end of the Garden Route, is famous for its large herds of elephant, buffalo and black rhino, and incorporates a coastal belt of giant dunes and islands that are home to Cape gannets and African penguins.

❸ **Madikwe** is a conservation success story, and in the 1990s more than 10,000 large animals were released into the reserve. Operating as a high-income, low-impact destination and with a clutch of luxury lodges, game viewing without the crowds can be very rewarding here.

❹ **Pilansberg** is a man-made reserve which has been stocked with large populations of big animals, which can be easily seen in the woodlands and on the savannahs. The environment is excellent for birdwatching too.

❺ **Hluhluwe-Imfolozo** has varied landscapes supporting a number of animals but is most famous for successfully bringing back both white and black rhino from the brink of extinction and this is the best place in Africa to see them.

Tip...

While the best national parks are some distance from Cape Town, there are a number of private game reserves that are home to large animals within striking distance of Cape Town (see page 73).

Festivals & events

Celebrations are a serious business in Cape Town, and during the summer months you'll be hard pressed to find a free weekend. Street carnivals and festivals compete with cultural and sporting events, and food and wine are also an important part of the Cape Town calendar. Cape Town is the undisputed pink capital of Africa so the gay community hosts a number of party events throughout the year. Islamic holidays are celebrated across Cape Town as the majority of Cape Coloureds are Muslim, while the Christian holidays are celebrated by other communities.

January

J&B Metropolitan Handicap (last Saturday) South Africa's major horse racing event at Kenilworth Race Course, where everyone is expected to dress up. The 2009 theme was glitz and glam. There's a marquee village, jet setters arrive by helicopter, and there's plenty of TV coverage for the fashion (jbmet.co.za).

Karnaval (2 January) This carnival, also known as Kaapse Klopse, is staged by the Cape Coloured community and begins in Bo-Kaap and ends up near the Green Point Stadium. It includes a procession of competing minstrel bands, complete with painted faces, straw boaters and bright satin suits.

February

Cape Town Pride (last two weeks) The biggest gay event in town, offering parties, literary events, picnics, karaoke competitions, beauty pageants and ending with a parade on the final Saturday with floats and decorated convertibles around Green Point, culminating in a street party in De Waterkant (capetownpride.co.za).

March

Cape Argus Pick 'n' Pay Cycle Tour (second Sunday) The world's largest timed cycling event taking an impressive 109-km route around Table Mountain and along the shores of the peninsula. It's open to international cyclists and attracts some 40,000 participants each year. It's South Africa's favourite family event and cyclists are supported by Cape Town's residents along the entire route (cycletour.co.za).

Cape Town Carnival (third weekend) New to the mother city, this annual event will be first held in 2010. Copying the model of the Rio Carnival, it will include a 350-m procession of floats, dancers and musicians on Beach Road in Mouille Point and there will numerous balls, beach and street parties over the weekend (capetowncarnival.com).

Cape Town Festival (third weekend)
This is an entertaining week-long arts and cultural festival at various venues, with a main stage in Company's Garden and ending with a street party in Long Street. It features many Cape Town home-grown musicians (capetownfestival.co.za).

April

Cape Town International Jazz Festival
(first weekend)
Held at the Cape Town International Convention Centre (CTICC), where five stages host a huge array of local and international jazz artists and on one night there's a free concert in Greenmarket Square. This celebrated event now attracts in excess of 30,000 people (capetownjazzfest.com).

Old Mutual Two Oceans Marathon (first Saturday)
Dubbed as one of the most beautiful marathons in the world, which runs on a 56-km route around the Cape Peninsula, this attracts over 26,000 runners for the full and half marathon and number of fun runs, and again is open to international competitors (twooceansmarathon.org.za).

Pink Loerie Mardi Gras (last week)
Cape Town's gay community gravitates to Knysna for a week of partying, and other events like mountain biking and boat rides, and it ends with a colourful carnival. Knysna's shops and restaurants join in the fun as they are decorated in pink (pinkloeriemardigras.co.za).

Taste of the Cape (first week)
On a playing field off Kloofnek Road, this offers the experience of trying some selected mini-plates of food from the city's top gourmet restaurants and the white marquees are beautifully lit at night. Buy a book of coupons and a wine glass and wander around the stalls (tasteofcapetown.com).

A ballerina preparing for the Cape Town Carnival.

May

Cape Times V&A Waterfront Wine Affair
(second week)
Over 350 wines produced by 95 of the leading local wineries are accompanied by food specially prepared by the participating V&A Waterfront restaurants. Local and imported cheeses, oysters, olives, pestos and preserves accompany the top Chenin Blancs, Steens, Pinotages and Cabernets (waterfront.co.za).

Good Food & Wine Show (second weekend)
At the Cape Town International Convention Centre (CTICC), this celebrates gourmet food and good wine, with tastings and Cape Town's best restaurants serving up tempting mini-plates, plus hands-on cooking experiences and demonstrations from celebrity BBC chefs from the UK (gourmetsa.co.za).

About the region

Sexpo (second weekend)
The world's largest health, sexuality and lifestyle show at the Cape Town International Convention Centre (CTICC) attracts a staggering 35,000 each year for shopping, shows, food and wine, even pole-dancing lessons (sexpo.co.za).

June

Cape Town Book Fair (mid-June)
The Cape Town International Convention Centre (CTICC) is filled with hundreds of thousands of books during this popular fair, which features both South African and international publishers. Events include author talks and children's reading sessions and some good discounts on books can be found (capetownbookfair.com).

July

Encounters Documentary Film Festival
(first two weeks)
Films are screened at Nu Metro at the V&A Waterfront and there's a packed programme of documentary shorts and full-length films from around the world, including some topical films made in South Africa. Many are followed by panel discussions (encounters.co.za).

Franschhoek Bastille Festival (second weekend)
Don a beret and join Franschhoek's residents to celebrate Bastille Day, with a food and wine marquee, barrel rolling and chefs and waiter races, a French film festival and a masked ball (franschhoek.org.za/festivals).

Knysna Oyster Festival (early July)
Oysters and whisky and wine tasting, an oyster shucking competition, sporting events like a marathon, boat races and cycle race, children's entertainment, and gourmet food in the town's restaurants. It attracts over 65,000 people, mostly from Cape Town, over 10 days (oysterfestival.co.za).

August

Arise Cape Town Fashion Week (mid-August)
Runway shows at the Cape Town International Convention Centre (CTICC) showcase young and established designers from across Africa, which conclude with a dazzling display of evening wear. The sponsor, Arise is a stylish magazine on African fashion (africanfashionint.com).

Stellenbosch Food & Wine Show (first week)
Held in the Paul Roos Centre, this is a showcase of the Cape Winelands with over 500 wines to taste and buy, food stalls, wine and food pairing evenings, live music, fashion shows, chef demonstrations and children's entertainment. There's a shuttle bus service from Cape Town (wineroute.co.za).

Nils Berg at the Cape Town International Jazz Festival.

September

Cape Town Comedy Festival (last two weeks)
Held at the Baxter Theatre, this features over 160 local and international acts on several stages, while at the V&A Waterfront street performers entertain visitors (comedyfestival.co.za).

Chelsea Festival at Kirstenbosch
(early September)
The best time to see the flowers in full bloom, special events here include gardening talks, flower arranging contests, and fine art exhibitions, but the real reason to come is to see Kirstenbosch's entry to the Chelsea Flower Show in London, for which they have won countless gold medals (sanbi.org).

Hermanus Whale Festival (third weekend)
This popular event marks the beginning of the calving season of southern right whales, when there is excellent land-based whale watching over Walker Bay from the cliff-tops in Hermanus. This is an easy day trip from Cape Town and features live music, a craft market and a marquee displaying exhibits on whales. A whale-crier blows his horn when he spots a whale (whalefestival.co.za).

Out in Africa Festival (mid-September)
Gay and lesbian film festival, with screenings at Nu Metro at the V&A Waterfront showing world cinema. It started in 1994 to celebrate the clause in the new South African constitution prohibiting discrimination on the grounds of sexual orientation (oia.co.za).

Paarl Cultivaria Festival (late September)
This kicks off with a black tie dinner for 1000 people on a very long table on Paarl's main street, and includes live music performances, wine-tasting, food stalls, art exhibitions and a children's activity centre (cultivaria.com).

October

Cape Town International Kite Festival
(second week)
Africa's biggest celebration of kite-flying on Muizenburg Beach with acrobatic kite displays, giant inflatables, craft market, kiddie's rides, kite-making workshop and food stalls. An excellent family day out (capementalhealth.co.za/kite).

November

Cape Times/Discovery Health Big Walk
(second Sunday)
This is the world's largest timed walk, which started in 1903 and now attracts 25,000 participants on walks from 5-80 km. Most people are on sponsored walks and the event raises a large amount for community charities (bigwalk.co.za).

December

Kirstenbosch Summer Concerts
(every Sunday until March)
This is a perfect way to enjoy the gardens with a picnic on the lawns; the concerts vary from rock, folk and jazz to classical and opera. A popular venue for international stars (sanbi.org).

Mother City Queer Project (mid-December)
One of the city's biggest annual gay-themed parties, which attracts thousands of revellers, in a different venue each year with a different fancy dress theme. There's a no costume, no entry policy so as you can imagine it's a colourful and fun event (mcqp.co.za).

Obz Festival (first weekend)
A huge street party in Observatory with stalls, live music, DJs and all-night parties. It showcases South African alternative music and is popular with students from the University of Cape Town (UCT) (obzfestival.com).

Sleeping

Cape Town and its environs offer a wide variety of accommodation from top-of-the-range five-star hotels, to more personable guesthouses or B&Bs, affordable holiday self-catering flats aimed at families, and dormitory beds or camping for budget travellers. Comprehensive accommodation information can be found on the regional tourism websites listed in each area. The whole region is a popular domestic holiday destination so you should always book well in advance over summer and to some extent at Easter too. In every budget, there are plenty of independent properties that have individual charm, but for those who prefer the anonymity of a large hotel, there are also a number of quality South African chains.

Overall, the quality of accommodation is very high in every budget, but you do generally get what you pay for. A double in a five-star hotel can cost upwards of R4000 per night but for this you will get super luxury furnishings and facilities and impeccable service. In a boutique hotel or top-class guesthouse rates are in the region of R2000, in a chain hotel R1000, in a B&B R500-700, while a bed in a dorm will cost as little as R100. Make sure you keep a copy of all correspondence and reconfirm your bookings once you arrive in the country.

Constantia Uitsig Spa.

Hotels

The variety of hotels in the region is very comprehensive, and there are some delightful family-run and country hotels, boutique hotels with stylish interiors in the cities and towns and, for those who enjoy the anonymity of a large hotel, chains like Southern Sun, Protea and City Lodge. Cape Town's grand old dame is the five-star Mount Nelson Hotel (see page 115), which is set in leafy parkland in the Gardens area with great views of Table Mountain. Also at the luxury end are the crop of smart modern hotels at the V&A Waterfront, which now includes Africa's only six-star hotel, the

Eccentric room at Daddy Long Legs Hotel, Long Street.

One&Only (see page 118). Across the city are some fine boutique hotels, many in the suburbs in the City Bowl, in Green Point and Sea Point, and there are also a few good options in the southern suburbs, but these are some distance from the city centre so you'll need a car. In the city centre, at the end of the highway in Foreshore, is a clutch of gleaming tower hotels; the first you are likely to see is the imposing blue glass Westin Grand at the end of the N1/N2. There are a number of fairly new affordable edgy hotels, the Daddy Long Legs and Grand Daddy (see pages 114 and 116) art hotels being fine examples, along and around Long Street, designed to appeal to a youthful fashionable visitor with an interest in nightlife. At the Grand Daddy, there is also the option of sleeping in an Airstream trailer on the roof.

On the Cape Peninsula, Camps Bay has a few exclusive options and is the holiday playground for the rich and famous. The well heeled can also look

at renting a house here. The other peninsula towns have a range of holiday accommodation but as the peninsula is usually explored on a day trip by foreign visitors, these are of more appeal to domestic visitors. The exception is Constantia, where some of Cape Town's best hotels in restored wine estates can be found, and Hout Bay which boasts a couple of new stylish hotels. The Winelands offers some superb luxury accommodation on the wine estates, which often feature top-class restaurants and other facilities like spas or golf courses. The towns along the Garden Route too offer quality hotels, from modern beach holiday properties to fine luxury country houses.

Guesthouses

Guesthouses can offer some of the most characterful accommodation in South Africa, with

About the region

interesting places springing up in both cities and small towns. They are smaller and, in most cases, cheaper than hotels, though standards obviously vary enormously; much of what you'll get has to do with the character of the owners and the location of the homes. Some are simple practical overnight rooms, while at the more luxurious end, rooms may be in historic homes filled with antiques, and offering impeccable service. Breakfast is almost always included and, in some, evening meals can be prepared if you phone ahead. There are many dotted around Cape Town's suburbs, and Swellendam en route to the Garden Route has some fine options set in beautifully restored Cape Dutch buildings if you want to break your drive.

Recommended websites

For guesthouses try the **Guest House Association of Southern Africa** (ghasa.co.za) or **Portfolio Collection**, a private agency with carefully selected mid-range properties (portfoliocollection.com); for self-catering flats try **Cape Homes** (capehomes.co.za), or **Cape Letting** (capeletting.com); while **Backpacking South Africa** (backpackingsouthafrica.co.za) and **Coast to Coast** (coastingafrica.com) list all South Africa's backpackers hotels. A good resource for all accommodation is **Sleeping Out** (sleeping-out.co.za) and **AA Travel Guides** (aatravel.co.za); the latter awards the AA Travel American Express Accommodation Awards to South African establishments each year.

Bed & breakfast

B&B accommodation is hugely popular in South Africa; even the smallest town has private homes that rent out rooms. Local tourist offices are the best source of information for finding B&Bs. Assuming you get on with your hosts, they can offer a valuable insight into local life. In rural areas, farmhouse B&Bs are often in beautiful settings where guests will have access to a garden and swimming pool as well as to hikes and horse riding. Increasingly, some establishments are providing TVs, air conditioning or fans, and have separate entrances for those who want more privacy away from the owners. The breakfasts are almost always good and large enough to fill you up for the day. Full English breakfasts are usually served but it is increasingly common to have a choice of continental breakfast or even a traditional South African breakfast of *boerewors*, mince on toast and mealie porridge.

Backpacker hostels

Backpacker hostels are the cheapest form of accommodation, and a bed in a dormitory will cost as little as R90 a night. Some also have budget double rooms with or without bathrooms, while others have space to pitch a tent in the garden. While hostel standards can obviously vary, stiff competition means that most hostels are clean and have good facilities. You can usually expect a self-catering kitchen, hot showers, a TV/DVD room and internet access. Many hostels also have bars and offer meals or nightly *braais*, plus a garden and a swimming pool. Most hostels are a good source of travel information and many act as booking agents for the Baz Bus, budget safari tours and car hire. On the whole, hostels are very safe and security is not a problem. Your fellow travellers remain the greatest threat, especially in dormitories in the busy city hostels. On Cape Town's Long Street, there are a number of cheap backpackers convenient for the nightclubs, and many more are

Above: Camping in the Hottentots-Holland Mountains.
Opposite page: La Fontaine.

dotted around the suburbs. There are also good established backpackers in Stellenbosch and Swellendam and many more along the Garden Route which are linked by the daily Baz Bus.

Camping & self-catering resorts

Camping is the cheapest and most flexible way of seeing South Africa; every town has a municipal campsite, there are rest camps in the national parks and nature reserves, and there is a string of resorts along the Garden Route. Even the most basic site will have a clean washblock with hot water, plus electric points and lighting, and *braai* facilities, with charcoal, wood and firelighters available in campsite shops. Additionally, some have basic

chalet accommodation; these vary in quality and facilities, from basic *rondavels* with bunks, to chalets with a couple of bedrooms and fully equipped kitchens, and may feature swimming pools and restaurants too. However, at the most popular tourist spots, these can get very busy and are best avoided in peak season.

It's a fact...

All accommodation in South Africa is graded a star value by the Tourism Grading Council of South Africa and the website has comprehensive lists in all categories; tourismgrading.co.za.

Eating & drinking

Cape Town and the region is a foodie's heaven and residents take eating out seriously. Cape Town in particular has experienced a boom in top-class restaurants, from traditional Cape Malay cooking to cordon bleu seafood, all at incredibly good prices. Some of the best restaurants in the country are found in the Winelands, many of which are part of historic wine estates. Franschhoek has a particularly good reputation, with a number of excellent French restaurants, while the Garden Route offers fresh, good-value seafood. South African cuisine is generally meat based – to *braai* (BBQ) is a national pastime – but thanks to Cape Town's cosmopolitanism, every international cuisine is represented.

South African cuisine

South African food tends to be fairly regional, although a ubiquitous love of meat unites the country. In and around Cape Town visitors will find many restaurants offering Cape Malay cuisine, a blend of sweet and spicy curries and meat dishes cooked with dried fruit. Seafood along the coast is excellent and usually very good value. Portuguese influences, thanks to neighbouring Mozambique, are strong – spicy peri-peri chicken or Mozambiquan prawns are widespread. Meat,

Top: Salmon salad at Catharina's at Steenberg, Constantia.
Above: Caroline's Fine Wines.

however, is universal and South Africa offers plenty of opportunities to try an assortment of game, from popular ostrich or springbok to more acquired tastes such as crocodile or warthog. One local meat product which travellers invariably come across is *biltong* – a heavily salted and spiced sun-dried meat, usually made from beef but sometimes made from game such as ostrich, kudu or impala, and which is chewed as a snack. The staple diet for much of the black South African population is a stiff maize porridge known as pap, served with a stew. Pap tends to be rather bland, although the accompanying stews are often quite tasty. There are several restaurants in Cape Town and around which are popular with tourists to try an assortment of African food from all over the continent.

South Africa is a major player in the international wine market and produces a wide range of excellent wines. The Cape Winelands have the best-known labels but there are a number of other wine regions dotted around the country. Unlike France, wine is rated not by region, but by the variety and quality of the grape, and by the producer. South Africa also produces a range of good beer. Major names include Black Label, Castle and Amstel. Windhoek, from Namibia, is also widely available and more popular than some of the South African beers. Home-brewed beer, made from sorghum or maize, is widely drunk by the African population. It has a thick head, is very potent and not very palatable to the uninitiated. Bitter is harder to come by, although a good local variety is brewed at Mitchell's Brewery in Knysna and Cape Town and can be found at outlets along the Garden Route. Bottled mineral water and a good range of fruit juices are available – the Ceres and Liquifruit brands are the best. Another popular drink is rooibos tea, literally red bush tea. This is a caffeine-free tea with a smoky flavour, usually served with sugar or honey, and is grown in the Western Cape.

Supermarkets usually have a similar selection of groceries to that found in Europe. South Africa is a

It's a fact...

No liquor may be sold on Sundays (and public holidays) except in licensed bars and restaurants. The standard shop selling alcohol is known as a bottle store. Supermarkets do not sell beer or spirits and stop selling wine at 2000.

Cape dishes

Bobotie A Cape Malay dish similar to shepherd's pie but with a savoury custard topping instead of mashed potatoes, and the mince stew is mixed with fruit. Some consider it as South Africa's national dish.

Boerewors A coarse, thick sausage made from beef or game meat and usually cooked in a spiral on the braai. The word is a combination of 'farmer' and 'sausage' in Afrikaans.

Bredie The Afrikaans word for 'stew', this is usually made with mutton, cinnamon, chilli and cloves and is cooked for a very long time and is traditionally served with saffron rice. *Waterblommetjie bredie* is meat cooked with the flower of the Cape pondweed (tastes a bit like green beans).

Cape brandy pudding Also known as Tipsy Tart, this warming winter pudding was probably concocted soon after brandy was distilled in the Cape in 1672. Dates and nuts are added to this syrupy dish.

Frikkadels Beef or lamb meatballs, usually made with nutmeg and coriander and baked or deep fried.

Koeksisters A popular Cape Coloured sweet snack, which is (sometimes) platted, made of deep fried sugary dough and then coated in honey and cinnamon.

Malva pudding A traditional caramelized Cape dessert made with apricot jam and sponge and usually served with custard. Many restaurants have this on the menu, and a twist is to soak the sponge in dessert wine.

Melktart A variation of a baked custard tart, with a biscuit shell and dusted with cinnamon. Popular at *braais* (after all the meat) and often served in cafés.

Potbrood A traditional yeasty bread cooked with honey in a cast-iron covered pot over the coals. Another accompaniment to a *braai*.

Potjiekos Stews cooked over coals in three-legged cast iron pots of the same name; they are thought to come from the Voortrekkers who hooked the pots under their wagons, and then heated them up over the fire at night.

great source of fresh fruit and vegetables, though some are seasonal so the price changes accordingly. Meat is generally significantly cheaper than in Europe. There are several large supermarket chains (Woolworths is always a good bet for quality fresh groceries) and most feature extensive counters for pre-prepared food, hot meals, pizzas, sandwiches and sushi. The region has plenty of farmers' markets for tasty homemade goodies, organic vegetables, wine and olives.

Braais

One of the first local terms you are likely to learn will be *braai*, which quite simply means barbecue. The *braai* is incredibly popular, part of the South African way of life, and every campsite, back garden and picnic spot has a *braai* pit. Given the excellent range of meat available, learning how to cook good food on a *braai* is an art that needs to be mastered quickly, especially if you are self-catering, and is part of the fun of eating in South Africa. Once you have established a core of heat using firelighters and wood or charcoal (charcoal is more eco-friendly and less smoky but wood makes for a wonderful fire), wrap up potatoes, sweet potatoes, squash, butternut, etc, in heavy-duty foil and cook them in the coals for an hour or so. Set beside a good piece of meat, with a sauce and a cold beer, and you will be living the South African dream. To check whether your *braai* is the right heat to cook on, hold your hand over the *braai* grill and count to 10. If you have to pull your hand back before 10 it's too hot, any later than 10 then it's too cold.

When & where to eat

Informal family restaurants are open all day from breakfast to late at night. The more formal specialist restaurants are generally open for lunch 1200-1500 and dinner from 1800. Kitchens usually close about 2200 but earlier in the smaller towns. The day begins with a healthy or traditional fry-up breakfast and leisurely brunches are popular at weekends. In smaller guesthouses you may be offered a more traditional South African breakfast of pap and *boerewors* or mince on toast. Exotic coffee accompanied by a muffin or pastry, is the norm mid-morning, and a lingering lunch on a wine estate on a sunny day is an unbeatable experience. Sundowners are popular – Camps Bay on the peninsula being the über cool spot for cocktails – but any bar overlooking the ocean will suffice. In a good restaurant it's always advisable to book dinner, and you can expect excellent service (waiting is a respectable job in South Africa) from staff who can talk you through the menu, reel off the specials and recommend wine. Additionally there may be the option to choose wine from the cellar, and at seafood restaurants select your platter from the chilled cabinet.

Restaurants are prolific, but hotspots in Cape Town include the area around Long and Kloof streets, the V&A Waterfront (there are over 80 places to eat here and they hold their own annual awards), Green Point and Sea Point, and all the shopping malls feature a number of restaurants. The five-star hotels are a good option for a special treat. Victoria Road in Camps Bay has a popular strip of restaurants, and around the Cape Peninsula

Tip...

A great starting point for choosing a restaurant is buying the latest edition of Eat Out (eatout. co.za), which features South Africa's best choice of restaurants and is available at CNA and Exclusive Books. Alternatively, dining-out.co.za provides hundreds of reviews and contact details of restaurants throughout the region.

are a number of excellent restaurants to stop at for lunch on a day tour, or dine in luxury at one of the Constantia estates. The Winelands has countless gourmet restaurants next to the vines where food is paired with wine, though few are open in the evening and booking for lunch is essential. Franschhoek is dubbed South Africa's 'gastronomic capital' thanks to its main street lined with French and nouveau cuisine eateries, which attract some of the world's best chefs. The Garden Route towns feature a good choice, often in historical hotels and Knysna is another celebrated culinary centre with top-class restaurants popular with wealthy local holidaymakers. The town is also famed for its oysters, which are cultivated in the lagoon. Along the coast, there are also affordable informal family restaurants, but even these usually offer seafood.

What the locals say

Where I eat seafood in Cape Town depends on what I feel like. You can't beat the tin pot of a kilo of steamed mussels at Den Anker or Chef Pon's prawns with chilli and basil, and Solly at Miller's Thumb cooks the most perfect seared tuna. For sushi, Tank is deservedly recommended, but the many cheap and cheerful Japanese- and Chinese-run spots around Sea Point can be equally as good.

Leanne Guild, Cape Town tour operator.

Tip...

The Southern African Sustainable Seafood Initiative (SASSI) (T079-499 8795, wwfsassi.co.za) has an SMS service that tells you whether the fish you are about to order is legal and sustainable (on the green list) or not (on the red list). SMS the name of the fish and the instant reply will tell you. Also look for the SASSI labels when buying fish.

Grapes from the Cape

White wine varieties

Cape Riesling (Crouchen Blanc)
A shy bearer which can produce quality white wines with a delicate yet fruity bouquet and sharp grassy aroma.

Chardonnay
A native of Burgundy, this variety is widely planted throughout the Cape Winelands. Locally, much experimentation has taken place with barrel fermentation and oak ageing, and excellent wines in a number of styles are being produced. It's also used in some of the base wines from which Cap Classique sparkling wines are made as well as in white blends.

Chenin Blanc (Steen)
The most widely cultivated variety in the Cape characterized by its versatility and fruitiness, Chenin Blanc produces good natural wines covering the whole spectrum from sweet to dry, as well as sherry and sparkling wine. It is also used for distilling brandy and spirits.

Colombar(d)
Planted in the Breede River region, this variety produces quality wines with a good acid content ensuring fresh, interesting and fruity flavours.

Gewürztraminer
A delicate aromatic flavour with an easily identifiable rose-petal fragrance, which is usually used to produce a light, off-dry wine.

Muscat d'Alexandrie (Hanepoot)
One of the world's most widely planted and versatile varieties, locally it was probably developed from 'Spaanse Dryven' (Spanish Grape) cuttings introduced to South Africa by Jan van Riebeeck in the 1650s. Nowhere else does it form such a high percentage of a country's total grape harvest as in South Africa, where it is used especially for dessert wine, as well as natural wine and raisins. Hanepoot delivers a strong, flowery bouquet and intense honey flavour.

Muscadel
Belonging to the Muscat family and used chiefly in dessert wines, this gives an intense, raisin-like bouquet and was historically associated with the famous Constantia dessert wines. Red and white grapes grow mainly in the Breede River region.

Nouvelle
This grape, a crossing of Semillon and Cape Riesling, was developed in South Africa by Stellenbosch University. While plantings remain tiny they are increasing, mainly for inclusion in blends.

Sauvignon Blanc
These wines have a distinctive green peppery or grassy character, and are often aged in wood (sometimes labelled Blanc Fumé). Extensively planted in the 18th century, South African Sauvignon Blanc is popular internationally.

Semillon
Produces a full yet subtle wine with little acid; often used in blends. Locally, some outstanding wooded varietal wines have been produced from this grape variety which once represented 93% of all Cape vines but now accounts for only about 1%.

Weisser Riesling (Rhine Riesling)
Produces very full, flavourful wines with excellent fruit acids that develop well with bottle ageing. Wines have a honeyed spicy nose and a flowery sweetness.

Red wine varieties

Cabernet Sauvignon
Grown across the Cape, it's also the foremost variety of the Bordeaux region of France, and produces full, spicy top-class wines that develop well with age. As in Bordeaux, it may be blended with Merlot.

Cinsaut
This can be used to blend with Cabernet to produce reasonably priced early drinking wines, or as quality wine for brandy distilling. It is also often used for rosé, port and jerepigo wines.

Gamay (Noir)
Mainly light red wines in the nouveau style are made of this grape in France's Beaujolais region. Several reds are made locally in a similar early drinking style.

Merlot
Traditionally used as a blending partner to add softness and breadth to Cabernet Sauvignon, this is now increasingly being bottled as a varietal wine, with some superb results. It's being planted in ever-increasing quantities, particularly around Stellenbosch and Paarl.

Pinot Noir
The king of Burgundy but notoriously difficult to grow elsewhere, though this variety is now producing excellent wines in the cooler viticultural areas of South Africa. Wines tend to be lighter in colour with earthy flavours and aromas. A large proportion is used in Cap Classique sparkling wines.

Pinotage
A local cross between Pinot Noir and Cinsaut, this variety is unique to South Africa, and can produce complex and fruity wines with age but is also often very drinkable when young. The 'Cape blend' is an evolving term which generally denotes a red blend with Pinotage as a component making up 30-70% of the wine.

Roobernet
A 1960s local cross between Cabernet Sauvignon and Pontac, it has an unusual (for reds) grassy character and withstands diseases particularly well. It can be made into a cultivar wine, also a good blending partner, particularly in combination with Pinotage for a uniquely South African blend.

Ruby Cabernet
A Californian cross between Carignan and Cabernet Sauvignon, this prolific producer is suited to warmer areas.

Shiraz
A noble variety of French origin, which is better known as Syrah elsewhere, this yields deep purple smoky and spicy wines, which develop a complex character with age.

Souzào
Originally from Portugal, this is one of the traditional port varieties. Its high fruit sugar content and strongly pigmented skin give taste and colour.

Tinta Barocca
Considered one of the best varieties for the production of port in South Africa, this produces earthy, organic red wines and is excellent for blending.

Entertainment

Bars & clubs

Most clubs get going around 2200 and at weekends stay open as late as 0400. The top end of Long Street features a number of popular bars and clubs with a youthful edge. Venues come and go, but pick up flyers in the cafés and waiting staff are always a good source of information. Clubs here tend to be a little grungy but are popular for dancing to hardcore house, Kwaito and trance music. Chrome and Hemisphere – the latter being 31 floors above the city – cater for a more sophisticated over 25s crowd. De Waterkant is where the gay and lesbian venues are, and the outside square in the Cape Quarter has a number of good restaurant/bars which open until late. The neon-lit 'strip' along Victoria Road in Camps Bay features many trendy restaurants and cocktail bars, where DJs entertain. Bars in five-star hotels are popular for after-work drinks and sundowners. The few British-style pubs offer homely pub grub and are principal venues for watching sport and are lively when important rugby matches are on. Central Stellenbosch has a good selection of nightlife for the young-at-heart thanks to the town's large student population. The towns along the Garden Route feature restaurant/bars catering to holidaymakers, Knysna has a few clubs and the Knysna Quays is a popular after-dark venue.

Live jazz at the Green Dolphin, V&A Waterfront.

Children

Children will enjoy attractions such as the Two Oceans Aquarium, which has kid's activities, and outdoor adventures like riding the cableway to the top of Table Mountain or seeing the penguins at Boulders Beach. The long promenade that stretches around Mouille Point and Sea Point is perfect for bracing family walks and features playgrounds, a mini-golf course, a maze, a kid's train, and the Sea Point open-air swimming pool. The Amphitheatre at the V&A Waterfront, and the Artscape and Baxter theatres often run children's events during the school holidays, and the Planetarium has shows specifically for five to 10 year-olds at the weekend. Around the Cape Peninsula and along the Garden Route are family-orientated beaches and teenagers may want to try surfing. On the peninsula, Imhoff Farm, which offers pony and camel rides, the World of Birds and the Cape Point Ostrich Farm will appeal.

Cinema

The two major cinema groups are Nu Metro (numetro.co.za), and Ster-Kinekor (sterkinekor.com). Multi-screen cinemas are found in the shopping malls including Century City, the V&A Waterfront and Cavendish Square. The latter two also have a separate Cinema Nouveau, which screens international and art-house films. For film festivals, see page 50. Cape Town's most enjoyable cinema, showing independent international films in a historic building that used to be a ballroom, is the Labia in Gardens. The cafe is licensed, so you can take your glass of wine into the movie. Cinemas are in the larger shopping malls along the Garden Route and Knysna has the independent Knysna Movie House.

Gay & lesbian

Cape Town is South Africa's pink capital, though Knysna too has a burgeoning scene and hosts the Pink Lourie Mardi Gras (see page 49). The Pink Map of Cape Town, available at the tourist offices, lists gay-friendly/oriented accommodation, restaurants and nightlife, tour operators, and even health spas and launderettes. There are a number of festivals on during the year (see page 48) and the in-spot for gay and lesbian bars and clubs is De Waterkant.

Music

Classical & opera
Artscape is the main venue where Cape Town Opera and the Cape Philharmonic Orchestra perform. The latter also occasionally plays in the City Hall to make use of its fine Edwardian organ. The University of Stellenbosch Symphony Orchestra plays at Endler Hall on the university campus, Kirstenbosch holds Sunday breakfasts with chamber music in winter, and there are rousing choral performances in St George's Cathedral. Traditional African music features in the tourist-orientated restaurants such as Mama Africa or Moyo in the Winelands.

Contemporary
The Kirstenbosch summer concert programme features concerts varying from rock and jazz to classical in an idyllic setting where you can picnic on the lawns. The Cape Town International Jazz Festival (see page 49) is a huge crowd puller, the Green Dolphin has nightly jazz accompanied by dinner, and there are many other lounge-style bars hosting live jazz. The Winchester Mansions Hotel has live jazz with brunch on Sundays. The clubs on Long Street occasionally have live music, but for local indie-rock and Kwaito bands head to Mercury Live & Lounge or The Assembly. Live bands also perform in bars in Stellenbosch and Knysna.

Theatre & dance
Cape Town City Ballet performs at Artscape and, during summer, at Maynardville Open-Air Theatre, which is also a venue for Shakespeare plays. Artscape and the Baxter Theatre have a year-round programme of plays, musicals and comedy. Cape Town's nicest theatre – the Theatre on the Bay in Camps Bay – has lovely designed 'curtain' architecture, and is well known for home-grown comedies and musicals. On Broadway is a popular gay-friendly dinner theatre, which hosts comedy and entertaining drag acts. The Spier Wine Estate sometimes has performances in its outdoor amphitheatre. The Knysna Playhouse is a venue for children's and adult theatre and music, as are the Barnyard theatres in Franschhoek, Mossel Bay and Plettenberg Bay.

Tip…

All tickets for events can be booked online at Computicket (computicket.com), which also has kiosks in the shopping malls and in Checkers supermarkets.

Shopping

Cape Town and the region is a shopper's Mecca and the giant shopping malls alone could consume days of your time. Every modern convenience, the latest fashion, South Africa's famed gold and diamond jewellery, and international brands are available and tourists have the added advantage of claiming the VAT back on items taken out of the country. There is a variety of quality souvenirs to choose from, as well as distinct African-inspired home decor items, and crafts and curios from across the African continent. Quality varies depending on where you buy from; the top-end shops and galleries will have the best pieces at a premium price, while the curio shops and markets have the lower-grade items but, as you long as you look over them carefully for flaws, you can often come away with a bargain.

In central Cape Town and in the region's towns, there is usually a string of South African chain shops along a main high street, but the best shops are usually found at out-of-town malls where you'll need a car. In Cape Town malls include the giant Canal Walk and Cavendish Square, as well as the numerous shops at Victoria Wharf at the V&A Waterfront. Elsewhere, Somerset Mall in Somerset West is the principal mall serving the Winelands, and the Garden Route Mall is on the N2 near Mossel Bay, but there are numerous others. These don't just feature shops, but banks, post offices, restaurants, cinemas and other entertainment. For food and drink, South Africa doesn't feature large open-air markets, but everything can be found under one roof in the supermarkets, and there are some

Tip...

Shops are open Monday to Friday 0900-1730, Saturday 0900-1300. The larger malls open every day and stay open much later; in Cape Town as late as 2100.

Above: Victoria Wharf shopping centre, Victoria & Alfred Waterfront.
Opposite page: A painter of recycled cans in Khayelitsha township.

specialist markets throughout the region. Wine can be bought directly from the estates, or from specialist wine shops who can give advice and can arrange international shipping. Clothes vary from international luxury brands like Burberry or Jimmy Choo in Victoria Wharf's Fashion Mall, to home-grown South African designers for contemporary and African-inspired clothes, and standard chain stores (Woolworths is well regarded for its quality clothing and food; it's very similar to the UK's Marks & Spencer). South Africa is well known for its quality diamonds and gold (the Clock Tower at the V&A Waterfront has a clutch of world-class jewellers) and investing in these means the VAT reclaim (see below) can be quite considerable.

Tip...

All prices are fixed. The exception is the curio markets, which usually feature traders from all over Africa and you are just as likely to hear Portuguese, Kiswahili, Hausa or French spoken as English. A bout of good-humoured haggling is expected.

Souvenirs

Items to look out for in the region's shops and markets include wire and beadwork sculptures and accessories and crafts made from recycled items, many of which are made by township cooperatives. There are also wooden carvings (often animals), masks, statues and the like, many of which come from East and West Africa, textiles including batiks and West African cloth, paintings of African village scenes or animals, and decorated ostrich eggs. The top-end galleries sell valuable African artworks and there are many talented South African artists and sculptors. Books too make a good souvenir, and there are numerous coffee-table books full of photographs of South Africa's evocative scenery and wildlife. The national chain Exclusive Books carries the best range. African music can be found in the national chain Musica, or speciality shops like The African Music Store (see page 131) on Long Street in Cape Town.

VAT refunds

Tourists can reclaim the 14% VAT on purchases bought in South Africa whose total value exceeds R250. You can do this when departing, at the VAT reclaim desks at airports in Johannesburg and Cape Town. Refunds are given by cheque in South African rand, which can be paid into home bank accounts (or at the airports cashed for rand at the bureaux de change). Goods need to be shown to the refund officer as proof of purchase with VAT receipts, so be sure to ask for these when you buy something, and at the airport this needs to be done before you check in your luggage. Refunds only apply to items taken out of the country and not on services rendered, such as accommodation or goods consumed or used within the country. For example, if you are buying clothes, keep the shop tags on them to prove that you haven't worn them in South Africa and you'll get the tax back. You can also go to the pre-processing office at the Clock Tower at the V&A Waterfront, where you will be required to submit all the receipts to be checked off against goods you will be exporting from South Africa, as well as presenting your passport and air ticket. They will stamp your receipts for verification but cannot give out refunds. This still has to be done at the airport on departure. For more information visit taxrefunds.co.za.

Activities & tours

Adventure tours

There are numerous adventure or adrenalin activities in the region. The fearless can try abseiling off Table Mountain or the highest bungee jump (216 m) in the world at the Bloukrans River Bridge between Plettenberg Bay and Tsitsikamma National Park, where there is also a cable slide across the gorge. In Cape Town, Downhill Adventures (see page 133) is an established operator that organizes a number of activities for the active, including sand-boarding and mountain biking. Other operators arrange kloofing, or canyoning, which involves hiking, boulder-hopping and swimming along mountain rivers. One of the most popular kloofing trips is to the Kamikaze Kanyon in the mountains above Gordon's Bay just outside Cape Town. Paragliding can be tried off Lion's Head or from Wilderness on the Garden Route. The Cape's strong winds have made it a very popular site for kiteboarding. The best spot is Dolphin Beach at Table View, north of the city centre where winds are strong and waves perfect for jumping.

Birdwatching

With over 700 species of bird recorded in South Africa, birdwatching has become a popular pastime that is easily combined with hiking. The Western

Cape offers excellent opportunities and enthusiasts will find a variety of reserves. Habitats include coastal fynbos, forest and wetlands and long stretches of rocky and sandy shoreline. Endemics seen in the Table Mountain National Park and Kirstenbosch include the Cape sugarbird, orange-breasted sunbird and Cape siskin. The rare Hottentot button-quail and Knysna warbler are also present. Due to the warm Agulhas current and the cold Benguela current meeting just offshore of the Cape, a great upwelling is formed creating a feeding ground for many seabirds. At least 20 pelagic species have been recorded on the coast including three species of albatross.

Above: Kitesurfing in front of Table Bay. Opposite page: The orange-breasted sunbird.

Boat tours

There are numerous boat trips in the region from a short water taxi across the V&A Waterfront to houseboat holidays on the Knysna lagoon. In Cape Town, from the V&A Waterfront, there are more than 20 boats of varying types and sizes operating from Quay 5, the Pierhead or the Clock Tower. You can choose from a sail on a schooner to Camps Bay, a guided tour of the working harbour, a sunset cruise with champagne, or a fast inflatable jet boat ride. There are short daily tours from Hout Bay Harbour to see the seals on Duiker Island, and boat tours from Simon's Town around the harbour area, which include a special visit to the naval dockyard, and longer trips to Seal Island and Cape Point. There are all manner of boating excursions available along the Garden Route. All the towns offer whale- and dolphin-watching excursions, as well as deep-sea fishing, and in some, shark cage diving trips, and on the lagoons and wetlands rowing boats and canoes can be rented. The Knysna Lagoon can be explored

by yacht, paddle boat, houseboat and the popular ferry that crosses the lagoon to the Featherbed Nature Reserve. Fishing is popular along the coast and the most common catches are mako shark, long-fin tuna and yellowtail, but there are strict rules governing all types of fishing. The simplest way of dealing with permits and regulations is through a charter company.

Cultural tours

With its wealth of history, Cape Town has a number of museums and historical buildings and these can be explored on a leisurely walk around the city centre or on a guided tour. There are many tour operators that can organize day tours around the Cape Peninsula and to the Winelands and the standard of guiding is very high in South Africa so these should be considered if you don't want to self-drive. The region's Apartheid history can be explored from the excursion to Robben Island, at

About the region

the District Six Museum, and by taking an informative tour to the townships on the Cape Flats, which give an insight into how segregation divided communities and the reality of living in the townships today. Elsewhere walking tours can be arranged in historic Stellenbosch, and a visit to Mossel Bay's Bartolomeu Dias Museum Complex is a good place to learn about the coast's maritime history.

Cycling

Cape Town is well equipped for mountain bikers and tour operators rent out mountain bikes and equipment and arrange mountain-biking

excursions, including the popular Table Mountain double descent (90% downhill). Some organize day tours from Cape Town to both the Cape Peninsula and the Winelands and take bikes for an hour or two of cycling. Many nature reserves and wilderness areas along the Garden Route have increased their accessibility for mountain bikes, with some excellent routes suitable for all levels of fitness, and in particular there are some excellent trails in the forests around Knysna and guided trips are on offer. Bikes can be hired in the Winelands for leisurely rides around the wine estates. The Cape Argus Pick 'n' Pay Cycle Tour (see page 48) is the biggest cycling event in South Africa and is open to international participants.

Bike riding on Signal Hill.

Diving

The convergence of two major ocean
environments provides the coast with a particularly
rich and diverse marine flora and fauna. The
Agulhas current continually sweeps warm
water down from the subtropical Indian Ocean
and meets the cold nutrient-rich waters of the
Atlantic, creating a marvellous selection of marine
ecosystems. The Cape waters are cold but are
often very clear and good for wreck and kelp
diving. The sea life is prolific and the sighting
of playful and inquisitive seals and shy sharks
(dogfish) is common. The best season for diving
is during the winter months when the weather
ensures the sea is flat as the prevailing winds
blow offshore. Water temperatures are 12-18°C;
visibility is usually 5-10 m. When the winds
change direction in the summer months visibility
can be reduced to almost zero. A number of dive
companies also specialize in great white shark
cage dives (see page 135). Knysna has a good
wreck dive and Plettenberg Bay has soft coral
reefs and a sheltered location. Home to dolphins
and seals, the bay also acts as a nursery to the
endangered southern right whales, which come to
calve in winter and spring (July-November). If the
Cape waters are too cold, you can dive in the tanks
of the Two Oceans Aquarium (page 106), at the V&A
Waterfront. The tank is surprisingly large, with
inquisitive ragged-tooth sharks, stingrays, turtles
and large predator fish.

Historic vineyards in the Constantia Valley.

Food & wine

Capetonians are unashamed foodies and apart
from a staggering array of excellent restaurants,
there are a number of food and wine festivals
throughout the year (see page 48). The city and the
smaller towns regularly feature deli's and farmers'
markets selling the likes of cheese, olives, olive oil,
chutneys and relishes all produced locally. The
Winelands is South Africa's oldest and most

beautiful wine-producing area and the most
popular tourist destination in the province after
Cape Town itself. There are several wine routes
criss-crossing the valleys, visiting hundreds of wine
estates, which open their doors for tastings, cellar
tours and sales. Many of them offer picnic baskets
to enjoy among the vines or feature gourmet
restaurants offering the experience of pairing wine
with food. Some also have luxury hotels in restored
estate buildings. Also check out Footprint's *Wine
Travel Guide to the World.*

About the region

Hiking

There are an enormous number of well-developed hiking trails in the region, many passing through areas of spectacular natural beauty. These range from pleasant afternoon strolls through nature reserves to challenging hikes in wilderness areas. In Cape Town you can climb from the city up Table Mountain and there are coastal trails around the Cape Peninsula. Along the Garden Route the Wilderness and Tsitsikamma national parks are ideal for short hikes. There are also a number of longer overnight trails along the coast, such as the famous Otter Trail (see page 251), which need to be booked months in advance as there is a maximum number of hikers permitted. A new initiative in South Africa is 'slack-packing' when hikers' luggage is transported ahead, and meals and overnights in hotels are included.

Spectator sports

South Africans are avid rugby, cricket and football watchers and the national teams are internationally acclaimed and since re-entering the international arena after being banned during Apartheid have had some resounding successes. In the southern suburb of Newlands is the famous Sahara Park Cape Town Test Match Ground. Despite considerable redevelopment, a few of the famous old oak trees remain and it is still possible to watch a game of cricket from a grassy bank with Table Mountain as a backdrop. Some of the public seats are very exposed – wear a hat and have plenty of sun cream to hand. International rugby games are played at the Western Province Rugby Football Union ground, also in Newlands, and like the cricket ground this has some spectacular views of the eastern side of Table Mountain. Avid sports fans can take tours of both the cricket ground and the rugby stadium (where they can run through the tunnel), see page 111. The 2010 FIFA South Africa World Cup™ matches allocated to Cape Town will be played in the new Green Point Stadium (see page 98).

Surfing

South Africa has quickly established itself as a major surfing hotspot and has some of the best waves in the world. There are, however, two drawbacks to surfing in South Africa. Firstly, the water is cold, especially around the Cape, and full-length wetsuits are generally essential. Second, there is a small risk of shark attack – but remember that attacks on surfers are very rare. Wherever you surf, be sure to listen to local advice, vital not just for safety but also for learning about the best surf spots. Cape Town has an ever-expanding surfing community with some excellent, reliable breaks on the Atlantic and False Bay beaches, but the whole southern coast is in fact dotted with good breaks. The many backpacker hostels along the coast are geared up for board rental, escorted surfaris and surfing lessons, and there are dedicated surf schools in Cape Town. Jeffrey's Bay – or J-Bay – on the south coast of the Eastern Cape and at the end of the Garden Route, is undoubtedly South Africa's surfing hotspot, known for its consistently good surf and host to the annual Billabong surf championships in July. This is also a good place to learn to surf, with a number of courses available and areas of reliable, small breaks perfect for beginners. Also check out Footprint's *Surfing the World*.

Swimming

The beaches on the Atlantic seaboard are almost always too cold to swim in – even during the hottest months the water temperatures rarely creep above 16°C. Camps Bay has a tidal pool and shady, grassy areas. Noordhoek is too rough for swimming, but is a great place for kite-flying or a horse ride. The beaches on the False Bay side of the Cape Peninsula are always a good 5°C warmer, and are perfectly pleasant for a dip during summer. Additionally, a number of beaches have artificial rock pools built by the water, which although rather murky can be perfect for paddling children. Sea Point Swimming Pool (see page 99), an outdoor

Surfer in Jeffrey's Bay.

Olympic-sized pool, is in a superb location and is built right on the rocks next to the ocean with glorious mountain and sea views. Water temperatures at beaches along the Garden Route are a comfortable 22°C in summer and there are plenty of sandy sheltered bays.

Wellbeing

Spas are big business in South Africa and they are just about mandatory in every luxury hotel in Cape Town, the Winelands and along the Garden Route. Many are internationally acclaimed and award winning; the Sanctuary Spa at the Twelve Apostles Hotel has won the World Travel Award as Leading Spa Resort in Africa. Most feature luxurious facilities like

hydrotherapy and treatment rooms, swimming pools and gyms. Some are in superb locations; many in the Winelands overlook the vines where there is the possibility of having a massage under an oak tree with a glass of wine. Visiting a spa is popular with men, and many offer specialized male treatments and double treatment rooms for couples.

Safari experiences

Aquila Private Game Reserve
Off the R46 south of Touws River, T021-431 8400,
aquilasafari.com.
Departs Cape Town at 0600, breakfast then a 3-hr game
drive, followed by a buffet lunch and return to Cape
Town, ℞1830 per person, ℞1100 if you're in your own car.

Set among 4500 ha of mountains, rivers, valleys and
kloofs which make up the southern Karoo highlands, this
is home to a wide range of species including lion, giraffe,
elephant, rhino, buffalo, black and blue wildebeest,
zebra, a variety of antelope, bat-eared fox, mountain
leopard, crocodile, ostrich, black-backed jackal and
hippo. It has the largest breeding herd of white rhino
in the Cape and, in February 2005, the first white rhino
was born at the reserve, thought to be the first rhino
born in the Cape for over 200 years. Aquila also has a
huge natural wetland, which is home to 172 species of
bird including several breeding pairs of the rare and
endangered black eagle. There is luxury accommodation
on the reserve, you can visit on a day safari, which
includes transfers from Cape Town, and other options
are horseback or quad-bike safaris.

Garden Route Game Lodge
7 km east of Albertinia off the N2, T028-735 1200,
grgamelodge.co.za.
Day visitors 0730-1630, 2-hr game drives 1100 and 1400,
℞350 per person.

This private game reserve has been stocked with a
number of species of large game including giraffe,
white rhino, lion, elephant, kudu, zebra, wildebeest and
buffalo. It's a popular overnight stay from Cape Town
in a convenient location off the N2 on the way to the
Garden Route. There is luxurious accommodation at the

Left: Giraffe at Garden Route Game Lodge.
Above: Kagga Kamma Private Game Reserve.
Opposite page: Plettenberg Bay Game Reserve.

lodge but day visitors are also welcome for game drives, which must be pre-booked, and lunch in the à la carte restaurant. As well as game drives, tours of the reptile centre are on offer where the resident herpetologist will share his knowledge of snakes, crocodiles and other cold-blooded creatures. You can also visit the cheetah-breeding centre.

Inverdoorn Game Reserve
Off the R356 north of Touws River,
T021-434 4639, inverdoorn.com.
Day tours include 2- to 3-hr game drive and lunch, ₱795 (children under 11 half price).

This is a private 10,000-ha game reserve specializing in 4WD game safaris to view its range of wildlife, which includes lion, rhino, buffalo, giraffe, zebra, wildebeest, eland, kudu and impala. There are wild cheetah, and also a breeding and rehabilitation centre where visitors can get close to the cats. The area is a typical Karoo landscape and quite beautiful to drive around, and is good for birdwatching, especially for raptors and vultures. Other activities on offer include hikes to San rock art, fishing and mountain biking. Accommodation is in a luxury lodge or visit for the day.

Kagga Kamma Private Game Reserve
Off the R303 north of Prince Alfred Hamlet,
T021-872 4343, kaggakamma.co.za.
Day trips include a rock art tour, guided quad-bike safari and lunch, ₱995 (Sep-Apr), ₱735 (May-Aug), per person.

This is on the fringe of the Cederberg Mountains north of Cape Town, and is a nature reserve devoted to the history of the San people, and the remarkable rocky landscape is dotted with their ancient rock art. The area is one of outstanding natural beauty and the best way of exploring

it is on foot. Resident anthropologists accompany visitors to rock art sites to explain their meaning, and are also very knowledgeable about the traditions, lifestyle and beliefs of the San. It is possible to go on game drives and quad-bike safaris in the reserve, which has a good variety of antelope including eland, gemsbok, bontebok, springbok and kudu. There are also lynx, caracal and leopard, but these are very elusive. Accommodation is in luxury cave suites hidden in the rocks or you can visit for the day.

Plettenberg Bay Private Game Reserve
12 km from Plett off the N2 on the R340,
T044-535 0000, rhinobasecamp.co.za.
2-hr game drives May-Sep 1100 and 1500, Oct-Apr 0830, 1000, 1100, 1230, 1500 and 1600, ₱345, children (under 12) ₱95; 2-hr horse safaris 1000 and 1500, ₱345 per person.

This is located on 2200 ha spread across the hills above the Garden Route coastline with good views of Plettenberg Bay and offers open 4WD safaris or guided horseback trails. The reserve boasts a diversity of natural biomes, including fynbos, grasslands and indigenous forests, and on the property is the natural confluence of the Keurbooms and Palmiet rivers. The reserve has been stocked with over 35 species of game, including lion, rhino, giraffe, hippo, crocodile, buffalo and a large variety of antelope; 101 species of bird have also been recorded. Accommodation is in a luxury lodge or visit for a game drive followed by a drink and light meal in the bar.

Contents

Cape Town

The sheer cliffs of Table Mountain.

Introduction

What to see in…

…one day
Start the day with ascent of **Table Mountain**, by foot or take the **Aerial Cableway**, and from the top get a grasp of the layout of Cape Town. Head to the **Two Oceans Aquarium** at the V&A Waterfront, then take the ferry to **Robben Island**. In the evening, enjoy an African eating experience at **Africa Café**, **Mama Africa** or **Marco's African Place**.

entral Cape Town is divided into a number of suburbs, each with its own character and atmosphere offering varied attractions to the visitor. The oldest part dating to the 1600s is the historical core around Company's Garden and the castle, while on the lower slopes of Signal Hill is the district of 17th-century artisan houses known as Bo-Kaap. Originally home to freed slaves, this remains a testimony of how slaves contributed greatly to the growth of Cape Town. Ringing the city are the pretty Victorian suburbs on the lower slopes of Table Mountain, from where there are jaw-dropping views of Table Bay, surpassed only by the incredible view from the top of the mountain itself. On the eastern slopes are the beautiful gardens at Kirstenbosch and, nestled beneath, the upmarket southern suburbs with their fine sandstone mansions and leafy gardens. The city's clutch of gleaming modern skyscrapers overlooking the busy working harbour are evidence of its prosperity in modern times, while the dazzling white luxury apartment blocks and hotels crowded on the lower slopes of Lion's Head in Green Point and Sea Point are proof of what a desirable place Cape Town is to live in and visit.

…a weekend or more
Visit the excellent museums around **Company's Garden** and in the **Castle of Good Hope**, or head for the shops and markets around quirky **Long Street**. Learn about Apartheid at the **District Six Museum** and on a township tour, and enjoy the peaceful gardens and sweeping views in lovely **Kirstenbosch**. Hit the shops in a giant mega-mall: **Victoria Wharf** or **Canal Walk**.

Victorian houses in Oranjezicht.

Essentials

❷ Getting around

On foot Cape Town's historical and commercial centre is concentrated in a small area and is easily explored on foot. Guided walking tours (see page 134) from Cape Town Tourism are also on offer. The V&A Waterfront and the promenade along Mouille Point and Sea Point are ideal for a stroll. The fit can walk up Table Mountain (see page 93).

By bus City Sightseeing Cape Town (T021-511 6000, citysightseeing.co.za, daily from 0830) are red, double-decker, open-top, hop-on hop-off buses. There are two routes; the Red Route has 13 stops and a bus comes by every 20 minutes, while the Blue Route has 13 stops and buses come by every 50 minutes. Audio-commentary is available in eight languages and there's a special kids' channel. The main ticket kiosk is outside the Two Oceans Aquarium at the V&A Waterfront, or buy tickets online and join anywhere on the routes. Stops include the Lower Cableway Station, Camps Bay, Kirstenbosch, all the city centre museums, and as far south as Hout Bay on the peninsula. A one-day ticket costs R120, children R60, and a two-day ticket is R200/R120. The buses are wheelchair friendly.

Integrated Bus Systems are being laid out along some main roads in Cape Town in line with requirements for the 2010 FIFA South Africa World Cup™. The first phase will be operational by 2010 when routes will link the airport and the West Coast suburbs with the city centre. Transport will be in large (bendy-like) buses in dedicated traffic lanes with stations, and will operate in a similar way to trams or light railways. Meanwhile, **Golden Arrow** buses depart from the city's bus station and follow major routes where bus stops are clearly denoted. Fares are from R4 for a short distance. Minibus taxis also ply the main roads and can be flagged

Below: City Sightseeing Bus. Opposite page: Rikki Taxi.

down, and while there is the danger of petty crime on the crowded vehicles, they can be used with caution and are cheap at around R4 for a short ride.

By taxi There are several ranks in the city centre including the train station, Greenmarket Square and Long Street. Elsewhere, call one in advance or ask your hotel or restaurant to do so. **Rikki Taxis** (T0861-745547, rikkis.co.za), buzz all over Cape Town. Shared people-carriers in London black cabs, they are cheaper than regular taxis, as they pick up other people along the route. Operating 24 hours, costs vary from R20 to R35 depending on the distance, and there are more than 20 Rikki free phones at some backpacker hostels, supermarkets and petrol stations. If you see one in the street, you can flag it down.

By train Cape Town has a network of metro commuter trains, run by **Cape Metrorail** (T0800-656463, capemetrorail.co.za) linking the suburbs/townships to the business districts. These trains are fine to use in rush hour (0700-0800 and 1600-1800), but are best avoided at quieter times due to safety issues and avoid the routes to the east, which pass through the Cape Flats. The exception is the route from the city to Simon's Town on the Cape Peninsula, which is marketed as a tourist route known as the **Southern Line** (page 172).

⊖ Bus station
Golden Arrow buses (T021-937 8800, gabs.co.za) depart from the bus station (0600-1900) next to the Grand Parade.

⊖ Train station
On the corner of Adderley and Strand streets; it's currently being refurbished. Metrorail (see above) and the long-distance rail services (see page 272) depart from here, as do long-distance buses (see pages 135 and 273).

⊖ ATM
Cash machines are available throughout the city at banks, shopping malls and petrol stations.

⊕ Hospital
Both the following private hospitals have emergency facilities (24-hr): **Netcare Christiaan Barnard Memorial Hospital** (181 Longmarket St, T021-480 6111), and **Cape Town Medi-clinic** (21 Hof St, Gardens, T021-464 5500, capetownmc.co.za).

⟳ Post office
The main post office is on Plein Street (T021-464 1754, sapo.co.za) and post offices are found in the shopping malls. There's a store locater on the website.

⊕ Tourist information
The main branch of **Cape Town Tourism** (The Pinnacle, corner of Burg and Castle streets, T021-487 6800, tourismcapetown.co.za, Mon-Fri 0800-1900, Sat 0830-1400, Sun 0900-1300, closes 1 hr earlier Apr-Sep) is an excellent source of information, and has a café, gift shop and internet access. There's also a desk for reservations in **South Africa National Parks** (sanparks.org). There are 18 other branches/ desks throughout the Cape, the most useful of which is at the Clock Tower at the V&A Waterfront (T021-405 4500, daily 0900-2100).

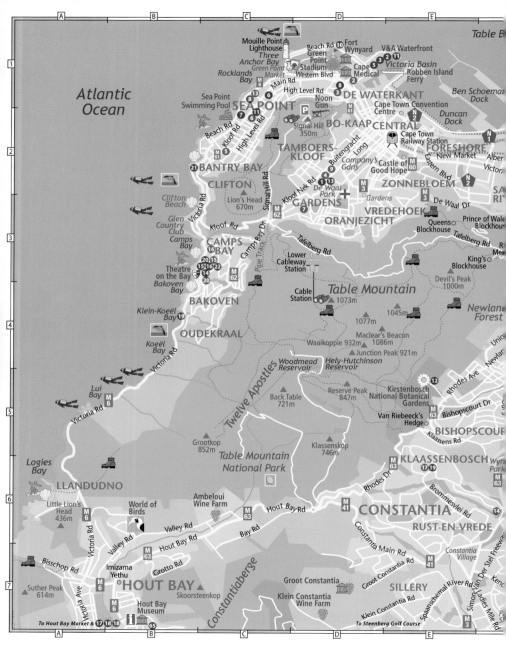

Cape Town listings

Sleeping
1 Andros *Corner Phyllis and Newlands roads* F5
2 Breakwater Lodge *Portswood Rd* D1
3 Brenwin Guest House *1 Thornhill Rd* D1
4 Cape Cadogan *5 Upper Union St* D2
5 Clarendon *67 Kloof Rd* C2
6 Glen *3 The Glen* C2
7 Kensington Place *38 Kensington Gardens* D3
8 Le Vendôme *20 London Rd* C2
9 Leeuwenvoet House *93 New Church St* D2
10 Radisson Blu *Beach Rd* D1
11 Table Bay *Quay 6* E1
12 Vineyard Hotel & Spa *Colinton Rd* F5
13 Winchester Mansions *221 Beach Rd* C2

From Cape Peninsula chapter (see page 160)
14 Alphen Hotel *Alphen Dr* F6
15 Bay *Victoria Rd* C3
16 Bay Atlantic Guest House *3 Berkley Rd* C3
17 Cellars-Hohenhort Hotel *93 Brommersvlei Rd* E6
18 Tintswalo Atlantic *2 km south of Hout Bay, off Chapman's Peak Dr* B7
19 Twelve Apostles *Victoria Rd* B4
20 Whale Cottage Guest House *57 Camps Bay Dr* C4

Eating & drinking
1 Arnold's *60 Kloof St* D2
2 Baia *Victoria Wharf* E1
3 Balducci's *Victoria Wharf* D1
4 Barristers Grill *Corner of Kildare and Main streets* F4
5 Belthazar *Victoria Wharf* D1
6 Café Erté *265 Main Rd* C1
7 La Perla *Corner of Church and Beach roads* C2
8 Miss K Food Café *65 Main Rd* D1
9 Myoga *Vineyard Hotel* F5
10 Obz Café *115 Lower Main Rd* G3
11 Posticino *323 Main Rd* C2
12 Silver Tree *Kirstenbosch National Botanical Gardens* E5
13 Yindee's *22 Camp St* D2

From Cape Peninsula chapter (see page 164)
14 Blues *Victoria Rd* C3
15 Codfather *Corner of Geneva Dr and The Drive* C3
16 Dizzy Jazz Café *41 The Drive* C3
17 Dunes *Hout Bay Beach* A7
18 Fish on the Rocks *Harbour Rd (beyond Snoekies Market)* B7
19 Greenhouse at Cellars *93 Brommersulei Rd* E5
20 Ocean Blue *Victoria Rd* C3
21 Salt *34 Victoria Rd* B2
22 Tuscany Beach *41 Victoria Rd* C3

City Bowl

From the Table Mountain Lower Cableway Station, you look out over the central residential suburbs of Tamboerskloof (Drummers' Ravine), Gardens, Oranjezicht (Orange View) and Vredehoek (Peaceful Corner). Together these form the City Bowl, a term inspired by the surrounding mountains. Closest to the mountain is Oranjezicht, a quiet district that was, up until 1900, a farm of the same name. On the boundary with Gardens, are the De Waal Park and Molteno Reservoir, originally built as a main water storage facility for the city in 1881, which now provides a peaceful wooded spot to enjoy a view of the city. In Vredehoek, the De Waal Drive (M3) brings rush-hour traffic into the top end of town from the southern suburbs and beyond, and this was the area in which many Jewish immigrants from Eastern Europe settled. Gardens is a lively neighbourhood with a choice of quality restaurants and guesthouses. Government Avenue is a delightful pedestrian route past Company's Garden and many of the city's main museums. This was the area where the Dutch East India Company first created fruit and vegetable gardens.

High-rises in the Central Business District (CBD).

South Africa Museum

25 Queen Victoria St, T021-481 3800, iziko org.za.
Open 1000-1700, ₨15, under 16s free,
free on public holidays, shop and café.
The City Sightseeing bus stops here.
Map: Central Cape Town, A5, p102.

This, the city's most established museum,
specializes in natural history, ethnography and
archaeology, and is a good place to take children.
There are extensive displays of the flora and fauna
of southern Africa, including the popular Whale
Well and interactive Shark World area, but the
highlight is the 'IQe – the Power of Rock Art'
exhibition. The exhibits focus on the significance
and symbolism of San rock art, and themes
explored include rainmaking and the significance
of animal imagery; the eland, for example, appears
more often than any other animal in San rock art,
and it holds a central role in all major rituals. There
is also a small display of pieces recovered from
Great Zimbabwe that illustrate its importance as
a trade centre – there are beads from Cambay, in
India, Chinese celadon ware, 13th-century Persian
pottery and Syrian glass from the 14th century.
The Stone Bones is an exhibition about the
fossilized skeletons found in the Karoo, which
date back 250 million years – predating dinosaurs.
There are life-sized reproductions of the reptile-like
creatures, including walk-around dioramas and
examples of the actual fossils.

Planetarium

Next door to the museum (see above),
T021-481 3900, iziko.org.za.
Show times vary depending on what's on;
check the website, ₨20, children ₨6,
adult chaperones at children's shows ₨10.
Map: Central Cape Town, A5, p102.

Presentations change every few months, but
usually a view of the current night sky is shown and
visitors receive a star map to find the constellations
and planets that are visible each month. Shows last
an hour and are fascinating. Children (aged 5-10)

Tip...

Every year in spring the South Africa Museum hosts
the excellent BBC Wildlife Photographer of the Year
exhibition. Contact the museum for exact dates.

will enjoy the Davy the Dragon show, which sends
Davy off into space to learn how to be the best
flying dragon ever.

Bertram House

Corner of Government Av and Orange St,
T021-424 9381, iziko.org.za.
Mon, Wed and Fri 1000-1700, entry by donation.
The City Sightseeing bus stops on Orange St.
Map: Central Cape Town, A5, p102.

This early 19th-century red-brick Georgian house
has a distinctly English feel to it. The building
houses a collection of porcelain, jewellery, silver
and English furniture, the majority of which was
bequeathed by Winifred Ann Lidderdale, an
important civic figure in Cape Town in the 1950s.
It was her desire to establish a house museum to
commemorate the British contribution to life at the
Cape. Downstairs the two drawing rooms contain
all the trappings of a bygone elegant age – card
tables, a Hepplewhite sofa, a square piano and
a fine harp. Three rooms have wallpaper from
London, a very expensive luxury for the period.

Jewish Museum

188 Hatfield St, T021-465 1546,
sajewishmuseum.co.za.
Sun-Thu 1000-1700, Fri 1000-1400, closed on
Jewish and public holidays, ₨35, children ₨15.
The City Sightseeing bus stops here.
Map: Central Cape Town, A6, p102.

Inside this excellent, contemporary museum is
a rich and rare collection of items depicting the
history of the Cape Town Hebrew congregation.
In 1841, 17 Jewish men assembled for the first time
in Cape Town to celebrate Yom Kippur. At the
meeting they set about the task of raising funds to

It's a fact...

Most museums are managed by Iziko Museums of Cape Town. Iziko in isiXhosa means 'hearth', which in a typical African homestead is the central place of activity and gathering. The word is used for the museums to represent a central place of a gathering together of South Africa's heritage.

Above: South African National Gallery.
Opposite page: Statue in Company's Garden.

build a synagogue, and in 1862 the foundation stone was laid for the first synagogue in Southern Africa. The following year the building was completed and furnished – quite a feat for such a small community at the time. On display upstairs are bronze Sabbath oil lamps, Chanukkah lamps, Bessamin spice containers, Torah scrolls, Kiddush cups and candlesticks. There is a beautiful stained-glass window depicting the Ten Commandments in Hebrew. From here a glass corridor leads you to a newer section of the museum that is devoted to the history of Jewish immigration to the Cape, mainly from Lithuania. A lot of thought has been put into the displays, which include photographs, immigration certificates, videos and a full reconstruction of a Lithuanian *shtetl*, or village. There are special displays outlining the stories of famous Jewish South Africans, including Helen Suzman, a former politician and anti-Apartheid activist. The museum complex also houses a library, café and bookshop.

Holocaust Centre

88 Hatfield St, T021-462 5553, ctholocaust.co.za. Sun-Thu 1000-1700, Fri 1000-1300, entry by donation. Next door to the Jewish Museum (see page 83).
Map: Central Cape Town, A6, p102.

This is an intelligent and shocking examination of the Holocaust and exhibits follow a historical route, starting with a look at anti-Semitism in Europe in previous centuries, and then leading to the rise of Nazism in Germany, the creation of ghettos, death camps and the Final Solution, and liberation at the end of the war. Video footage, photography, examples of Nazi propaganda and personal accounts of the Holocaust produce a vividly haunting and shocking display. The exhibits cleverly acknowledge South Africa's emergence from Apartheid and draw parallels between both injustices, as well as looking at the link between South Africa's Greyshirts (who were later assimilated into the National Party) and the Nazis. The local context is highlighted further at the end of the exhibition, with video accounts of Jews who survived the Holocaust and moved to Cape Town.

National Gallery

Government Av, T021-467 4660, iziko.org.za. Tue-Sun 1000-1700, R15, under 16s free. The City Sightseeing bus stops at the South African Museum, a couple of mins' walk away.
Map: Central Cape Town, B5, p102.

The National Gallery houses a permanent collection but also hosts some excellent temporary exhibitions that include the best of the country's contemporary art. The original collection was bequeathed to the nation in 1871 by Thomas Butterworth Bailey, and features a collection of 18th- and 19th-century British sporting scenes, portraits and Dutch paintings. Far more interesting are the changing exhibitions of contemporary South African art and photography. Check the website to see what's on. There's a good souvenir shop on site.

Rust en Vreugd

78 Buitenkant St, T021-464 3280, iziko.org.za.
Tue-Thu 1000-1700, entry by donation.
The City Sightseeing bus stops at the District
Six Museum, which is a 5-min walk away on
Buitenkant St.
Map: Central Cape Town, B6, p102.

A few hundred metres east of the National
Gallery, hidden behind a high whitewashed wall,
is this 18th-century mansion. It was declared
a historical monument in 1940, and was
subsequently restored to its original finery.
It houses six galleries displaying a collection
of watercolours, engravings and lithographs
depicting the history of the Cape. Of particular
note are Schouten's watercolour of van Riebeeck's
earth fort (1658), watercolours by Thomas Baines
of climbing Table Mountain, lithographs of Khoi
and Zulus by Angas, and a collection of cartoons
by Cruikshank depicting the first British settlers
arriving in the Cape.

Company's Garden

Government Av.
Open 0700-1900, closes 1800 Jun-Aug.
Walk from Adderley or Orange streets, the City
Sightseeing bus stops at St George's Cathedral,
the museums and Orange St.
Map: Central Cape Town, B5, p102.

Across Orange Street from the entrance to the
Mount Nelson Hotel is the top end of Government
Avenue, a delightful pedestrian route past many of
the city's main museums. Originally sheltered by
lemon trees, it is now lined with oaks and myrtle
hedges, and is one of Cape Town's most popular

Tip...

Parking for all the sights in and around Company's
Garden, can be found on and around Queen Victoria
St and Buitenkant St or there is a multi-storey car
park in Mandela Rhodes Place on the corner of
Adderley and Wale streets.

The grey squirrels living amongst the oak trees were introduced from America by Cecil Rhodes.

walks. It was declared a national monument in 1937. Running alongside Government Avenue are the peaceful Company's Garden, situated on the site of Jan van Riebeeck's original vegetable garden, which was created in 1652 to grow produce for settlers and ships bound for the East. It is now a small botanical garden, with lawns, a variety of labelled trees, ponds filled with Japanese koi and a small aviary. The grey squirrels living amongst the oak trees were introduced from America by Cecil Rhodes. There are also a couple of statues here: opposite the South African Public Library at the lower end of the garden, is the oldest statue in Cape Town, that of Sir George Grey, governor of the Cape from 1854 to 1862. Close by is a statue of Cecil Rhodes, pointing northwards in a rather unfortunate flat-handed gesture, with an inscription reading, "Your hinterland is there", a reminder of his ambition to paint the map pink from the Cape to Cairo. There is a café in the garden, serving drinks and snacks beneath the trees.

South African Public Library

5 Queen Victoria St, behind St George's Cathedral, T021-424 6320, nlsa.ac.za.
Mon, Tue, Thu, Fri 0900-1700, Wed 1000-1700. Walk from Adderley St, the City Sightseeing bus stops at St George's Cathedral.
Map: Central Cape Town, C5, p102.

Adjoining the gardens is the South African Public Library, which opened in 1818. It is the country's oldest national reference library and was one of the first free libraries in the world. Today it houses an important collection of books covering South Africa's history. The building also has a bookshop and an internet café.

Houses of Parliament

Entry via Parliament St gate, T021-403 2266, parliament.gov.za.
The City Sightseeing bus stops at St George's Cathedral
Map: Central Cape Town, C5, p102.

From Adderley Street, walk up Bureau Street and turn right into Parliament Street. On the other side of the avenue are the Houses of Parliament. The building was completed in 1885, and when the Union was formed in 1910 it became the seat for the national parliament. In front of the building is a marble statue of Queen Victoria, erected by public subscription in honour of her Golden Jubilee. It was unveiled in 1890.

Public gallery tickets are available during parliamentary sessions (Jan-Jun); overseas visitors must present their passports. Phone ahead for tours of the chambers and Constitutional Assembly.

Houses of Parliament on Government Avenue.

St George's Cathedral

5 Wale St, T021-424 7360, stgeorgescathedral.com.
Mon-Fri 0800-1600 and during services in the evenings and at weekends.
The City Sightseeing bus stops here.
Map: Central Cape Town, C5, p102.

The last building on Government Avenue and on the corner of Wale Street is St George's Cathedral, best known for being Archbishop Desmond Tutu's territory from 1986 until 1996 (see box, right). It is from here that he led over 30,000 people to City Hall to mark the end of Apartheid, and where he coined the now universal phrase 'Rainbow Nation'. The building was designed by Sir Herbert Baker in the early 20th century. Inside, some of the early memorial tablets have been preserved, while over the top of the stairs leading to the crypt is a memorial to Lady D'Urban, wife of Sir Benjamin D'Urban, the Governor of the Cape from 1834 to 1838. The Great North window is a fine piece of stained glass depicting the pioneers of the Anglican church. There is a small café, The Crypt, open during the day for light snacks and breakfasts.

Slave Lodge

Corner Adderley and Wale streets, T021-460 8242, iziko.org.za.
Mon-Sat 1000-1700, R15, children under 16 free.
The City Sightseeing bus stops at St George's Cathedral.
Map: Central Cape Town, C5, p102.

The second oldest building in Cape Town (after the castle) has had a varied history, but its most significant role was as a slave lodge for the VOC (see page 29) – between 1679 and 1811 the building housed up to 1000 slaves. Local indigenous groups were protected by the VOC from being enslaved so most slaves were consequently imported from Madagascar, India and Indonesia, creating the most culturally varied slave society in the world. Conditions at the lodge were appalling and up to 20% of the slaves died every year. It has now been

Desmond Tutu

The former Anglican Archbishop of Cape Town, Desmond Tutu is accepted as an influential and respected figure far beyond the borders of South Africa. His powerful oration and his simple but brave defiance of the Apartheid state impressed the world, which won him the Nobel Peace Prize in 1984. After Apartheid, Tutu chaired the hearings of the Truth and Reconciliation Committee in 1996 and argued forcibly that the policy of granting amnesty to all who admitted their crimes was an important step in healing the nation's scars. In recent years, he has used his voice in international conflict resolution, and in 2007, along with Nelson Mandela and Graça Machel, he convened a group of world leaders known as the Elders, to contribute their wisdom, independent leadership and integrity to tackle some of the world's toughest problems. Nelson Mandela once said of him, "sometimes strident, often tender, never afraid and seldom without humour, Desmond Tutu's voice will always be the voice of the voiceless".

developed into a museum charting the history of the building and slavery in South Africa. At the entrance to the exhibition is a slick cinema room showing a 15-minute film on the history of slavery in the Cape, highlighting the rules under which slaves lived, the conditions in which they were imported and sold, and the fundamental role slavery played in the success of building Cape Town. Beyond here, the museum has a series of displays, including a model of a slave ship and images and sounds of what life was like in the lodge.

Around the region

Groote Kerk

Behind the Slave Lodge, off Bureau St,
T021-422 0569, grootekerk.org.za.
Open 1000-1900, free guided tours available.
The City Sightseeing bus stops at St George's
Cathedral.
Map: Central Cape Town, C5, p102.

Nearby is one of Cape Town's older corners, Church
Square, site of the Groote Kerk. Up until 1834 the
square was used as a venue for the auctioning of
slaves from the Slave Lodge. All transactions took
place under a tree – a concrete plaque marks the old
tree's position. The Groote Kerk was the first church
of the Dutch Reformed faith to be built in South
Africa (building started in 1678 and it was
consecrated in 1704). The present church, built
between 1836 and 1841, is a somewhat dull, grey
building designed and constructed by Hermann
Schutte after a fire had destroyed most of the
original. Many of the old gravestones were built into
the base of the church walls, the most elaborate of
which is the tombstone of Baron van Rheede van
Oudtshoorn. Inside, more early tombstones and
family vaults are set into the floor, while on the walls
are the coats of arms of early Cape families. Two of
the Cape's early governors are buried here – Simon
van der Stel (1679-1699) and Ryk Tulbagh (1751-1771).

District Six Museum

25A Buitenkant St, T021-466 7200, districtsix.co.za.
Mon 0900-1500, Tue-Sat 0900-1600, R15
(all international visitors of all ages). There is a
small café and a bookshop in the museum.
The City Sightseeing bus stops here.
Map: Central Cape Town, C7, p102.

This small museum, housed in a former Methodist
Church, is one of Cape Town's most powerful
exhibitions and gives a fascinating glimpse of
the inanity of Apartheid. District Six was once
the vibrant, cosmopolitan heart of Cape Town,
a largely coloured inner city suburb renowned for
its jazz scene. In February 1966, P W Botha, then
Minister of Community Development, formally
proclaimed District Six a 'white' group area.
Over the next 15 years, an estimated 60,000
people were given notice to leave their homes
and were moved to the new townships on the
Cape Flats. The area was razed, and to this day
remains largely undeveloped.

The museum contains a lively collection of
photographs, articles and personal accounts
depicting life before and after the removals.
Highlights include a large map covering most
of the ground floor on which ex-residents have
marked their homes and local sights. The Name
Cloth is particularly poignant: a 1½-m-wide length
of cloth has been provided for ex-residents to write
down their comments, part of which hangs by the
entrance. It has grown to over 1 km, and features
some moving thoughts. A display in the back
room looks at the forced removals from the
Kirstenbosch area.

City Hall & Grand Parade

Darling St.
Map: Central Cape Town, D6, p102.

From Adderley Street, a short walk down Darling
Street will take you to the City Hall and the Grand
Parade. The latter is the largest open space in Cape
Town and was originally used for garrison parades
before the castle was completed. In 1994, after his
release from prison, Nelson Mandela made his first
speech from City Hall to over 100,000 people. Today
the oak-lined parade is used as a car park and on the
edge are some informal market stalls during the
week. It is presently being re-landscaped in
preparation for the 2010 FIFA South Africa World
Cup™, when it will serve as the city's principal
fan-park. The neoclassical City Hall, built to celebrate
Queen Victoria's Golden Jubilee, overlooks the
parade. Its clock tower is a half-size replica of Big Ben
in London. In 1979 the municipal government
moved to a new Civic Centre on the Foreshore, a
dominant tower block which straddles Hertzog
Boulevard. The hall is now the headquarters of the
Cape Town Symphony Orchestra and houses the
City Library (Mon-Fri 0900-1800, Sat 0900-1400).

Market on Grand Parade in front of the City Hall.

Castle of Good Hope

Buitenkant St, entry from the Grand Parade side,
T021-464 1260, castleofgoodhope.co.za, iziko.org.za.
Open 0930-1600, ₨20, children (5-16) ₨10, half price
on Sun, free guided tours Mon-Sat 1100, 1200 and
1400, café. The City Sightseeing bus stops here.
Map: Central Cape Town, D7, p102.

Beyond the Grand Parade, on Darling Street, is the
main entrance of South Africa's oldest colonial
building, the Castle of Good Hope. Work was
started in 1666 by Commander Zacharias
Wagenaer and completed in 1679. Its original
purpose was for the Dutch East India Company to
defend the Cape from rival European powers, and
today it is an imposing sight. Under the British, the
castle served as government headquarters and
since 1917 it has been the headquarters of the
South African Defence Force, Western Cape.

Today the castle is home to three museums.
The William Fehr Collection is one of South Africa's
finest displays of furnishings reflecting the social
and political history of the Cape. There are
landscapes by John Thomas Baines and William

Huggins, 17th-century Japanese porcelain and
18th-century Indonesian furniture. Upstairs is an
absurdly huge dining table which seats 104, in a
room still used for state dinners. More furniture in
the Secunde's House recreates the conditions
under which an official for the Dutch East India
Company would have lived in the 17th, 18th and
early 19th centuries. The third museum is the
Military Museum, a rather indifferent collection
depicting the conflicts of early settlers.

The free guided tours are informative and fun,
and highlights include the torture chambers, cells,
views from the battlements and Dolphin Court,
where Lady Anne Barnard was supposedly seen
bathing in the nude by the sentries. When it was
built the castle was on the coast. All the land to
the north of here is reclaimed.

Tip...

Try to be at the castle at noon when there is a full
ceremonial changing of the guard, which coincides
with the firing of the Noon Gun from Signal Hill.

Adderley Street & Heerengracht

The City Sightseeing bus stops on Heerengracht and at the Cape Town International Convention Centre (CTICC).
Map: Central Cape Town, D5/G5, p102.

Adderley Street is one of the city's busiest shopping areas, and is sadly marred by a number of 1960s and 1970s eyesores, but it does still boast some impressive bank buildings. On the corner of Darling Street is the Standard Bank Building (1880), a grand structure built shortly after the diamond wealth from Kimberley began to reach Cape Town. Diagonally across is the equally impressive Barclays Bank Building (1933), a fine Ceres sandstone building which was the last major work by Sir Herbert Baker in South Africa. At the corner of Adderley Street and Strand Street stands a modern shopping mall complex, the Golden Acre. On the lower level of the complex the remains of an aqueduct and a reservoir dating from 1663 can be viewed.

Continuing down towards the docks, Adderley Street passes Cape Town Railway Station and becomes Heerengracht. At the junction with Hans Strijdom Street is a large roundabout with a central fountain and a bronze statue of Jan van Riebeeck, given to the city by Cecil Rhodes in 1899. At the bottom end of Heerengracht on the Foreshore are statues of Bartholomeu Dias and Maria van Riebeeck, donated respectively by the Portuguese and Dutch governments in 1952 for Cape Town's tercentenary celebrations. The palm trees here once graced a marine promenade in this area, a further indication of how much additional land has been reclaimed from Table Bay over the years. At the end of Heerengracht, on the corner of Coen Steytler Street, is the Cape Town International Convention Centre (CTICC).

The palm trees here once graced a marine promenade in this area, a further indication of how much additional land has been reclaimed from Table Bay over the years.

Greenmarket Square

A couple of blocks south of the junction of Strand Street and St George's Mall, the City Sightseeing bus stops at Cape Town Tourism; the square is a 2-min walk up Burg St.
Map: Central Cape Town, D5, p102.

This has long been a meeting place, and during the 19th century it became a vegetable market. In 1834 it took on the significant role of being the site where the declaration of the freeing of all slaves was made. Today it remains a popular meeting place, with a busy daily market selling African crafts, jewellery and clothes. Most of the buildings around the square reflect the city's history. Dominating one side is the Park Inn Hotel, housed in what was once the headquarters of Shell Oil – note the shell motifs on its exterior. Next to the Tudor Hotel is the second oldest building on the square – the Metropolitan Methodist Church (1876). This, the only high Victorian church in Cape Town, has a tall spire decorated with an unusual series of miniature grotesques. The church was designed by Charles Freeman and is regarded as one of the finest in the country. If you walk out of the square past the Methodist church to Church Street, you'll come to the area between Burg and Long streets, which is the venue for an antiques market (Mon-Sat).

Above: Beaded wire souvenirs for sale in Greenmarket Square.
Opposite page: Gold of Africa Museum.

Old Town House

In Greenmarket Sq, diagonally opposite the Tudor Hotel, T021-481 3933, iziko.org.za. Mon-Fri 1000-1700, Sat 1000-1600, entry by donation.
Map: Central Cape Town, C5/D5, p102.

Originally built in 1755 to house the town guard, this became the first town hall in 1840 when Cape Town became a municipality. Much of the exterior remains unchanged, and with its decorative plaster mouldings and fine curved fanlights, it is one of the best-preserved Cape baroque exteriors in the city. The first electric light in Cape Town was switched on in the Old House on 13 April 1895. Today the white double-storeyed building houses the Michaelis Collection of Flemish and Dutch paintings, as well as the Courtyard Café which serves snacks. At the entrance to the house is a circle set into the floor which marks the spot from which all distances to and from Cape Town are measured.

Koopmans-De Wet House

Strand St, T021-4813935, iziko.org.za. Tue-Thu 1000-1700, ℞10, under 16s free.
The City Sightseeing bus stops at Cape Town Tourism and the Gold Museum on Strand St, both a couple of mins' walk away.
Map: Central Cape Town, E5, p102.

Just off St George's Mall, a pedestrianized road lined with shops and cafés, is the delightfully peaceful Koopmans-De Wet House. The house is named in memory of Marie Koopmans-De Wet, a prominent figure in cultured Cape Society who lived here between 1834 and 1906. The inside has been restored to reflect the period of her grandparents who lived here in the late 18th century. Though not too cluttered, there is a fascinating collection of· furnishings which gives the house a special tranquil feel. Look out for the early map of the Cape coastline at the head of the stairs, dating from 1730. At the back of the house are a shaded courtyard and the original stables with the slave quarters above.

Tip...

In the courtyard of the Gold Museum is the Gold Restaurant (T021-421 4653, goldrestaurant.co.za, daily 1000-2300), which serves good South African cuisine, and if you are visiting for dinner, evening guided tours are available of the museum for ℞40 per person which includes a glass of wine sprinkled with gold leaf.

Gold of Africa Museum

96 Strand St, T021-405 1540, goldofafrica.com. Mon-Sat 0930-1700, ℞25, children ℞15.
The City Sightseeing bus stops here.
Map: Central Cape Town, E4, p102.

A few blocks west of Koopmans-De Wit House is the Lutheran Church, and next door is the Martin Melck House, now home to the Gold of Africa Museum. Originally the house served as a clandestine Lutheran church, as in the 18th century the Dutch authorities refused to tolerate any churches other than the Dutch Reformed Church. The present museum houses a slick display of the history of gold mining, outlining the first mining by Egyptians in 2400 BC and the subsequent development of trade networks across Africa. There are comprehensive displays of 19th- and 20th-century gold artworks from Mali, Ghana and Senegal, including jewellery, masks, hair ornaments and statuettes. Downstairs there's a shop and workshop where you can watch goldsmiths at work.

Around the region

Long Street

The City Sightseeing bus (but only the Blue Route) runs along Long St.
Map: Central Cape Town, A4/F4, p102.

One of the trendiest stretches in Cape Town, Long Street gets particularly lively at night. Lined with street cafés, fashionable shops, bars, clubs and backpacker hostels, it has a distinctly youthful feel

about it, although a clutch of new boutique hotels, posh apartment complexes and upmarket restaurants are injecting the area with a new sophisticated edge. Long Street is also home to some fine old city buildings. One of Cape Town's late Victorian gems is at No 117, now an eclectic home decor and gift shop called Imagenius. On the outside is an unusual cylindrical turret with curved windows; inside is a fine cast-iron spiral staircase leading to a balustraded gallery.

The Slave Church Museum

40 Long St, T021-423 6755.
Mon-Fri 0900-1600, free.
Map: Central Cape Town, C4, p102.

This is the oldest mission church in South Africa, built between 1802 and 1804 as the mother church for missionary work carried out in rural areas. Fortunately the building was saved from demolition in 1977 and restored to its present fine form. Though utilized by directors and members of the South African Missionary Society, it was more commonly used for religious and literacy instruction of slaves in Cape Town. Inside are displays of missionary work throughout the Cape, and behind the pulpit are displays showing early cash accounts and receipts for transactions such as the transfer of slaves.

Heritage Square

Two blocks north of Long St, the entrance is on Shortmarket St.
Map: Central Cape Town, D4, p102.

This renovated block of 17th- and 18th-century townhouses, includes the city's oldest blacksmiths, but is better known for its excellent restaurants and the Cape Heritage Hotel (see page 114). In the centre is a cobbled courtyard holding the Cape's oldest living grape vine, which was planted in 1781.

Left: Building in Long Street.
Opposite page: View of Table Mountain from across Table Bay.

Table Mountain National Park

Map: Cape Town, p80.

Rising a sheer 1073 m from the coastal plain, Cape Town is defined by Table Mountain and it dominates almost every view of the city. Its sharp slopes and level top make it one of the world's best-known city backdrops. For centuries, it was the first sight of Cape Town afforded to seafarers, and today its size continues to astonish visitors. But it is the mountain's wilderness, bang in the middle of a bustling conurbation, that makes the biggest impression. The Table Mountain National Park encompasses the entire peninsula stretching from here to Cape Point. The most popular ascent of the mountain directly above the City Bowl is described below; other parts of the park are covered later (see page 148).

The dizzying trip to the top in the Aerial Cableway is one of Cape Town's highlights. The first cableway was built in 1929, and since then has had three upgrades, the latest being in 1997. It's estimated to have carried up some 18 million people to date. There are two cars, each carrying up to 65 passengers, and as you ride up the floor rotates, allowing a full 360° view. Journey time is just under five minutes. There is the Table Mountain Café at the top station, which also has a deli for takeaway sandwiches, cheese and sushi platters and other light meals. An extensive network of paths has been laid out, allowing walks of various lengths, leading to different lookout points with stunning views of the City Bowl, Cape Flats, Robben Island and back along the peninsula. There are also free guided walks daily at 1000 and 1200.

Hiking The most popular hiking route starts 1½ km beyond the Lower Cableway Station and follows a course up Platteklip Gorge; there's another path from Kirstenbosch. Both take about two to three hours to the top, and are fairly tough and should not be taken lightly. The fog (the

It's a fact...

Halfway along the road up Signal Hill you pass **Lion's Head**, a popular hiking spot. In the 17th century the peak was known as *Leeuwen Kop* (Lion's Head) by the Dutch, and Signal Hill was known as *Leeuwen Staart* (Lion's Tail), as the shape resembles a crouching lion.

famous 'Table Cloth') and rain can descend without warning, so never climb alone and inform someone of which route you're taking. In poor weather don't rely on the Cableway being open to take you back down, so allow enough daylight hours to make the descent on foot.

Take a waterproof jacket, hat, sunscreen, sunglasses, plenty of water, energy snacks, and put the mountain rescue number in your phone (T10177).

Signal Hill Signal Hill's summit offers spectacular views of the city, the Twelve Apostles and the ocean. You can drive to the 350-m summit, and watching the sun dip into the Atlantic from this viewpoint with a cold sundowner in hand is a highlight of a visit to Cape Town. From the town centre, follow signs for the Lower Cableway Station and take a right at Kloof Nek opposite the turning for the cableway station.

Aerial Cableway

Tafelberg Rd, information line T021-424 8181, tablemountain.net.

First car up 0830, last car down 1800-2200 depending on the time of year, phone or check the website for up-to-the-minute times and, given Cape Town's unpredictable weather, if the cableway is open or not. The cableway is closed for annual maintenance for 2 weeks end Jul/beginning Aug (see website for dates).

Return adult ₱145, children 4-18 ₱76, family ticket, 2 adults and 2 children ₱370; one-way ticket, adult ₱74, children 4-18 ₱38, under 4s go free. Because of the weather factor, tickets cannot be pre-booked; in summer (Dec-Jan) this can mean queues.

To get to the Lower Cableway Station; you can drive and parking is along Tafelberg Rd, go by taxi and there is a taxi rank at the station when you come back down, by Rikki taxi, by the City Sightseeing bus, or by regular Golden Arrow bus from the city centre to Camps Bay and get off at Kloof Nek, from where it is a 1½-km walk up Tafelberg Rd to the station.

Tip...

Check the website for special offers, like two for the price of one on summer evenings to watch the sunset.

Western suburbs

Bo-Kaap, De Waterkant, Green Point and Sea Point, the closest residential areas to the city, are undergoing rapid transformation in line with the new Green Point Stadium and related infrastructure. First up, Bo-Kaap, a charming area of artisan houses painted in bright colours, is the Islamic heart of the city. This then blends into the similar houses of De Waterkant, many of which have been restored as luxury homes in what has become a trendy area of decor shops, boutiques and restaurants centred around the Cape Quarter development. Somerset Road turns to Main Road in Green Point and continues on through Sea Point to Bantry Bay, Clifton and Camps Bay, the city's most exclusive suburbs. In 1923 the Union Government gave Green Point Common, today an invaluable green lung for the city, to the city council to use for recreational purposes.

Bo-Kaap

600 m west of the city along Wale St.
Map: Central Cape Town, C3, p102.

Bo-Kaap is one of the city's most interesting residential areas. It was developed in the 1760s and today feels a world away from the nearby business district. Here the streets are cobbled and tightly woven across the slopes of Signal Hill, and the closely packed houses are painted in bright hues of lime, pink and blue. The name means 'upper Cape' and it developed as a working-class district for freed slaves, who were mostly imported by the Dutch from Malaysia, Indonesia and other parts of Asia. These slaves were the forefathers of today's Cape Malay community in Bo-Kaap. It was they who introduced Islam into South Africa, and the Owal Mosque on Dorp Street, built in 1794, is the oldest mosque in the country. There are nine other mosques in the district and the air here rings with muezzin calls before the five daily prayers. Opposite the museum on Wale Street, Atlas Trading is a shop worth stopping by to see the shelves stacked with relishes and pickles and at the back the wooden boxes of spices used in Cape Malay cooking.

Bo-Kaap Museum (71 Wale St, T021-481 3939, iziko.org.za, Mon-Sat 1000-1700, R10, under 16s free) Housed in an attractive 18th-century house, this is dedicated to the Cape's Malay community and contains the furnishings of a wealthy 19th-century Muslim family. There are antique furnishings and Islamic heirlooms such as an old Koran and *tasbeh* beads set in front of the *mihrab* alcove, while the back room has displays dedicated to the input that slaves had in the economy and development of Cape Town. At the back is a community centre, with temporary photographic exhibitions. The

Above: Bo-Kaap, the Malay Quarter in Cape Town.
Opposite page: Lighthouse at Green Point.

house itself is one of the oldest buildings in Cape Town surviving in its original form. It was built by Jan de Waal for artisans in 1763 and it was here that Abu Bakr Effendi started the first Arabic school and wrote important articles on Islamic law. He originally came to Cape Town as a guest of the British government to try and settle religious differences amongst the Cape Muslims.

De Waterkant

From the city, follow Somerset Rd.
Map: Central Cape Town, E1, p102.

To the west, Bo-Kaap blends into the trendy De Waterkant – until fairly recently a run-down area of flaking bungalows – now Cape Town's most fashionable district, with beautifully restored Victorian homes painted in bright hues crammed into a tight grid of cobbled streets, climbing up towards Signal Hill. This is the city's main gay area, with excellent nightlife and a wide choice of super-trendy restaurants, bars and boutiques. Most of these are in the Cape Quarter (capequarter.co.za), a shopping/dining complex with a charming outside piazza with a central water feature and trees with twinkly lights. This is currently being extended to cover a large block from Waterkant Street to Somerset Road, and the Victorian façades on Somerset Road are being incorporated into the complex.

> **Tip...**
>
> You can do a great half-day tour of Bo-Kaap with Andulela Experience (see page 134), which includes a walkabout, a visit to the museum, a cookery class and lunch in a local family's home.

Green Point

Map: Central Cape Town, E1, p102.

About 500 m beyond De Waterkant, along Somerset Road, is the start of Green Point, where there was a large roundabout with a turning northeast to the V&A Waterfront. This has temporarily been taken out as the road development around the new Green Point Stadium is being built. This includes a new road being ploughed through from the stadium to the V&A Waterfront and an elevated roundabout, underneath which will be pedestrianized walkways. Part of Waterkant Street is being developed as a 'Golden Mile' from Cape Town Railway Station, which will be the city centre terminus for the new Integrated Rapid Transport (IRT), see page 43. Work on this will continue until 2010. At the time of writing the new Green Point Stadium for the 2010 FIFA South Africa World Cup™ was 85% complete and should be finished by the time you read this. Currently the area is teaming with the Team Green Point construction workers in their distinctive red and yellow uniforms decorated with football emblems. As a spin-off to being close to the stadium, there's presently a massive wave of development along Somerset/Main Road which runs from the centre of Green Point the length of Sea Point, and the buildings are developing into a series of high-rise apartment blocks and shopping and restaurant malls. Green Point Common to the left of the stadium is at the moment a pile of rubble but is being developed into sports fields and a new 18-hole golf course.

Mouille Point & Sea Point

Map: Central Cape Town, C1, p102.

Running parallel to Main Road is Beach Road which winds its way from the V&A Waterfront and around Mouille Point, where there is another smart row of apartment blocks and the red and white candy-striped Green Point Lighthouse. This is the oldest working lighthouse on the South African coast, built by Herman Schutte (a German

builder) in 1824 and electrified in 1929. From Green Point, both Main Road and Beach Road then continue on their parallel journey through Sea Point and merge on their way to Clifton. There's a pleasant promenade the length of Beach Road, which is intercepted by short stretches of beach and has an adjoining strip of park where there are a few attractions for children such as a mini-train, mini-golf and playgrounds. Primarily it's a place where local people jog, rollerblade or walk their dogs and there are good views of Table Bay and some surf spots below the promenade wall. The beach is unsafe for swimming, although there are a couple of rock pools: Graaf's Pool and Milton's Pool.

It's a fact...

The new state-of-the-art Green Point Stadium will be 52 m high and will accommodate 68,000 spectators, have an underground car park for 1200 cars and be surrounded by 60 ha of parkland. There was some controversy about the fact they built the new stadium on South Africa's oldest golf course and not directly on the site of the old stadium. The reason they did this was because in its new location every television shot of it will have Table Mountain as a backdrop. There couldn't be better publicity for Cape Town.

The centre of Sea Point on Main Road has a bit of a scruffy reputation, but the numerous new developments are giving it a facelift and bringing in a number of upmarket shops and restaurants.

Sea Point swimming pool (Beach Rd T021-434 3341, Oct-Apr 0700-1900, May-Sep 0830-1700, R10, children R6) is seen by some (probably Cape Town people) as being the most stunning location for a public swimming pool in the world. Indeed, it is a sparkling bright blue outdoor Olympic-sized pool built right on the rocks next to the ocean with superb mountain and sea views. It has two splash pools for kids and a springboard diving pool.

Motorbike hire

There are a number of places to hire motorbikes around the city and they are a great way to get around in summer but remember you'll need a licence. **Cape Town Scooter** (T082-450 9722, capetownscooter.co.za), rents out scooters and delivers to your hotel, and **La Dolce Vita Biking** (T083-528 0897, la-dolce-vita.co.za), rents out scooters from their shop at 13 Kloof Nek Rd, Gardens. **Cape Sidecar Adventures** (2 Glengariff Rd, Sea Point, T021-434 9855, sidecars.co.za), rents out vintage ex-Chinese Red Army motorbikes with sidecars, and **Harley Davidson Cape Town** (9 Somerset Rd, Green Point, T021-446 2999, harley-davidson-capetown.com), rents out Harleys and provides route maps for day tours.

Green Point Stadium.

Victoria & Alfred Waterfront

The V&A Waterfront derives its name from the two harbour basins around which it was developed, and was named after Queen Victoria and her son Alfred. In the 1980s, it was completely redeveloped as a leisure, shopping and eating attraction, which today gets more than 10 million visitors a year. A number of original buildings remain around the basins and are an interesting diversion from the razzmatazz of the shops and restaurants. It also remains a working harbour, which provides much of the area's real charm. There are boat companies along Quay 5 offering all manner of cruises, from short half-hour harbour tours to two-hour sails to Camps Bay by schooner.

Over the years and with growing popularity, the quality of shops has shifted upmarket. The majority now sell clothes, souvenirs, jewellery and specialist items. In November 2007, a whole new extension of Victoria Wharf was opened, with a fashion gallery featuring the likes of Gucci, Jimmy Choo and Burberry. There are now more than 70 restaurants, not to mention Africa's first and only six-star hotel.

Clock Tower

Map: Central Cape Town, H1/H2, p102.

At the narrow entrance to the Alfred Basin, on the Berties Landing side, is the original Clock Tower, built in 1882 to house the port captain's office. This is in the form of a red octagonal Gothic-style tower and stands just in front of the Clock Tower Centre, a modern mall with a collection of shops, offices and restaurants. Next to the Clock Tower is the Nelson Mandela Gateway to Robben Island (see page 106), from where you catch the main ferry to the island. Just below look out for Cape fur seals on a landing. This side of the Waterfront is connected to the bulk of the area by a swing bridge, which swings open every 10 minutes to allow boats to pass underneath.

Union Castle Building

Map: Central Cape Town, H1, p102.

On the opposite side of the swing bridge, the stocky square building known as Union Castle Building (1919) was designed by the firm of architects owned by Sir Herbert Baker. The Union Steamship Company and the Castle Line both ran monthly mail ships between

Essentials

❷ **Getting there** A bus runs from outside the railway station in the city centre or there's a Golden Arrow bus service that runs along Beach Road in Sea Point and Green Point to the V&A. City Sightseeing (see page 78) has its ticket office outside the aquarium.

❸ **ATM** These can be found throughout the complex and there are many foreign exchange desks.

❶ **Tourist information** There is a tourist information office (T021-405 4500, tourismcapetown.co.za, daily 0900-2100) in the Clock Tower Centre across the swing bridge from the main development. They stock a good selection of maps and guides for the whole country; there are also desks for car hire and safari companies, and a SANParks booking desk. A full list of all the shops, amenities and attractions can be found at waterfront. co.za, and printed guides can be picked up throughout the V&A. For more information, call T021-408 7600.

Tip...

There are several multi-storey car parks. The one underneath Victoria Wharf is the most expensive (R10 per hr); the other car parks are half the price.

Clock Tower and Swing Bridge, V&A Waterfront.

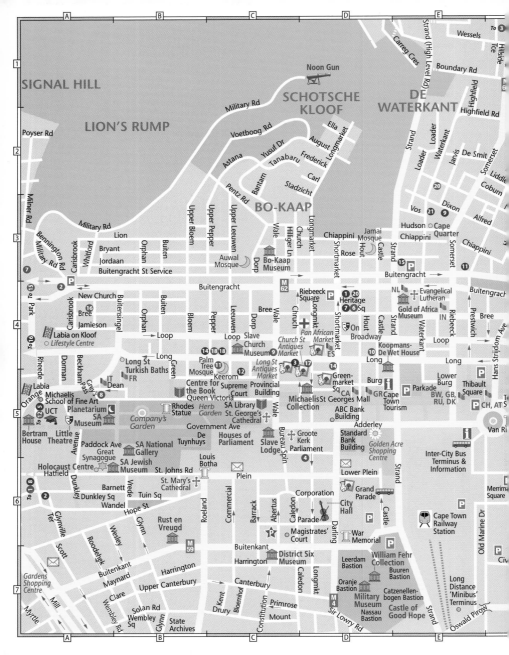

Central Cape Town listings

❶ Sleeping

1 Ashanti Lodge *11 Hof St* A6
2 Backpacker *74 New Church St* A4
3 Big Blue *7 Vesperdene Rd* F1
4 Cape Diamond *Corner of Longmarket and Parliament streets* D5
5 Cape Grace *West Quay Rd* G2
6 Cape Heritage Hotel *90 Bree St* D4
7 Cape Milner *2a Milner Rd* A3
8 Cape Town Hollow *88 Queen Victoria St* A5
9 Daddy Long Legs *134 Long St* C4
10 Grand Daddy *38 Long St* D4
11 Long St Backpackers *209 Long St* C4
12 Mount Nelson Hotel *76 Orange St* A5
13 One&Only *Dock Rd* F1
14 Park Inn *10 Greenmarket Sq* D4
15 Parker Cottage *3 Carstens St* A3
16 Protea Hotel Fire and Ice *Corner of New Church and Victoria streets* A4
17 Tudor Hotel *Greenmarket Sq* D4
18 Urban Chic *Corner of Long and Pepper streets* C4
19 Victoria & Alfred *Pierhead* H1
20 Village Lodge *49 Napier St* E2
21 Westin Grand Cape Town Arabella Quays *Convention Sq* G4

❶ Eating & drinking

1 Africa Café *Heritage Sq* D4
2 Aubergine *39 Barnet St* A6
3 Café Mozart *37 Church St* C4
4 Café San Marco *Victoria Wharf* H1
5 Cape Colony *Mount Nelson Hotel, 76 Orange St* A5
6 Cape Town fish market *Victoria Wharf* H1
7 Caveau *Heritage Sq* D4
8 Chef Pon's Asian Kitchen *12 Mill St* A6
9 Chenin *Cape Quarter* E3
10 Den Anker *Pierhead* H1
11 Fireman's Arms *25 Mechau St* E3
12 Five Flies *14 Keerom St* C4
13 Hildebrand *Pierhead* H1
14 Mama Africa *178 Long St* C4
15 Marco's African Place *15 Rose St* E3
16 Miller's Thumb *10b Kloof Nek Rd* A4
17 Mitchell's Brewery *East Pier Rd* H1
18 Mr Pickwicks *158 Long St* C4
19 Quay Four *Quay 4* H1
20 Savoy Cabbage *Heritage Sq* D4
21 Tank *Cape Quarter* E3

Cape Town Harbour

Construction began in 1860, when Prince Alfred, Queen Victoria's second son, tipped the first load of stone to start the building of the breakwater for Cape Town's harbour, which became known as the Alfred Basin. No sooner had the first basin been completed than diamonds and gold were discovered in South Africa, and over the next 40 years Cape Town and the docks were to change beyond recognition. In 1900 work began on a new breakwater which would protect an area of 27 sq km. After five years' work the Victoria Basin was opened. This new basin was able to shelter the new generation of ships using Table Bay. A third basin was created to the east of Victoria Basin in 1932. The next phase of growth was an ambitious one, and it was only completed in 1945. The project involved the dredging of Table Bay and the reclaiming of land. The spoil from the dredging provided 140 sq km of landfill, known as Foreshore. This new land extends from the present-day railway station to Duncan Dock. As you walk or drive around Cape Town today, remember that just over 50 years ago the sea came up to the main railway station.

Britain and South Africa in the late 19th century. In 1900 they amalgamated and from then on mail was delivered every week. The last Union Castle ship to sail to England with the mail was the *Windsor Castle* in 1977. Upstairs is the Maritime Museum (T021-405 2880, iziko.org.za, daily 1000-1700, entry by donation), a collection of model ships and objects associated with the era of mail ships. It also holds an archive of over 19,000 photographs of ships that visited Cape Town from the 1920s to the 1960s. Nearby is the museum ship, the *SAS Somerset*, a boom defence vessel that is permanently moored for public viewing.

Nobel Square

nobelsquare.com.
Map: Central Cape Town, G1, p102.

South of the Spier hotel, this opened on 16 December 2006, the Day of Reconciliation, and pays tribute to South Africa's four Nobel Peace Prize laureates – the late Nkosi Albert Luthuli (1961), Archbishop Desmond Tutu (1984) and FW de Klerk and Nelson Mandela who jointly won it in 1993. Slightly larger than life-size statues of the four formidable men stand next to each other with a backdrop of Table Mountain and, in front of the sculptures, the Laureates' preferred quotations engraved in their chosen language. In the middle of the square, the Peace and Democracy sculpture – a narrative work of a jumble of people and faces on top of each other – represents the contribution made by women and children to the attainment of peace in South Africa.

Time Ball Tower

Map: Central Cape Town, H1, p102.

Heading west, on the other side of Dock Road, is the 1894 Time Ball Tower; its purpose was to act as an accurate reference for ships' navigators who set their clocks as the ball on the roof fell. Correct time was vital for navigators to be able to determine precise longitude. Beside the tower is a 110-year-old dragon tree, *Dracaeno draco*, from the Canary Islands, and next to the tree is the original harbour master's residence (1860).

THE MOST VISITED DESTINATION
IN SOUTH AFRICA.*

Here's a working harbour and the gateway to Robben Island; home to sunbathing seals, African buskers, cosmopolitan restaurants and over 450 international and local shops. Set against the backdrop of Table Mountain, it's a truly sophisticated mix of African culture and Victorian tradition.

For more information, call V&A Waterfront on **+27 (0) 21 408 7600 or visit** **www.waterfront.co.za**

The V&A Waterfront is the most visited attraction by international visitors to the Western Cape - 2004 SATOUR.

Around the region

Two Oceans Aquarium

Entrance is on Dock Rd, by the Waterfront Craft Market, T021-418 3823, aquarium.co.za. 0930-1800, ₨85, children (4-13) ₨40 (14-17) ₨65, under 4s free. Map: Central Cape Town, G1, p102.

Focusing on the unique Cape marine environment created by the merging of the Atlantic and Indian Oceans, this aquarium is the top attraction at the V&A Waterfront. The display begins with a walk through the Indian Ocean, where you'll follow a route past tanks filled with a multitude of colourful fish, turtles, seahorses and octopuses. Highlights include giant spider crabs and phosphorescent jellyfish floating in a mesmerizing circular current. Then you walk past touch pools, where children can pick up spiky starfish and slimy sea slugs. Free puppet shows and face painting keep children busy at the Alpha Activity Centre in the basement. The main wall here looks out into the water of the actual harbour, and you can watch Cape fur seals dart and dive before the glass. The seals are fed at 1100 and 1400. Upstairs is a vast tank holding the Kelp Forest, an extraordinary tangle of giant kelp that sways drunkenly in the artificial tides. The highlight is the Predators exhibit, a circular tank complete with glass tunnel, holding ragged-tooth sharks, eagle rays, turtles and some impressively large hunting fish. There are daily feeds at 1500 and, with an Open Water diving certificate, you can arrange to dive with the sharks.

Cape Medical Museum

City Hospital Complex, Portswood Rd, T021-418 5663, Tue-Fri 0900-1600, entry by donation. Map: Central Cape Town, D1, p102.

Close by the Waterfront, at the City Hospital Complex on Portswood Road, the medical achievements of South Africa's doctors are celebrated in this interesting display. There are turn-of-the-20th-century reconstructions of a consulting room and dispensary, dentist's room, operating theatre and hospital ward plus a collection of medical instruments.

Robben Island

The Nelson Mandela Gateway at the Clock Tower Centre is the embarkation and disembarkation point for tours, T021-413 4220, robben-island.org.za. An air-conditioned catamaran completes the half-hour journey to the island. Tickets cost ₨180, under 18s ₨90. Departures are daily at 0900, 1100, 1300 and 1500, and the whole excursion lasts 3½ hrs. You must remain with your guide throughout the tour.

The Nelson Mandela Gateway houses a shop, the ticket office and a small museum (open 0730-2100) with photographic and interactive displays on Apartheid and the rise of African nationalism.
    Lying 12 km off Green Point's shores, Robben Island is best known as the notorious prison that

Two Oceans Aquarium.

Former inmate Dr James Marsh outside Robben Island prison.

held many of the ANC's most prominent members, including Nelson Mandela and Walter Sisulu. It was originally named by the Dutch, after the term for seals, 'rob' – actually a misnomer as none are found here. The island's history of occupation started in 1806, when John Murray was granted permission by the British to conduct whaling from the island. During this period the authorities started to use the island as a dumping ground for common convicts; these were brought back to the mainland in 1843, and their accommodation was deemed suitable only for lepers and the mentally ill. These were in turn moved to the mainland between 1913 and 1931, and the island entered a new era as a military base during the Second World War. In 1960 the military passed control of the island over to the Department of Prisons, and it remained a prison until 1996. On 1 December 1999 the island was declared a World Heritage Site by UNESCO.

Robben Island's effectiveness as a prison did not rest simply with the fact that escape was virtually impossible. The authorities anticipated that the idea of 'out of sight, out of mind' would be particularly applicable here, and to a certain extent they were correct. Certainly, its isolation did much to break the spirit of political prisoners, not least Robert Sobukwe's. Sobukwe, the leader of the Pan African Congress, was kept in solitary confinement for nine years. Other political prisoners were spared that at least, although in 1971 they were separated from common-law prisoners, as they were deemed a 'bad' influence. Conditions were harsh, with forced hard labour and routine beatings. Much of the daily running of the maximum security prison was designed to reinforce racial divisions: all the wardens, and none of the prisoners, were white; black prisoners, unlike those deemed coloured, had to wear short trousers and were given smaller food rations. Contact with the outside world was virtually

non-existent – visitors had to apply for permission six months in advance and were allowed to stay for just half an hour. Newspapers were banned and letters were limited to one every six months.

Yet despite these measures, the B-Section, which housed Mandela and other major political prisoners, became the international focus of the fight against Apartheid. The last political prisoners left the island in 1991.

Tours begin with a 45-minute drive around the key sites, including Sobukwe's house, the lime quarry where Mandela was forced to work, the leper cemetery and the houses of former wardens. Tours around the prison are conducted by ex-political prisoners, who paint a vivid picture of prison life here.

It's a fact…

As a prison, the area was strictly protected allowing the fish and bird populations to flourish. There are over 100 species of bird on the island, and it is an important breeding site for African penguins.

Tip…

Be sure to book a day ahead (or several days in peak season) as tickets sell out quickly, and always phone first to see if the ferry is running in bad weather.

Southern suburbs

Primarily encompassing the more affluent residential areas of Cape Town, the suburbs, stretching southeast from the centre, are an interesting diversion to the usual tourist spots. Although a car is the best way to visit them, it's possible to reach all by train – the metro service between the city centre and Simon's Town runs through the suburbs. There is the option of buying a hop-on, hop-off train ticket on this line as part of the Southern Line tourism initiative (see page 172 for more details). This area supports many of Cape Town's best schools, as well as the impressive University of Cape Town campus with its ivy-covered sandstone buildings designed by acclaimed architect Herbert Baker, on land donated to the city by Cecil Rhodes. As such the nearby cheaper residential areas of Observatory and Woodstock are home to a large student population living in rented accommodation. The main road that runs through these areas is the M3, which eventually makes it way down through the embassy belt of Bishopscourt and the lush Constantia Valley to the towns on the False Bay coast.

Woodstock & Observatory

Map: Cape Town, F2, p80.

The first suburb, Woodstock, is a mixed commercial and residential area, historically a working-class coloured district. Today it is somewhat run down and depressing, although the back streets are an attractive mesh of Victorian bungalows. Observatory is an area of tightly packed houses, narrow streets and student hangouts. Being close to the university, there is a good range of trendy bars, cafés and restaurants catering for a mixed scene of students, bohemian types and backpackers. The observatory after which the suburb is named is where Station Road intersects Liesbeeck Parkway. The first Astronomer Royal to work at the Royal Observatory was also a clergyman, the Reverend Fearon Fellowes. Aside from making astronomical observations the observatory was responsible for accurate standard time in South Africa. It has also been an important meteorological centre and has a seismograph which records earthquakes around the world. Observatory is also where you'll find the Groot Schuur Hospital on Main Road, the site of the world's first heart transplant, performed by Professor Christiaan Barnard.

Neighbourgoods Market

Held on a Saturday morning and hugely popular, this farmers' market (375 Albert Rd, Woodstock, T021-448 1438, neighbourgoodsmarket.co.za, Sat 0900-1400) is in a restored biscuit factory now known as the Old Biscuit Mill. The stalls sell organic veggies, homemade bread, pastries, cupcakes, chutneys, jams, goat's cheese, chocolate and many more delicious goodies. Other stalls serve meals like Indian curries, Mexican wraps, Greek kebabs, sushi and pizza, accompanied by a glass of fizz or a bloody Mary.

Heart of Cape Town Museum

Groot Schuur Hospital, Main Rd, Observatory, T021-404 1967, heartofcapetown.co.za.
2-hr guided tours run daily at 0900, 1100, 1300 and 1500 and must be pre-booked, ℝ200, children (10-16) ℝ100, under 10 free. The museum has a minibus, transport to and from hotels is ℝ50 per person.
Map: Cape Town, F3, p80.

This commemorates the world's first heart transplant and has a number of rooms including the two adjoining theatres that were used for the transplant, which took place in 1967 (the last four digits of the museum's telephone number). The informative tours

The popular Neigbourgoods Market, Woodstock.

Memorial to British imperialist Cecil Rhodes.

go a long way to recreate the tension of the night of December 2, and the eerie waxwork figures of Barnard and his team are brought to life with a sound track of clinking scalpels. The heart came from a traffic accident victim, 25-year-old Denise Darvell, and was transplanted to 54-year-old Louis Washkansky, who was suffering from a heart that was reduced to a third of its pumping capacity. The operation took almost nine hours. When the heart started beating in Washkansky, Barnard's first words were 'Dit gaan werk' ('it's going to work'). Quite incredibly, Washkansky's wife drove past the accident that killed Darvell on her way to see her dying husband in Groot Schuur, so the museum also commemorates Darvell's life.

Mowbray, Rosebank & Rondebosch

Map: Cape Town, G3/G4, p80.

The next suburbs of Mowbray, Rosebank and Rondebosch lie just below the University of Cape Town. Mowbray was originally known as Driekoppen, or three heads, after the murder by three slaves of a European foreman and his wife in 1724. On their capture they were beheaded and their heads

impaled on stakes at the farm entrance to act as a deterrent. Rondebosch, conversely, has for some time been associated with education. Aside from the university, several important schools were founded in the district. The area was also important from a practical point of view: in 1656 Van Riebeeck realized that Company's Garden was exposed to a damaging southeast wind. His first choice of a more sheltered spot was Rondebosch. This proved a success and a grain storage barn was built. Early accounts describe the area as wild country, with the farmers frequently losing livestock to hyenas, lions and leopards – an image that is hard to imagine as you sit in the evening rush hour on Rhodes Drive. Also in Rondebosch are Groot Schuur, the Prime Minister's official residence, Westbrooke, home of the State President and Rustenburg, the original residence of the Cape Governor over 200 years ago .

Irma Stern Museum (Cecil Rd, Rosebank, T021-685 5686, irmastern.co.za, Tue-Sat 1000-1700, R10, under 16s R5) Irma Stern was one of South Africa's pioneering artists and her lovely house displays a mixture of her own works, a collection of artefacts from across Africa and some fine pieces of antique furniture from overseas, including 17th-century Spanish chairs, 19th-century German oak furniture and Swiss Mardi Gras masks. Her portraits are particularly poignant and those of her close friends are superb, while her religious art is rather more disturbing. Stern's studio, complete with paint brushes and palettes, has been left as it was when she died. From Rosebank station it is a three-block walk; there's a map on the website.

Rhodes Memorial (off Rhodes Drive, by the Rondesbosch turning, T021-689 9151, rhodesmemorial.co.za, Nov-Apr 0700-1900, May-Oct 0800-1800) The imposing granite memorial to Cecil John Rhodes (Cape Prime Minister from 1890 to 1896) was designed by Francis Masey and Sir Herbert Baker. Four bronze lions flank a wide flight of steps which lead up to a Greek Temple. The temple houses an immense bronze head of Rhodes, wrought by JM Swan. Above the head are the words "slave to the spirit and life work of Cecil John Rhodes who loved and served South Africa". At the base of the steps (one for each year of his short 49-year life) is an immense bronze mounted figure of *Physical Energy* given to South Africa by GF Watts, a well-regarded sculptor of the time; the original stands in Hyde Park, London. Other than the memorial, the great attraction here is the magnificent view of the Cape Flats and the southern suburbs. Behind the memorial are a number of popular trails leading up the slopes of Devil's Peak. The only way to get here is by car, it's clearly signposted off the M3.

Newlands

Boundary Rd, Newlands, T021-659 6700, newlandstours.co.za.
Pre-booked tours run Mon-Fri 0900-1700, from ₨44, children (under 16) ₨28.
A few mins' walk from Newlands Station.
Map: Cape Town, F4, p80.

The suburb of Newlands backs right up to the slopes of Table Mountain and is probably best known for being the home to **Western Province Rugby Union** and the beautiful Newlands cricket Test Ground

now known as **Sahara Park**. The first official rugby match at Newlands was played in 1890 and the stadium was a venue for 1995 World Cup matches. The first recorded cricket match in Africa took place between officers in the British army in Cape Town in 1808, and the Newlands cricket oval opened in 1888. In 2003 it hosted the Cricket World Cup opening match. There are a number of options here run by Newlands Tours. You can visit the rugby stadium and enter through the players' entrance, see the changing rooms and surgery and run through the players' tunnel. At the cricket ground you can walk across the pitch and visit the scorer's and third umpire's booths. Both these can be combined with a tour of the **South African Rugby Museum**, a somewhat chaotic collection which commemorates the history of the sport in the country and is also home to the Currie Cup, the premier domestic competition trophy. Of interest are the early radio commentaries, and highlights of great South African rugby moments are shown on TV.

Josephine Mill (13 Boundary Rd, Newlands, T021-686 4939, josephinemill.co.za, Mon-Fri 1000-1600, Sat 1000-1400, ₨10, milling demonstrations Mon-Fri 1100 and 1500, ₨20), on the opposite side of the road to Newlands, a few minutes' walk from Newlands Station, is the only surviving watermill in Cape Town. It has been restored as a working flour mill; note the massive iron waterwheel. The building is in the style of a Cornish red-brick mill, built by a Swede, Jacob Letterstedt in 1840, and named in honour of his Crown Princess, Josephine. The mill is tucked away near the rugby stadium and has a shop selling organic stone-milled flour and bread and a peaceful tea garden and deli.

Kirstenbosch National Botanical Gardens

Kirstenbosch, 13 km from the city centre, is South Africa's oldest, largest and most exquisite botanical garden. The gardens stretch up the eastern slopes of Table Mountain, merging seamlessly with the fynbos of the steep slopes above. Cecil Rhodes bought Kirstenbosch farm in 1895 and promptly presented the site to the people of Cape Town with the intention that it become a botanical garden. It was not until 1913 that it was proclaimed a National Botanical Garden – the Anglo-Boer War had caused the delay. The first director of the gardens was Professor Harold Pearson, who died just three years after the garden's creation. A granite Celtic cross marks his grave in the Cycad garden. There is a fitting epitaph: "If ye seek his monument, look around you." The real development was under Professor RH Compton, who cared for the gardens for 34 years. The herbarium, named after him, houses over 250,000 specimens, including many rare plants.

A great deal of time and effort has been put into making the gardens accessible to the general public, ensuring they provide pleasure for both serious botanists and families enjoying a day out on the slopes of Table Mountain. For a sense of the past, it is worth visiting what is known as van Riebeeck's Hedge. Back in 1660 a hedge of wild almond trees (*Brabejum stellatifolium*) was planted by van Riebeeck as part of a physical boundary to try and prevent cattle rustling. Segments still remain today within the garden. The Skeleton Path can be followed all the way to the summit of Table Mountain. It starts off as a stepped path, but becomes fairly steep near the top. It involves a climb up a rocky waterfall; take special care in the wet season.

Perhaps the most enjoyable way of experiencing the gardens is at one of the Sunday sunset concerts held throughout summer (see page 48). Also available for a small fee are eco-adventure tours, and tours by motorized golf cart. Just beyond the entrance is a shop and café

on the courtyard terrace. The café serves overpriced sandwiches and cakes; better value and with far nicer views is the Silver Tree and Fynbos Deli inside the gardens, which serves good meals (until 2200). And, for a reasonable price, you can have a ready-made picnic with wine and join the Capetonians on the lush lawns.

Essentials

Rhodes Dr, Newlands, T021-799 8783, sanbi.org.
Sep-Mar 0800-1900, Apr-Aug 0800-1800,
R32, children (6-17) R10.
The easiest way of getting here is by car, or there are trains to the nearest station at Mowbray, and from here there is an erratic bus service or a very long walk. Alternatively, the City Sightseeing buses stop here.
Map: Cape Town, E5, p80.

Five of the best

Kirstenbosch gardens

❶ The **Peninsula Garden** displays many of the 2500 fynbos and other species found on the Cape Peninsula, some of which occur nowhere else on earth.

❷ The **Water-wise Garden** shows gardeners how to conserve water while still having a lush and colourful garden. Principles like soil preparation, creating shade and grouping plants according to their water needs are explained.

❸ The **Fragrance Garden** features aromatic plants with unusual textures. Also known as the Braille Trail, they have been grown at waist height to enable blind visitors to touch and smell them and signage boards are in Braille. On a warm day, when the volatile oils are released by the plants, there are some lovely aromas.

❹ The **Dell** is the oldest and arguably most attractive part of Kirstenbosch planted with shade-loving vegetation like ferns and cycads. There is a beautifully shaded path snaking along a stream and this is where to come on a hot day.

❺ The **Medicinal Plants Garden** displays indigenous South African herbs used by the Khoi and San peoples in the treatment of a variety of ailments. The plants' uses are identified on plaques.

Sleeping

Cape Cadogan ℞℞℞℞
5 Upper Union St, Tamboerskloof, T021-480 8080, capecadogan.com.
Map: Cape Town, D2, p80.
Ultra-elegant 2-storey mansion with 12 rooms, spacious with grass mat flooring, private terraces, subtle lighting and decor, large four-poster beds, interesting touches like driftwood chandeliers, fabulous bathrooms, some with enormous stone walk-in showers for two. Shady courtyard with small pool, all-white dining room with pleasant breezes. Also has four one-bed self-catering mews houses to rent just off Kloof Street.

Cape Heritage Hotel ℞℞℞℞
90 Bree St, Heritage Sq, T021-424 4646, capeheritage.co.za.
Map: Central Cape Town, D4, p102.
Charming hotel set in a rambling renovated town house dating from the late 17th century. The 17 huge rooms are individually styled, with muted coloured walls (avocado, rust-red, eggshell blue) and contemporary decor

Tip...

Several agencies specialize in medium- and long-term holiday lets of private homes, self-catering flats or home swaps. These are good value for families or groups. Try capehomes.co.za, or capeletting.com.

but retain the high teak ceilings and yellowwood floors. Breakfast is served under a historical vine in the courtyard, or in the airy black-and-white breakfast room. Good location close to Long Street. Friendly management.

Cape Milner ℞℞℞℞
2a Milner Rd, Tamboerskloof, T021-426 1101, capemilner.com.
Map: Central Cape Town, A3, p102.
Fashionable business-oriented hotel, popular with media types, with 57 rooms in a modern building with neutral pale grey decor and slick dark wood furniture, flat-screen TVs with satellite and Wi-Fi. The lovely pool area has a sun deck, small infinity pool and cocktail bar. It's a popular local meeting place and has a decent restaurant serving good Capetonian cuisine.

Cape Town Hollow ℞℞℞℞
88 Queen Victoria St, T021-423 1260, capetownhollow.co.za.
Map: Central Cape Town, A5, p102.
A pleasant newish hotel overlooking Company's Garden with 56 rooms and all-white comfortable furnishings, spacious bathrooms, air conditioning, TV and fantastic views of the mountain from front-facing rooms. There's a small, sunny pool deck on first floor, some gym equipment, conference centre, spa and a

smart Italian restaurant on the ground floor with adjoining bar, which has Wi-Fi.

The Grand Daddy ℞℞℞℞
38 Long St, T021-424 7247, thegranddaddy.co.za.
Map: Central Cape Town, D4, p102.
Long Street's newest and most eccentric boutique hotel, with 45 double rooms. Like its sister hotel, Daddy Long Legs (see page 116), it is decorated throughout by local artists and the design element is simply stunning. Talk of the town are the seven vintage Airstream trailers on the roof that are again individually theme decorated. The Daddy Cool bar is a sexy and stylish cocktail bar and the Showroom Café offers good food with an organic and low-calorie slant.

Kensington Place ℞℞℞℞
38 Kensington Gardens, Higgovale, T021-424 4744, kensingtonplace.co.za.
Map: Cape Town, D3, p80.
Cape Town's original boutique hotel in a quiet, leafy area. Small and well run with excellent and friendly service. Eight beautiful and good-sized rooms, each individually styled with Afro-chic furnishings, big bathrooms, lots of light from the large windows, great views over the city, bar, small pool and tropical gardens, breakfast served on a leafy veranda, excellent restaurant.

Mount Nelson Hotel.

Mount Nelson Hotel ℞℞℞℞
76 Orange St, Gardens, T021-483 1737, mountnelsonhotel.co.za.
Map: Central Cape Town, A5, p102.
Cape Town's famous colonial hotel with 131 luxurious rooms and 31 'Oasis' garden suites. Emphasis is on traditional decor – lots of floral fabrics, antique-style furniture, heavy curtains, but all in bright, airy colours. Set in beautiful landscaped parkland with heated swimming pool, tennis courts, squash court and beauty centre. The celebrated Cape Colony Restaurant serves Cape specialities and contemporary fare to live jazz, and there's the trendy Planet Champagne Bar.

Urban Chic ℞℞℞℞
Corner of Long and Pepper streets, T021-426 6119, urbanchic.co.za.
Map: Central Cape Town, C4, p102.
Italian-owned hotel in a trendy corner block with 20 rooms spread over several floors (prices rise the higher you go, as the views of the mountain improve), with beautiful, airy decor, pale colours, modern art on the walls,

and large stone-clad bathrooms. Stylish bar attached, and on the 1st floor is the Gallery Café with a large fusion menu, for-sale art on the walls and a covered balcony over Long Street.

Westin Grand Cape Town Arabella Quays ℞℞℞℞
Convention Sq, Lower Long St, T021-412 9999, starwoodhotels.com.
Map: Central Cape Town, G4, p102.
A fairly new addition to the city, this huge grey glass structure overlooks the convention centre and has 483 rooms, in modern and minimalist style, with massive beds, floor-to-ceiling windows, stone bathrooms with double showers with jets, satellite TV, and internet. Facilities include popular rooftop spa, gym and pool, five restaurants and bars, and service is impressively swift and efficient.

Leeuwenvoet House ℞℞℞
93 New Church St, Tamboerskloof, T021-424 1133, leeuwenvoet.co.za.
Map: Cape Town, D2, p80.
Pronounced Loo-en-Foot, this historical guesthouse has 12 double rooms, all with traditional, attractive decor, air conditioning, TV and telephone, and some have Victorian baths. Excellent health and full English breakfasts, heated swimming pool, bar, off-street secure parking, close to shops and restaurants but retains a peaceful atmosphere.

Parker Cottage ℞℞℞
3 Carstens St, Tamboerskloof, T021-424 6445, parkercottage.co.za.
Map: Central Cape Town, A3, p102.
Award-winning B&B, stylish and atmospheric set in two restored Victorian bungalows, nine bedrooms, bathrooms with claw-foot baths, some have fireplaces, polished wood floors, lots of antiques, flamboyant colours with a Victorian touch, good breakfasts, bar, friendly service, gay-friendly and an easy stroll to restaurants on Kloof Street. It incorporates eco-friendly aspects like solar heating and a water-wise garden.

Park Inn ℞℞℞
10 Greenmarket Sq, T021-423 2050, parkinn-capetown.com.
Map: Central Cape Town, D4, p102.
Good central location set in the historic Shell building right on bustling Greenmarket Square. Some 166 rooms with pleasant neutral decor and functional, attractive bathrooms (shower only). Small pool deck with sauna and gym with view of Table Mountain, good steak restaurant – The Famous Butcher's Grill – on the ground floor with tables overlooking the market, plus pleasant, if dark, cigar bar. Excellent service, secure parking, a practical, comfortable choice.

Listings

Cape Diamond ℞℞
Corner of Longmarket and Parliament streets, T021-461 2519, capediamondhotel.co.za.
Map: Central Cape Town, D5, p102.
In a great location just round the corner from Government Avenue and a short walk from Long Street and set in a restored art deco diamond dealership with 60 double rooms and three self-catering apartments, with contemporary decor, and the occasional splash of bright colour. Rooftop jacuzzi, bar, Patat restaurant specializing in Cape cuisine, owner-run, great value.

Daddy Long Legs ℞℞
134 Long St, T021-422 3074, daddylonglegs.co.za.
Map: Central Cape Town, C4, p102.
South Africa's first art hotel with 13 rooms spread across a town house, offering funky, artistic rooms – each is individually themed and designed, with walls covered in art-works. Rooms are small, but the stylish, original decor makes up for it. Breakfast is offered in the café downstairs. Good value and refreshingly different. Also offers self-catering apartments on Long Street, with exposed brick walls and polished wood floors.

Protea Hotel Fire and Ice ℞℞
Corner of New Church and Victoria streets, T021-488 2555, proteahotels.co.za.
Map: Central Cape Town, A4, p102.
Fashionable place with spacious modern lobby with trendy cocktail bar, swinging chairs, restaurant specializing in gourmet burgers and a cheeky smoking room where seats are fashioned as coffins. Rooms are small but neat with all mod cons. The unique pool here has one wall that forms part of the restaurant. Room prices work in the same way as budget airlines – price goes up as availability goes down.

Tudor Hotel ℞℞
Greenmarket Sq, T021-424 1335, tudorhotel.co.za.
Map: Central Cape Town, D4, p102.
This historic building, right on bustling Greenmarket Squate, has 26 rooms, choice of doubles and family rooms, with TV, some air conditioned, modern with contemporary decor, trendy bathrooms with shower. A generous continental breakfast is served in the stylish downstairs café, off-street parking ℞60 per day. A great location with friendly staff.

The Backpacker ℞℞-℞
74 New Church St, T021-423 4530, backpackers.co.za.
Map: Central Cape Town, A4, p102.
Cape Town's first hostel and today one of the most comfortable and best run in town. Set across several houses with spotless dorms, doubles and singles. Polished wood floors, upmarket decor, tiled courtyard and linked gardens with pool, lovely bar with TV, meals and snacks served throughout the day, one of the best backpacker travel centres around.

A room at the Daddy Long Legs Hotel.

Ashanti Lodge ℝ
11 Hof St, Gardens,
T021-423 8721, ashanti.co.za.
Map: Central Cape Town,
A6, p102.
One of Cape Town's best-known
and most popular hostels, not
least for its party atmosphere.
Dorms and doubles in huge old
house with polished wooden
floors, high ceilings, large
windows and communal
balconies. There's a courtyard
and small pool and a couple of
spaces for camping. Lively bar
serving good snacks, with pool
table and satellite TV, plus good
booking centre, internet access
and DVD room. Also has a
guesthouse (ℝℝ) nearby with
smart en suite double rooms
and spotless kitchen.

Long St Backpackers ℝ
209 Long St, T021-423 0615,
longstreetbackpackers.co.za.
Map: Central Cape Town,
C4, p102.
Sociable, vaguely pretentious
hostel spread around leafy
courtyard, 80 beds in small
dorms and doubles which feel
cramped, fully equipped kitchen,
TV/video lounge, pool room,
internet access, travel centre, free
pickup, great mosaics in some of
the bathrooms. Good security
with 24-hour police camera
opposite. Lively atmosphere,
occasional parties organized
and weekly communal *braais*;
can be noisy.

Western suburbs

Le Vendôme ℝℝℝℝ
20 London Rd, Sea Point,
T021-430 1200, le-vendome.co.za.
Map: Cape Town, C2, p80.
A large, well-designed luxury
hotel with a French theme and
traditional and very comfortable
rooms and suites with air
conditioning, TV and internet
facilities, attractive courtyard
with pool, one restaurant
overlooks the pool and serves
snacks and lunch, the other is for
fine dining. Secure parking.

Radisson Blu ℝℝℝℝ
Beach Rd, Granger Bay,
T021-441 3000,
radissonblu.com/hotel-capetown.
Map: Cape Town, D1, p80.
A large, quality hotel in an
unbeatable location right on the
ocean's edge and a short walk
from the V&A Waterfront. All 177
rooms are spacious with sunny
decor and crisp white linen and
have all mod cons including Wi-Fi.

Tobago's restaurant and bar is
very popular for sundowners and
outside tables, there's a stunning
infinity pool and a state-of-the-art
spa and fitness centre.

Winchester Mansions ℝℝℝℝ
221 Beach Rd, Sea Point,
T021-434 2351, winchester.co.za.
Map: Cape Town, C2, p80.
A well-run family hotel with 76
rooms with TV, bathroom with
separate shower, some with
views of the Atlantic. Pleasant
pool deck and Ginkgo Spa. All
rooms overlook a large courtyard
where meals are served beneath
the palms. Also has Harvey's
restaurant, offering fusion cuisine
and jazz brunches on Sundays.

The Clarendon ℝℝℝ
67 Kloof Rd, Sea Point,
T021-439 3224, clarendon.co.za.
Map: Cape Town, C2, p80.
Luxurious Italian-style guesthouse
with 10 spacious rooms spread
across main house and gardens,
plus extra house further up the

street. Rooms are large and grandly furnished with posh bathrooms, some with great views of Lion's Head. Attractive garden with large pool shaded by banana trees, breakfast served on terrace, beautiful lounge, off-street parking.

Village Lodge ℝℝℝ
49 Napier St, De Waterkant, T021-421 1106, thevillagelodge.com.
Map: Central Cape Town, E2, p102.
Relative newcomer to the area, offering 15 double rooms spread across two converted houses. Decor is trendy greys and white, with shimmery black stone bathrooms (shower only), some with air conditioning, all M-Net TV, but they feel a little cramped. Attractive restaurant, Soho, attached, serving Thai food in slick black surrounds, and there's a rooftop pool with mountain views. Also has cottages and apartments in the area.

Brenwin Guest House ℝℝ
1 Thornhill Rd, Green Point, T021-434 0220, brenwin.co.za.
Map: Cape Town, D1, p80.
Guesthouse with 13 large, well-appointed rooms with en suite bathrooms, wooden floors, simple, airy decor, sunny breakfast room, shady patio overlooking tidy tropical garden with swimming pool and loungers, within easy walking distance of the Waterfront. Also rents out three self-catering apartments each sleeping four.

The Glen ℝℝ
3 The Glen, Sea Point, T021-439 0086, glenhotel.co.za.
Map: Cape Town, C2, p80.
Gay boutique hotel in an Italian-style villa with views of Signal Hill, with classy decor and super-trendy stone bathrooms, some of which have double showers, tropical garden with palm trees and pool, Moroccan-themed steam room with splash pool, secure parking, special rates out of season.

Big Blue ℝ
7 Vesperdene Rd, Green Point, T021-439 0807, bigbluebackpackers.hostel.com.
Map: Central Cape Town, F1, p102.
An airy backpacker hostel set in a gorgeous mansion dating from 1885, with 86 beds in spacious dorms, single and double rooms (some with en suite), all with polished floors, high ceilings, ceiling fans, yellow and orange walls and framed pictures. Pleasant breakfast room, bar with outdoor section leading on to small pool, internet café, travel centre, TV room, spotless kitchen.

V&A Waterfront

Cape Grace ℝℝℝℝ
West Quay Rd, T021-410 7100, capegrace.com.
Map: Central Cape Town, G2, p102.
This has become one of the most luxurious hotels in Cape Town and is just a short walk from the shops and restaurants, with 122 spacious, comfortable rooms with all mod cons, traditional and plush decor, balconies have views of the waterfront or the mountain. Service and food is excellent, with two bars and a celebrated waterfront restaurant. Attractive swimming pool and deck with bar opens out from the restaurant and there's a lovely rooftop spa.

One&Only ℝℝℝℝ
Dock Rd, T021-431 5215, oneandonlyresorts.com.
Map: Central Cape Town, F1, p102.
This 131 room super luxury hotel is Sol Kerzner's (of Sun City fame) new offering and Africa's first six-star hotel and, as you can imagine, it is stunning. All spacious rooms have balconies or terraces overlooking Table Mountain or the ocean; two islands in the marina have a clutch of villas, and if you are in this league you can park your yacht outside. There's also a vast heated swimming pool (the largest in Cape Town) and a tranquil spa. The giant lobby

Tip…

Generally hotels at the V&A Waterfront are aimed at the high-spending foreign visitor, and all are expensive. For cheaper accommodation within walking distance of the Waterfront, although not at night, consider Green Point, above.

has a cocktail bar, which is also used for high tea, a branch of famed Japanese restaurant Nobu, and Gordon Ramsey's gourmet Maze restaurant.

Table Bay ƦƦƦƦ
Quay 6, T021-780 7878, suninternational.co.za.
Map: Cape Town, E1, p80.
Enormous luxury offering from the Sun International Group, 329 top-notch rooms. What they lack in character they make up for in facilities and comfort. Large pool and sun deck, health club and spa, bar and good restaurant. Expensive by Cape Town standards, efficient service but feels ostentatious (note the sculpture by the main entrance commemorating the stays of celebrities and politicians).

Victoria & Alfred ƦƦƦƦ
Pierhead, Waterfront, T021-419 6677, vahotel.co.za.
Map: Central Cape Town, H1, p102.
Stylishly converted warehouse with 96 rooms, spacious with cool and comfortable furnishings, king-size beds,

air conditiong, TV with DVD player, minibar, dramatic mountain views, large marble and stone bathrooms with separate WC, some rooms have jacuzzis on the balconies. Excellent restaurant serving seafood and steaks, fashionable, airy bar attached. Friendly and efficient service.

Breakwater Lodge ƦƦ
Portswood Rd, Waterfront, T021-406 1911, proteahotels.com, breakwaterlodge.co.za.
Map: Cape Town, D1, p80.
This hotel, managed by the Protea group, fills what was once the notorious Breakwater Prison (1859) and is today aimed at the tour group market. The 268 rooms are fairly small but comfortable, with functional decor. Cheaper rooms share a shower and toilet with the neighbouring room. Two restaurants, bar, conference centre. Overpriced for what you get but cheapest option in the Waterfront.

Southern suburbs

Andros ƦƦƦƦ
Corner Phyllis and Newlands roads, Upper Claremont, T021-797 9777, andros.co.za.
Map: Cape Town, F5, p80.
Grand old Cape Dutch house built in 1908 by Herbert Baker set in neat parkland, elegant and homely ambience, with eight well-appointed rooms

with TV, bathrooms, underfloor heating, white and cream decor, smart breakfast room, terrace and swimming pool, gym, sauna and beauty treatments on offer. Picnic hampers and meals arranged on request. Swiss-owned, several languages spoken.

Vineyard Hotel & Spa ƦƦƦƦ
Colinton Rd, off Protea Rd, Newlands, T021-657 4500, vineyard.co.za.
Map: Cape Town, F5, p80.
This hotel has 175 air-conditioned rooms with Wi-Fi set around an 18th-century house; the decor is a mix of Cape Dutch with yellowwood furniture and modern features. The oldest part was originally built as a country house for Lady Anne Barnard in 1799. There are indoor and outdoor heated pools, two restaurants, two cafés, spa and gym. A new wing of rooms is presently under construction.

Eating

City Bowl

Africa Café RRR

Heritage Sq, 108 Shortmarket St, T021-422 0221, africacafe.co.za.
Mon-Sat 1830-2300.
Map: Central Cape Town, D4, p102.
African-themed restaurant geared at tour groups, offering an excellent introduction to the continent's cuisines. The menu is a set 'feast' and includes 13 dishes from around Africa, such as Egyptian-smoked fish, Kenyan patties, Cape Malay mango chicken curry and springbok stew. The price includes as many dishes you like, as well as coffee and dessert.

Aubergine RRR

39 Barnet St, Gardens, T021-465 4909, aubergine.co.za.
Tue-Fri 1200-1400, Mon-Sat 1900-2230.
Map: Central Cape Town, A6, p102.
Sophisticated and award-winning menu, with a modern slant on classical European dishes such as foie gras and quail, excellent wine list. One of the best restaurants in town, with a stylish shaded courtyard, lounge/bar, and good service, and the three- to five- course degustation menu is an elaborate affair when wine is paired to food.

Cape Colony RRR

Mount Nelson Hotel, 76 Orange St, T021-483 1000, mountnelson.co.za.
Daily 1830-2300.
Map: Central Cape Town, A5, p102.
One of Cape Town's finest restaurants in the impressive setting of the Mount Nelson. Dishes are a mix of traditional British (think sensible roasts) and Cape classics, such as Bo-Kaap chicken and prawn curry, plus lots of game. Impeccable service, live jazz most evenings.

Five Flies RRR

14 Keerom St, T021-424 4442, fiveflies.co.za.
Mon-Fri 1200-1500, daily 1900-2300.
Map: Central Cape Town, C4, p102.
A long-standing local favourite in a historic setting, with a lovely string of dining rooms, and excellent two- or four-course menu of traditional food with a modern slant, which is best known for its meat and fish dishes. The preferred haunt of lawyers and judges but also attracts well-heeled media types.

La Perla RRR

Corner of Church and Beach roads, Sea Point, T021-434 9538, laperla.co.za.
Open 1000-2300.
Map: Cape Town, C2, p80.
Opened in 1969 (some of the elderly waiters in their white starched shirts have been

Tip...

The Mount Nelson Hotel serves elaborate cream teas in the lounge and on the terrace every afternoon for R150 (under 12's, R75) from 1430-1730. This is a fabulous experience and bookings are essential.

Gourmet food at Aubergine restaurant.

there since then), but recently completely refurbished, this is a long-term Sea Point favourite, with an extensive Italian menu with over 200 dishes specializing in seafood, with excellent antipasti, plenty of vegetarian options, and wonderful desserts. Outside seats overlook the ocean.

Miller's Thumb ℝℝℝ
10b Kloof Nek Rd, T021-424 3838.
Tue-Fri 1230-1430,
Mon-Sat 1830-2230.
Map: Central Cape Town,
A4, p102.
Beloved by locals, bookings essential, this place serves delicious and good-value seafood, plus steaks and some veggie choices, lots of spices and a Creole or Mozambique twist on some dishes. A friendly and a laid-back place.

Savoy Cabbage ℝℝℝ
Heritage Sq, 101 Hout St,
T021-424 2626,
savoycabbage.co.za.
Mon-Fri 1200-1430,
Mon-Sat 1900-2230.
Map: Central Cape Town,
D4, p102.
Widely regarded as one of the best restaurants in Cape Town, serving beautifully prepared contemporary South African cuisine. The menu changes daily, and includes dishes such as gemsbok carpaccio, free-range duck breast and a gorgeous soft-centred chocolate pudding.

Good wine list too, especially on reds. Booking essential.

Tank ℝℝℝ
Cape Quarter, Waterkant St,
De Waterkant, T021-419 0007,
the-tank.co.za.
Open 1100-late.
Map: Central Cape Town,
E3, p102.
Airy, super-fashionable seafood restaurant serving the best-rated sushi in the city with attractive tables spilling out onto the piazza. Inside, tables are dotted around two rooms, with a huge central aquarium. Good menu with daily specials, but slightly pretentious clientele.

Caveau ℝℝ
Heritage Sq, 92 Bree St,
T021-422 1367, caveau.co.za.
Mon-Sat 0800-late.
Map: Central Cape Town,
D4, p102.
Laid-back, stylish deli and restaurant with stone-clad walls, comfy banquettes and tables overlooking Bree Street. Menu changes daily, but includes tapas, excellent cheese and meat platters, salads and adventurous mains, and on Tuesday evening there is a sushi and wine pairing event.

Chenin ℝℝ
Cape Quarter, Waterkant St,
De Waterkant, T021-425 2200,
cheninrestaurant.co.za.
Mon-Sat 0900-late.
Map: Central Cape Town,
E3, p102.
Wine bar with tables leading onto the Cape Quarter piazza, serving a wide range of wines accompanied by excellent seafood (the mussels in white wine and cream are especially good), steaks and burgers. Cosy interior, dishes can be ordered in large or small portions.

Mama Africa ℝℝ
178 Long St, T021-424 8634,
mamaafricarest.net.
Mon-Sat 1900-late.
Map: Central Cape Town,
C4, p102.
Popular restaurant and bar serving 'traditional' African dishes often with great live music. Looking a little faded around the edges, but remains popular with tourists, and the food is tasty, despite the notoriously slow service. Centrepiece is a bright green carved Mamba-shaped bar.

Marco's African Place ℝℝ
15 Rose St, T021-423 5412,
marcosafricanplace.co.za.
Tue-Sat 1200-late,
Sun 1500-late.
Map: Central Cape Town,
E3, p102.
Good-value 'African' menu covering everything from

slow-roasted Karoo lamb to samp and beans, plus popular Pan-African platter with assortment of grilled game. Huge place with a friendly atmosphere, tasty starters but main courses can be disappointing. Live music in the evening when a cover charge is added to the bill.

Posticino ℞℞
323 Main Rd, Sea Point, T021-439 4014, posticino.co.za. 1200-2300.
Map: Cape Town, C2, p80.
Popular with local residents and always has a buzzy atmosphere, this good-value Italian is well known for its thin-based pizzas and you can make up your own pasta sauce. Sit on the terrace in summer and bag a table next to the fire in winter.

Yindee's ℞℞
22 Camp St, Tamboerskloof, T021-422 1012.
Mon-Fri 1230-1430,
Mon-Sat 1830-2300.
Map: Cape Town, D2, p80.
An excellent Thai restaurant serving authentic spicy curries, stir-fries, soups and unusual deep-fried coconut ice cream for dessert. Served in a sprawling Victorian house with traditional low tables. Service can be very slow, but the place is always popular, so book ahead.

Chef Pon's Asian Kitchen ℞℞-℞
12 Mill St, Gardens, T021-465 5846, chefponsasiankitchen.co.za.
Open 1700-2200.
Map: Central Cape Town, A6, p102.
There's a long menu of favourite dishes from across Asia, and everything arrives freshly cooked and sizzling hot but it's the Thai food that wins hands down. Decor is simple and dark, but cosy on a winter's night, and lingering after your meal is discouraged if they need the table (which they frequently do).

Cafés
Arnold's
60 Kloof St, Gardens, T021-424 4344, arnolds.co.za.
Mon-Fri 0645-2300,
Sat-Sun 0800-2300.
Map: Cape Town, D2, p80.
Popular and bustling good-value spot on busy Kloof Street, good salads, pasta, burgers and more substantial meals like ostrich steak. Fast, friendly service, happy hour 1630-1830, may have to queue for a table at weekends for the legendary cooked breakfasts, which include unusual items like warthog ribs.

Café Erté
265 Main Rd, Sea Point, T021-434 6624, cafeerte.com.
Open 1000-0400.
Map: Cape Town, C1, p80.
Tiny but trendy café/bar playing loud trance and techno, serves a vegetarian-only menu of salads,

sandwiches and snacks, plus cocktails and shooters, and has several internet terminals. There are a few tables outside and it's very noticeable thanks to the blue neon lighting.

Café Mozart
37 Church St, T021-424-3774.
Mon-Fri 0700-1700,
Sat 0800-1500.
Map: Central Cape Town, C4, p102.
With tables spilling out on to the pedestrianized Church Street among the stalls of Church Street Antiques Market, this 30-year-old café serves excellent breakfasts, filled baguettes and croissants, and teas with finger sandwiches and cakes. Inside are deep-set leather couches and Wi-Fi access.

Fireman's Arms
25 Mechau St, T021-419 0207, firemansarms.co.za.
Mon-Sat 1200-2300.
Map: Central Cape Town, E3, p102.
Historic pub set in what was Cape Town's first fire station built in 1864, still complete with fire pole and fireman's hats. Best known as a place to watch sports and it gets packed out on rugby match days. Good homely menu of pub grub like liver and onions or bangers and mash.

Miss K Food Café
65 Main Rd, Green Point,
T021-439 9559, missk.co.za.
Tue-Sun 0730-1700.
Map: Cape Town, D1, p80.
A fashionable hangout for
breakfast is this all-white café
and on a Sunday morning
expect to queue. Later in the day
light meals include buffet salads,
home-made pies and decadent
creamy cakes and tarts. Not
licensed but you can BYO.

Mr Pickwicks
158 Long St, T021-423 3710.
Mon-Sat 0830-late.
Map: Central Cape Town,
C4, p102.
Trendy spot, a favourite with
pierced and tattooed Long
Street locals, serving the best
milkshakes in town, plus
baguettes, pasta, toasties and
healthy salads. Licensed and
stays open to the early hours,
pumps out loud funk and dance

tunes. Also sells tickets to
Cape Town's major club nights
and gigs.

V&A Waterfront

Baia ℞℞℞
Victoria Wharf, T021-421 0935.
Open 1200-1500, 1900-2300.
Map: Cape Town, E1, p80.
Fine seafood restaurant spread
over four terraces with moody,
stylish decor and lighting. Very
smart (and expensive) venue,
delicious seafood dishes
following a Mozambique
theme – try the spicy beer-
baked prawns. Very stylish with
views of Table Mountain, slightly
erratic service. Book ahead.

Belthazar ℞℞℞
Victoria Wharf, T021-421 3753,
belthazar.co.za.
Daily 1200-2300.
Map: Cape Town, D1, p80.
Top-of-the-range steakhouse
with tables overlooking the
harbour. Excellent Karan dry-
and wet-cured steaks, plus a
range of seafood and with a
staggering 600 South African
wines to choose from, including
100 wines by the glass – this
claims to be the world's largest
wine bar.

Fireman's Arms.

Cape Town Fish Market ℝℝℝ
Victoria Wharf, T021-413 5977, ctfm.co.za.
1100-2300.
Map: Central Cape Town, H1, p102.
Fish restaurant where you can build your own platter from items in the chilled cabinet, but the reason to come here is the revolving sushi bar, serving excellent sushi and sashimi. Decor is in a fishing harbour theme – nets, buoys, etc – with blue neon lighting. There are now other branches around the country.

Den Anker ℝℝℝ
Pierhead, T021-419 0249, denanker.co.za.
Open 0900-2300.
Map: Central Cape Town, H1, p102.
Popular Belgian restaurant and bar with a continental feel, high ceiling flying the various duchy flags, airy bar, views across Alfred Basin of Table Mountain, civilized atmosphere. Good menu serving French and Belgian dishes, lots of seafood and an impressive selection of imported bottle beers.

Balducci's ℝℝ
Victoria Wharf, T021-421 6002, balduccis.co.za.
Open 0900-2230.
Map: Cape Town, D1, p80.
Popular and elegant restaurant with seats overlooking the harbour serving some inventive international cuisine. Good choice of pasta dishes and mains ranging from ostrich steak and luxury lamb burgers, to confit de canard and blackened kingklip. Service is slick with a welcoming maître d' and there's an impressive list of wine and cocktails.

Hildebrand ℝℝ
Pierhead, T021-425 3385, hildebrand.co.za.
Open 1100-2300.
Map: Central Cape Town, H1, p102.
Well-established Italian seafood place right on the harbour's edge, offering superb handmade pasta and good antipasto platters, plus traditional Italian desserts. The chateaubriand is flamed at your table. Good reputation, but touristy given the location.

Quay Four ℝℝ
Quay 4, T021-419 2008, quay4.co.za.
Open 1000-late.
Map: Central Cape Town, H1, p102.
Popular relaxed pub on the downstairs deck and a more formal seafood restaurant upstairs (1800-2230), with great views over the Waterfront, seafood is the focus but also has grills and vegetarian options. Best known for its calamari and fish and chips served in giant frying pans and beer on tap.

Cafés
Café San Marco
Victoria Wharf, T021-418 5434.
Open 0830-2230.
Map: Central Cape Town, H1, p102.
In a good location with al fresco tables with views of the mountain and occasional street performers at the Waterfront, serving a full menu of coffees and alcoholic drinks, enormous salads, stuffed paninis and gelato ice cream.

Mitchell's Brewery
East Pier Rd, T021-419 5074.
Open 1100-2300.
Map: Central Cape Town, H1, p102.
English-style wood panelled pub that brews its own beer including bitter and stout, which are not common in South Africa. Upstairs, sports are shown on TV and there's simple pub fare on offer. **The Ferryman's Tavern** (T021-419 7748, ferrymans.co.za) next door is an almost identical pub open the same hours.

Southern suburbs

Myoga ℝℝℝ
Vineyard Hotel, Colinton Rd, Newlands, T021-657 4545, vineyard.co.za.
Mon-Sat 1130-1500, 1830-2230.
Map: Cape Town, F5, p80.
A very smart award-winning hotel restaurant with a great global fusion menu run by acclaimed chef Mike Bassett. Lunch is buffet style with a weigh-by-plate

Entertainment

Mitchell's Brewery.

charging system and dinner is à la carte. The desserts are very creative – think violet ice cream with dissolving candy floss. Booking always advised.

Barristers Grill ℝℝ
Corner of Kildare and Main streets, Newlands, T021-671 7907, barristersgrill.co.za.
Mon-Sat 0930-2300, Sun 1130-2300.
Map: Cape Town, F4, p80.
A popular steakhouse that has expanded into a bistro/café during the day with plenty of al fresco tables. Great steaks and ribs, plus veggie choices and a good-value Sunday roast lunch. Still retains the mock-Tudor timber decor of a traditional steakhouse.

Silver Tree ℝℝ
Kirstenbosch National Botanical Gardens, T021-762 9585, kirstenboschrestaurant.com.
Open 0830-2200.
Map: Cape Town, E5, p80.

Lovely terrace with views of the gardens and mountain looming behind. Decent Cape menu, including a great sweet and spicy *bobotie*, butternut ravioli, ostrich burgers, plus breakfasts, sandwiches and salads and there's a carvery on Sunday. Also offers a picnic hamper service. There's access at night from the car park after the gardens have closed.

Cafés
Obz Café
115 Lower Main Rd, Observatory, T021-448 5555, obzcafe.co.za.
Open 0700-2400.
Map: Cape Town, G3, p80.
Popular student haunt open all day for light meals, coffee or cocktails, great salads and sandwiches, also has main meals in the evenings and occasional live music and comedy. Laid-back place with hubbly bubbly pipes and fat sofas.

Bars & clubs
Alba Lounge
Pier Head, V&A Waterfront, T021-425 3385, albalounge.co.za.
Open 1700-late.
Sophisticated cocktail lounge above the Hildebrand restaurant with a quiet ambience, comfortable couches and good harbour views. Food includes hot canapés or larger Italian meals, and the chocolate martini is to die for.

The Assembly
61 Harrington St, T021-465 7286, theassembly.co.za.
Fri-Sat 2100-0400.
This is a cavernous place in a converted loft with a very long bar, and features a mixed bag of music from DJs and live bands. Features include an old-fashioned (but useful) coat check and you can buy a pre-paid card for drinks.

The Bang Bang Club
70 Loop St, T021-426 2011, thebangbangclub.co.za.
Wed-Sat 2200-0400.
Upmarket spot with leather couches and banquettes, murals on the walls and

Tip...
There is plenty of nightlife around Long Street and this is the place to come for local live music and the latest dance sounds. The best source of advice on gigs and club nights is in the cafés on Long Street where you can pick up fliers.

mood-enhancing lighting, with upstairs VIP seating, downstairs dance floor, three bars, house and lounge music, attracts a fashionable (some posey) crowd and gets packed at weekends.

Buena Vista Social Café
Main Rd, Green Point, T021-433 0611, buenavista.co.za.
Mon-Fri 1200-0200,
Sat and Sun 1700-0200.
Cuban-themed bar and restaurant catering to a well-heeled crowd, with Latin music, live bands at the weekend, a nice balcony overlooking Main Road, great spot for sophisticated cocktails on a hot evening and has a mix of Cuban and Tex-Mex-style dishes.

Chrome
Pepper St, between Long and Loop streets, T021-422 3368, chromect.com.
Wed-Sun, doors open 2200.
One of Cape Town's newest clubs with lots of mirrors and neon aimed firmly at the serious dance crowd, mostly hip hop and R&B, large dance floor, sophisticated lighting and sound system, VIP lounges with smoother music, over 25s.

Hemisphere
ABSA Centre, 2 Riebeek St, T021-422 3368, hemisphere.org.za.
Thu and Sat doors open at 2200, Fri 1630 (for sundowners).
Super-sophisticated night spot in an incredible location on the 31st floor of the ABSA Centre with great night-time city views. Very attractive oval bar, glassed VIP section, plush furnishings and frequented by models and local celebs. Need to dress up and no under 25s.

Jo'burg
218 Long St, T021-422 0142, joburgbar.com.
Open 0900-0330.
Trendy bar with industrial decor serving pints and cocktails to a mixed crowd, gay-friendly, relaxed during the week but gets very busy at weekends when live bands play in the early evening followed by DJs who spin funky house and drum 'n' bass.

Oblivion
Corner 3rd Av and Chichester Rd, Harfield Village, between Claremont and Kenilworth, T021-671 8522, oblivion.co.za.
Open 1130-0200.
No under 23s. Laid-back wine bar and restaurant, which turns into a raucous dance venue later in the evening when the house DJ gets going, and has a good selection of snack platters, nachos and pizzas and an impressive wine list.

Rafiki's
13 Kloof Nek Rd, T021-426 4731, rafikis.co.za.
Open 1200-0200.
Popular bar overlooking Kloof Nek with a huge wrap-around balcony perfect for a sundowner. Relaxed atmosphere, friendly crowd, DJs and occasional live music in the evenings, and simple food like pizzas and burgers.

Tiger Tiger
The Atrium, Main Rd, Claremont, T021-683 2220, tigertiger.co.za.
Tue, Thu-Sat 2030-late.
Age restriction changes depending on the night – check the website. This is the Southern suburbs' most commercial and modern nightclub with several bars, plenty of seating areas, a large sunken dance floor and mainstream pop music. Attracts the odd local rugby or cricket star given its proximity to Newlands.

Zula
196 Long St, T021-424 2242, zulabar.co.za.
Tue-Sat 1200-late.
Fashionable bar and cocktail lounge with several small rooms, big sofas, hip-hop on most nights, great balcony overlooking Long Street, and occasional live music. Sells snacks like pizzas, burgers and nachos and non-alcoholic smoothies.

Cinema
Labia Cinema
68 Orange St, Gardens, T021-424 5927, labia.co.za.
This is perhaps Cape Town's most enjoyable cinema, showing independent international films in a historic building that used to be a ballroom, with a café serving

Cinema

The two major cinema groups showing mainstream Hollywood films are **Nu Metro** (numetro.co.za), and **Ster-Kinekor** (sterkinekor.com). New films are released on Friday. The websites and daily newspapers have full listings. There are multi-screen cinemas in all the large shopping malls including Canal Walk, the V&A Waterfront and Cavendish Square. The latter two also have a separate Cinema Nouveau, which screens international and art-house films (information and bookings also at Ster-Kinekor). For film festivals, see page 48.

Tip...

The area around De Waterkant is the focus of Cape Town's gay and lesbian scene, with a number of trendy bars and club. For details of gay festivals, see page 48.

good pre-movie snacks. A short walk away in the Lifestyle Centre on Kloof Street, the **Labia on Kloof** is the mainstream version, with two screens showing Hollywood releases. Both are licensed, so you can take your glass of wine into the movie.

Gay & lesbian
Bronx Action Bar
35 Somerset Rd, De Waterkant, T021-419 9216, bronx.co.za.
Open 2000-late.
Cape Town's best-known and most popular gay bar and club, gets packed out at weekends, mostly men but women welcome, live DJs spin out thumping techno every night except Mon when karaoke is on offer.

Café Manhattan
74 Upper Waterkant St, De Waterkant, T021-421 6666, manhattan.co.za.
Open 1000-late.
Cape Town's most established venue in a bright red building with a wrap-around balcony and long bar, popular with regulars, good varied food, especially the burgers, perfect venue to start an evening out in De Waterkant.

Loft Lounge
24 Napier St, De Waterkant, T021-425 2647, loftlounge.co.za.
Wed-Sun 1900-late.
Stylish and sophisticated gay and lesbian bar in a new building designed to look like an old converted warehouse to keep in with the architecture of the area, with plush couches and chaises longues, art from local artists on the walls, balcony, lounge music and DJs later in the night.

Music
Cape Philharmonic Orchestra
Artscape (see page 128), T021-410 9809, cpo.org.za.
Although based at Artscape where they accompany the Cape Town Opera and Cape Town City Ballet in season, the orchestra also plays symphonies in the City Hall where there is a fine organ.

Cape Town Opera
Artscape (see page 128), T021- 410 9807, capetownopera.co.za.
The acclaimed Cape Town Opera performs at Artscape and the season is usually from May to November, and includes at least one well known crowd-pleaser such as *Madam Butterfly*.

Green Dolphin
Pierhead, V&A Waterfront T021-421 7471, greendolphin.co.za.
Open 1200-1500, 1800-2400.
Established restaurant and jazz venue that opened in 1990, which features top local jazz groups that play in the evening while you eat. Bookings are advised. There's a varied international menu with lighter meals at lunchtime.

Kirstenbosch Summer Concerts
Kirstenbosch (see page 112), T021-799 8782, sanbi.org.
Nov-Mar every Sun at 1700.
Summer concerts from folk and jazz to classical and opera, and the odd international pop star, in an idyllic setting where you can picnic on the lawns. The

Tip...

All tickets for concerts, theatre, etc can be purchased online from Computicket (computicket.com), or from their kiosks in the larger shopping malls and branches of Checkers supermarkets.

Listings

programme is published at the beginning of October and ticket prices vary but include garden entry. The normal drill is to arrive mid-afternoon to bag your place with a picnic blanket near the stage. In winter (July–August) they hold Sunday breakfast (0930-1045) followed by a concert of chamber music (1100-1200) at the tea room for ฿140 per person including garden entry.

Mercury Live & Lounge
43 de Villiers St, T021-465 2106, mercuryl.co.za.
Wed, Fri, Sat 2100-late.
Live music venue and club nights, rock, punk and hip hop acts play regularly. Cape Town's leading live indie music venue, with a lively, young crowd but for popular bands you may have to queue so pre-booking tickets is advised.

The V&A Waterfront Amphitheatre
In front of Victoria Wharf, V&A Waterfront, T021-408 7600, waterfront.co.za.
This has free concerts and live performances, mainly jazz and local rock bands and some children's entertainment; daily at 1700 in summer, and on the weekends at 1600 in winter. Check the programme on the website.

Tip...

The **Cape Town City Ballet** (capetowncityballet.org.za) is South Africa's premier ballet company and performs around the country. In Cape Town, they usually perform at Artscape or the Baxter Theatre.

Theatre
Artscape
DF Malan St, Foreshore, T021-410 9800, artscape.co.za.
This is the city's major complex offering opera, ballet, theatre and music, with several stages and a main theatre seating 1500, plus bars and a restaurant.

Baxter Theatre
Main Rd, Rondebosch, T021-685 7880, baxter.co.za.
This has a long-established involvement in black theatre, and a good reputation for supporting community theatre and children's performances, but also draws international productions and musicals. It holds the excellent Cape Town Comedy Festival in September.

On Broadway
88 Shortmarket St, T021-424 1194, onbroadway.co.za.
A fun, intimate and gay-friendly supper theatre showing comedy, drag revues and cabaret and stays open late after the shows. There's a varied affordable menu with dishes like gourmet burgers or Cape Malay curries.

Shopping

Art & antiques
Church Street Antiques Market
Church St, between Long and Burg St.
Mon-Sat 0900-1400.
This clutch of stalls in a pedestrian-only area sells offbeat antiques, nautical equipment, crockery, jewellery and interesting junk. Non-shoppers can enjoy breakfast at one of the pavement tables at Café Mozart (see page 122).

Long Street Antiques Arcade
127 Long St, T021-423 3585.
Mon-Fri 0900-1600, Sat 0900-1400.
This is a rabbit warren of tiny shops selling old maps and prints dating back to the 1800s, medals, dusty cameras, clocks, jewellery, china, paintings and porcelain.

Books
Clarke's Bookshop
211 Long St, T021-423 5739, clarkesbooks.co.za.
Mon-Fri 0900-1700, Sat 0900-1300.
A mass of antiquarian, second-hand and new books in a muddled old shop, a must for any book lover, and also specializes in books on Southern Africa art.

Tip...

Look out for the *Antiques, Collectables and Africana* leaflet at the tourist offices, which is updated every year and lists good antique shops around Cape Town.

Select Books
232 Long St, T021-424 6955,
selectbooks.co.za.
Mon-Fri 0900-1700,
Sat 0900-1300.
This is something of a local
institution, with a pleasantly
ordered interior and vast range
of books on Southern Africa
including great contemporary
choices, and books on local flora
and fauna, and sport, especially
rugby and cricket.

Food & drink
Andiamo
Cape Quarter, 72 Waterkant St,
De Waterkant, T021-421 3687,
andiamo.co.za.
Open 0900-2230.
Loved by locals, this bustling deli
sells Mediterranean items, like
cured hams and cheese, olives,

Bookshop chains

CNA (cna.co.za) is a city-wide
chain of shops carrying a
reasonable stock of guide books,
glossy coffee-table publications,
maps and magazines as well
as stationery. **Exclusive Books**
(exclusivebooks.com) is a more
upmarket chain with excellent
branches at Victoria Wharf at the
V&A Waterfront and Cavendish
Square Mall, which have cafés.
They are particularly good for
maps, guidebooks and coffee-
table books on Cape Town
and Africa and carry a full
range of international
magazines and newspapers.

Exclusive Books.

Five of the best

Shopping malls

❶ **Canal Walk** (Century Blvd, Century City, Milnerton, T021-555 4444,
canalwalk.co.za, 0900-2100) Again with over 400 retail outlets, cinemas,
a large entertainment atrium, food court, restaurant piazza, this features
local chain stores as well as international brands.

❷ **Cavendish Square** (Dreyer St, Claremont, T021-657 5600, cavendish.
co.za, Mon-Sat 0900-1900, Sun 1000-1700) 230 stores, 20 restaurants,
cinemas, food court, the new Cavendish Connect section features
individual boutiques.

❸ **Clock Tower Centre** (V&A Waterfront, T021-408 7600, waterfront.
co.za, 0900-2100) Luxury shopping for watches, sunglasses, diamonds,
tanzanite and other fine jewellery, plus art galleries, specialist top-end
African curio shops, and the VAT refund desk is here.

❹ **Gardens Centre** (Mill St, Gardens, T021-465 1842,
gardensshoppingcentre.co.za, Mon-Fri 0900-1900, Sat 0900-1700,
Sun 0900-1400) Large branches of supermarkets and Woolworths, plus
85 specialist shops for homeware, fashion, decor and gifts.

❺ **Victoria Wharf** (V&A Waterfront, T021-408 7600, waterfront.co.za,
0900-2100) With over 400 upmarket shops, this is Cape Town's premier
shopping mall. There is a large branch of Woolworths, the Red Shed is full
of stalls selling jewellery and gifts, and there are many specialist shops
for curios, jewellery and local and international fashion.

oils, biscuits and baked goods as well a full range of meals at tables in the piazza.

Caroline's Fine Wine Cellar
62 Strand St, T021-419 8984, carolineswine.com.
Mon-Fri 0900-1730, Sat 0900-1300.
Stocks more than 1500 South African wines, plus other wines from all over the world, and the staff are predictably very knowledgeable. There's another branch in Victoria Wharf.

Giovanni's Deliworld
103 Main Rd, Green Point, T021-434 6593.
Open 0730-0900.
Cape Town's best and busiest deli, this is a favourite with regulars who come to chat at the coffee bar and buy the imported cheese, cold meats and olives, fresh bread and pastries and hard-to-come-

by groceries from Italy and the UK. The delicious ready meals can be eaten here or taken away.

Melissa's: The Food Shop
Victoria Wharf, T021-418 0138, melissas.co.za.
Open 0900-2100.
A range of branded home-made food in attractive packaging including cakes, bread and confectionery, herbs and spices, jams and pickles and there are ready-made meals to take away or light meals to eat in.

Markets
Greenmarket Square
Between Shortmarket and Longmarket streets.
Mon-Sat 0900-1600.
A lively curio and crafts market on a picturesque cobbled square, selling goods from across Africa, and flanked by several terrace cafés. Be prepared to take part in some cheerful haggling.

Green Point Market
Beside Green Point Stadium (although presently at a temporary spot on Green Point Common).
Sun 0800-1700.
A good mixture of curios neatly laid out for inspection, some food stalls, and plenty of buskers. Prices are lower during poor weather when there are fewer visitors.

Pan African Market
76 Long St, T021-426 4478.
Mon-Fri 0900-1700, Sat 0900-1500.
Two-storey centre set in a converted Victorian house, selling crafts from across the continent and good local crafts made from recycled material, plus beadwork and ceramics. The café offers African food, and there's a book shop and holistic healing area.

Tip...
Each of the suburbs has its own shopping complex with a branch of one of the major supermarket chains. For high-quality groceries head to Woolworths which is much the same as Marks & Spencer in Britain, with equivalent prices. Supermarkets are only licensed to sell wine (and not on a Sunday) so beer and other liquor is sold in bottle stores, usually close to, or attached to the supermarkets (again not on Sunday). Restaurants and bars do serve alcohol on Sunday.

The African Music Store.

Cape Town fashion

Long Street and Kloof Street in the City Bowl have become the powerhouse of Cape Town's fashion scene, and have a good choice of kooky boutiques selling one-offs and locally designed clothes and accessories. For better-known clothes chains, upmarket boutiques and international labels, head to the shopping malls. For designer clothes and accessories, Victoria Wharf's upstairs Fashion Mall features the likes of Paul Smith, Gucci and Armani. The most exclusive designer shop in Cape Town, and the only place in South Africa to sell labels such as Stella McCartney and Matthew Williamson, is the boutique in the One&Only hotel (see page 118).

Music

The African Music Store
134 Long St, T021-426 0857, africanmusicstore.co.za.
Mon-Fri 0900-1800,
Sat 0900-1400.
Stocks an excellent choice of albums by major Southern African artists as well as compilations and reggae. The staff are incredibly helpful and are happy to let you listen to any number of CDs before purchasing.

Musica
Dock Rd Complex, V&A Waterfront, Nobel Sq, T021-425 6300, musica.co.za.
Open 0900-2100.
This sells an extensive range of South African contemporary and African traditional music in an enormous restored dock building and you can listen before you buy. Other branches can be found in the shopping malls.

Souvenirs

African Image
52 Burg St, T021-423 8385, african-image.co.za.
Mon-Fri 0900-1700,
Sat 0900-1500.
Excellent alternative to the tired souvenir shops, this gallery sells contemporary African art, such as bags made from traditional weavings, beautiful baskets, old township signs, photography, plus quirky souvenirs like coke-bottle-top bags and chickens made from colourful plastic bags. Also has an outlet in Victoria Wharf.

Monkeybiz
65 Rose St, Bo-Kaap, T021-426 0636, monkeybiz.co.za.
Mon-Fri 0900-1700,
Sat 0900-1300.
Something of a local sensation, Monekybiz creates employment for women (many of them HIV positive) in the townships of Mandela Park and Khayelitsha. The women create beautiful and quirky one-off bead works, including figures, animals and accessories.

Out of This World
Victoria Wharf, T021-419 3246.
Open 0900-2100.
This has one of the more tasteful selections of the many African arts and crafts shops at the V&A Waterfront, and there's also carefully chosen ethnic interior decor items collected from around the world.

Streetwires
77 Shortmarket St, T021-426 2475, streetwires.co.za.
Mon-Fri 0900-1700,
Sat 0900-1300.
Another wire sculpture cooperative supporting local communities, which is a useful place to browse these interesting South African craft works without feeling under pressure from the usual street vendors. You can also meet the artists.

Activities & tours

Adventure tours
Abseil Africa
T021-424 4760,
abseilafrica.co.za.
Operates one of the world's highest and longest commercial abseils – 112 m down Table Mountain – R495 excluding cable car fee. Also runs day trips to other abseil points around the

Cape and kloofing (canyoning) trips, which involve hiking, boulder-hopping and swimming along mountain rivers.

Cabrinha
T021-556 7910, cabrinha.co.za.
The Cape's strong winds have made it a very popular site for kiteboarding. The best spot is

Dolphin Beach at Table View, north of the city centre where winds are strong and waves perfect for jumping. This company rents out equipment to experienced kiteboarders and offers two-hour lessons at Table View for R495 for beginners, and is affiliated to the International Kiteboarding Organization (IKO).

Surfing on Noordhoek Beach.

Downhill Adventures
Downhill Adventures, Shop 10 Overbeek Building corner Kloof, Long & Orange St, T021-422 0388, downhilladventures.com.
Guided hikes up Table Mountain; mountain biking such as the popular Table Mountain double descent, which is a 90% downhill trail around Devil's Peak;

Tip...

Surfing is a serious business in Cape Town, and there are excellent breaks catering for learners right through to experienced surf rats. Some of the best breaks are on Long Beach, Kommetjie, Noordhoek, Llandudno, Kalk Bay, Muizenberg and Bloubergstrand. To check out the local scene visit wavescape.co.za.

kiteboarding on Dolphin Beach in Table View; sandboarding on the dunes one hour north of Cape Town; and also surfing instruction and hire.

Homeland
305 Long St, T021-426 0294, homeland.co.za.
Mountain bike and helmet rentals cost ₨140 for 24 hours; cheaper rates the longer you hire. Also rents camping equipment, surf boards, paddle skis and wetsuits (essential) to experienced surfers.

Para-Pax
T082-881 4724 (mob), parapax.com.
Paragliding from Lion's Head is very popular, with gliders landing by the sea between Clifton and Camps Bay. Tandem flights cost ₨950 and include drinks and refreshments. Pick-up/drop-off from hotels is ₨100 extra and for ₨150 you get photos and video.

Skydive Cape Town
T082-800 6290 (mob), skydivecapetown.za.net.
Tandem jumps on the West Coast for ₨1450; extra ₨570 for video and photos. There are fantastic views back across to Cape Town and Robben Island.

Boat tours
There are more than 20 boats of varying types and sizes operating from Quay 5, the Pierhead or the Clock Tower at the V&A Waterfront. Just take a stroll around and the touts at the various kiosks will tell you what's on offer and when the next departure is. You can choose from a sail on a schooner to Camps Bay, a quick ferry trip across one of the docks, a guided tour of the working harbour, a sunset cruise with champagne, or a fast inflatable jet boat ride.

Tigresse
Quay 5, V&A Waterfront, T021-421 0909, tigresse.co.za.
Upmarket outfit with daily departures on luxury catamarans for a 1½-hour sail out to Table Bay; booking advised during peak periods. ₨110, ₨180 with champagne, discounts for children (4-12).

Waterfront Boat Company
Quay 5, V&A Waterfront, T021-418 5806, waterfrontboats.co.za.
Six boats to choose from including a large catamaran and stylish schooner called the *Spirit of Victoria*, and a range of boat tours including around (not to) Robben Island, whale watching, sunset and dinner cruises. Prices start from ₨200 for 1½-hour sunset cruise, jet boat from ₨350, one hour.

Cultural tours
If you don't have a car, the most popular day tours from Cape Town are the Cape Peninsula, the Winelands and the townships. Peninsula tours generally go

down the west side to Hout Bay and offer an optional boat trip to see the seals on Duiker Island, then go over Chapman's Peak Drive (if it's open) and into the Table Mountain National Park to Cape Point. They return to the city on the eastern side with a stop to see the penguins at Boulders Beach. Winelands tours take in about half a dozen vineyards in the Stellenbosch and Paarl regions. Township tours usually begin at the District Six Museum and continue to Langa and Khayelitsha, and companies work with the communities they visit, putting back some of the proceeds. If you want to combine a half-day township tour with the excursion to Robben Island, all operators will drop off at the ferry. For a full list of tour operators, visit tourismcapetown.co.za.

Andulela Experience
T021-790 2590, andulela.com.
This sensitive company offers very different interactive township tours that focus on music, poetry, jazz and soccer from ₽495, and a half-day visit to Bo-Kaap that includes a walking tour, a Cape Malay cookery lesson and lunch for ₽470.

Tip…
For information about city tours on open-top buses with City Sightseeing, visit citysightseeing. co.za, or see Getting around, page 78.

Cape Capers
T021-448 3117, tourcapers.co.za.
A range of trips, including half-day tours looking at Cape Town's slave history, District Six and Bo-Kaap tours and the Cape Care Route that goes to social and environmental projects on the Cape Flats. Tours start from ₽340.

Cape Rainbow Tours
T021-551 5465, caperainbow.com.
Tours are in many European languages and go to the townships, Winelands, Peninsula and, in season, to the West Coast to see the flowers and Hermanus to see the whales. Tours from ₽390.

Day Trippers
T021-511 4766, daytrippers.co.za.
Peninsula tours which include one or two hours of cycling at Cape Point, Winelands and township tours, and a guided hike up to the top of Table Mountain. Good value and fun, popular with backpackers. Tours start from ₽345.

Endeavour Safaris
T021-556 6114, endeavour-safaris.com.
This ground-breaking company offers assisted tours to the Cape Peninsula, Robben Island, District Six Museum, Table Mountain, Kirstenbosch and Winelands for the frail and physically challenged, with specially adapted vehicles and trained guides. They can also arrange tours for the deaf, blind and people needing oxygen or regular kidney dialysis. They can also organize longer tours, such as a six-day tour of Cape Town for the visually impaired that includes elements of sound and touch like African drumming and crushing grapes in the Winelands. Safaris across Southern Africa are also available.

Footsteps to Freedom
T083-452 1112, footstepsoffreedom.co.za.
Mon-Sat 1030-1330, ₽120, ₽60 children (under 12).
Starting at Cape Town Tourism, this is a walking tour of central Cape Town which goes to the Castle, District Six Museum and Company's Garden and can be combined with a township minibus tour later in the afternoon. English and German spoken, and it's the best way to learn about the city centre's historical past.

Friends of Dorothy
T021-465 1871, friendsofdorothytours.co.za.
Gay-friendly tours, including a Four Passes tour, Peninsula, Winelands and whale-watching trips and customized three- to five-day 'Over the Rainbow' tours of the Garden Route. Gay drivers and guides, maximum seven. Half-day tours start from ₽350.

Hylton Ross
T021-511 1784, hyltonross.com.
A full range of day tours, including Cape Point with optional boat ride to see the seals from Hout Bay, Winelands, township, and longer trips to the Garden Route.

Diving
The Cape waters are cold but are often clear and good for kelp diving and there are a number of interesting wrecks off the coast. The best season for diving is during the winter months when the weather ensures the sea is flat as the prevailing winds blow offshore. Water temperatures are 12-18°C; visibility is usually 5-10 m. When the winds change direction in the summer months however, visibility can be reduced to almost zero.

Dive Action
22 Carlisle St, Paarden Island, T021-511 0800, scubadivecapetown.co.za.
Full dive shop and training centre offering a range of wreck, shore and coral dives around the Cape.

Table Bay Diving
Quay 5, V&A Waterfront, T021-419 8822, tablebaydiving.com.
Dive charters and full range of PADI courses. Scuba and snorkelling gear for sale.

Helicopter flights
The Hopper
Quay 5, V&A Waterfront, T021-419 8951, thehopper.co.za.
The 15-minute flight goes along the coast to Camps Bay, then turns back through Kloof Nek to see the top of Table Mountain and the City Bowl; ₨500 per person. Longer 20-, 30- and 60-minute flights take in other parts of the peninsula.

The Huey Helicopter Co
Quay 5, V&A Waterfront, T021-419 4839, thehueyhelicopterco.com.
Flights in an ex-US Army Huey that served during the Vietnam War – as the sides are open this is more of an adrenalin activity. The 30-minute loop goes down as far as Noordhoek and across to False Bay and back over Constantia; ₨1800.

Tip...
Cape Town looks quite incredible from the air and a helicopter flight is a great way to get a grip of the geography of Table Mountain. Passengers are ferried by golf-cart from Quay 5 to the helipad beyond the Table Bay Hotel.

Shark cage diving

Offshore from Gansbaai, 165 km southeast of Cape Town, Dyer Island is an important breeding spot for African penguins and many other sea birds. On nearby Geyser Island there is a breeding Cape fur seal population thought to number 50,000. The area between the two islands is known as Shark Alley, as great white sharks are attracted to the plentiful food. Full-day excursions to Gansbaai for diving with great white sharks are available from Cape Town. People with a diving certificate can see them from an underwater cage, and non-divers can still do it, but they first have to spend a day doing a course. Expect to pay in the region of ₨1100 plus extra for transfers to and from Cape Town.

Shark Diving Unlimited, Gansbaai, T028-384 2787, sharkdivingunlimited.com.

Shark Lady, Kleinbaai, T028-312 3287, sharklady.co.za.

White Shark Adventures, Gansbaai, T028-384 1380, whitesharkadventures.com.

White Shark Diving Co, Kleinbaai, T021-461 1583 (Cape Town), sharkcagediving.co.za.

Transport

Daily long-distance buses head north up the N7 to Upington (13 hrs) and Windhoek (21 hrs) in Namibia, east along the N2 to George (7 hrs), Knysna (8 hrs), and Port Elizabeth (13 hrs), and northeast up the N1 to Johannesburg (20 hrs).

Contents

Noordhoek Beach, Cape Peninsula.

Cape Peninsula

Introduction

J utting 75 km out into the Atlantic Ocean, the Cape Peninsula has the Atlantic Seaboard along its west coast and False Bay along the east. At the northern end is Table Mountain overlooking Cape Town, and at the southern end is the Cape of Good Hope. Contrary to common belief, this is not the meeting place of the Atlantic and Indian oceans (that occurs at Cape Agulhas, some 200 km to the southeast). However, it is where ships begin to travel more eastward than southward, so rounding of the Cape in 1488 was a major milestone in the attempts to establish direct trade with the Far East. In 1578 Sir Francis Drake described the Cape Peninsula as "the fairest cape in the whole circumference of the globe", and most people would still agree with him. The rugged Table Mountain range serves as a spine, and is flanked by long sandy beaches, rocky coves and outcrops, trendy suburbs and quaint fishing villages, and is pounded by the ocean on all sides.

What to see in...

...one day
From Cape Town drive through the luxurious **Atlantic Seaboard** suburbs, and perhaps stop for breakfast in **Camps Bay**. In **Hout Bay** join a boat trip to see seals on **Duiker Island**, before driving around spectacular **Chapman's Peak**. Spend a couple of hours exploring the **Table Mountain National Park** and drive back to Cape Town via the scenic fishing villages on **False Bay** and the penguins at **Boulders Beach**.

...a weekend or more
Spend some leisurely time on the peninsula by visiting the museums in **Simon's Town**, hiking in the **Silvermine Reserve**, shopping at the quirky shops in **Kalk Bay**, or wine-tasting in **Constantia**. The beaches at **Clifton** and **Camps Bay** are perfect for long lazy days.

Cape of Good Hope.

Around the region

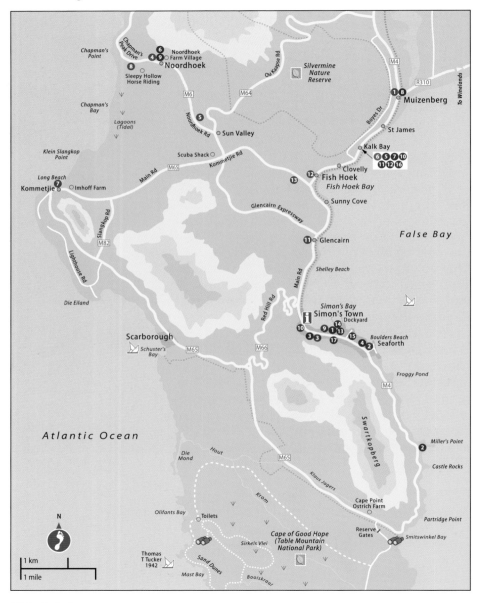

Chapman's Peak Drive

Chapman's Point

Noordhoek
Farm Village
Noordhoek

Sleepy Hollow
Horse Riding

Chapman's Bay

Lagoons (Tidal)

Klein Slangkop Point

Long Beach

Kommetjie

Imhoff Farm

Main Rd

Noordhoek Rd

Sun Valley

Kommetjie Rd

Scuba Shack

Ou Kaapse Rd

Silvermine Nature Reserve

Boyes Dr

M4

R310

To Winelands

Muizenberg

St James

Kalk Bay

Clovelly

Fish Hoek
Fish Hoek Bay

Sunny Cove

False Bay

Glencairn Expressway

Glencairn

Shelley Beach

Simon's Bay
Simon's Town
Dockyard

Boulders Beach
Seaforth

Froggy Pond

M4

Swartkopberg

Miller's Point

Castle Rocks

Scarborough

Schuster's Bay

Die Eiland

Slangkop Rd

Lighthouse Rd

M82

M65

M66

Red Hill Rd

Main Rd

Atlantic Ocean

N

Die Mond

Hout

Olifants Bay

Toilets

Krom

Klaus Jagers

M65

Cape Point Ostrich Farm

Reserve Gates

Partridge Point

Smitswinkel Bay

Thomas T Tucker 1942

Sand Dunes

Sirkels Vlei

Cape of Good Hope
(Table Mountain National Park)

Booiskraal

Mast Bay

1 km

1 mile

140 Cape Peninsula

Beach huts near Muizenberg.

Cape Peninsula listings

Atlantic Seaboard

The suburbs on the Atlantic Seaboard are the most exclusive in Cape Town and, with a mountainous background and views over the crashing ocean, some of the most beautiful. The beaches are glorious but alas the Atlantic is usually too cold for swimming. Nevertheless in summer they are extremely popular for sunbathing, sports and as places to come at the end of a Cape Town day to watch the sunset. Most visitors explore the peninsula by taking the coast roads from Cape Town down through the Atlantic Seaboard to Table Mountain National Park, and then return to the city via False Bay. This can be done under your own steam and a day's car hire is an ideal way to explore at your own pace; alternatively, all the tour operators offer the excursion – some take mountain bikes too, for a spot of cycling in the Table Mountain National Park. If self-driving you can go in either direction, but to see the seals on Duiker Island from Hout Bay you need to be there early in the day so it makes sense to head down the west coast first.

Clifton

Map: Cape Town, C3, p80.

Cape Town's best-known beaches stretch along Clifton, and are renowned as the playground of the young and wealthy; this is the place to see and be seen. Other than being hotpots of high society, Clifton's four sheltered beaches are stunning, perfect arches of powder-soft white sand sloping gently into turquoise water. The beaches, reached be a series of winding footpaths, are divided by rocky outcrops and are unimaginatively named First, Second, Third and Fourth. Each has a distinct character – if you're bronzed and beautiful, head to First beach. More demure visitors may feel more comfortable on Fourth, which is popular with families and has been an award-winning Blue Flag beach for many years now. The sunbathing and swimming are good on all the beaches and life guards are on duty, but note that the water is very cold – usually around 12°C. Most of the relatively small-scale, high-luxury development has been behind the beaches (some impressive houses can be glimpsed from the winding steps leading down).

Essentials

➒ Getting around The tour operators take the Atlantic Seaboard route on Cape Peninsula day tours, but a car is a logical option if you want to stop. Some minibus taxis from central Cape Town go as far as the police station in Camps Bay, and Golden Arrow buses (roughly one an hour) go to Hout Bay. The City Sightseeing bus (see page 78) goes as far as Hout Bay on its Blue Route via Kirstenbosch and the southern suburbs and then returns to Cape Town via Camps Bay, Sea Point and Green Point.

➒ ATM These can be found in all the towns and shopping malls.

➊ Tourist information There are several tourist offices around the peninsula and additional information can be found at capepointroute.co.za.

Tip...

Be warned that there is limited parking on the main road above the beaches in Clifton in high season, so get there early.

Clifton Beach.

Around the region

Camps Bay & the Twelve Apostles

Map: Cape Town, B3/B4, p80.

Following the coast south, you soon skirt around a hill and come out over Camps Bay, a long arch of sand backed by the Twelve Apostles. This is one of the most beautiful (and most photographed) beaches in the world and it also has Blue Flag status, but the calm cobalt water belies its chilliness. The sand is also less sheltered than at Clifton, and sunbathing here on a windy day can be painful. But there are other distractions: the beachfront is lined with excellent seafood restaurants, and a sundowner followed by a superb meal is quite the perfect ending to a day in Cape Town.

The drive between Camps Bay and Hout Bay runs along the slopes of the Twelve Apostles and is beautiful. Apart from the turning to Llandudno, there is no easy access to the coast until you reach Hout Bay. Llandudno itself is a small, exclusive settlement with only one road in and out, and a fine beach and excellent surf but again parking can be difficult on a sunny day.

Hout Bay

There is a fleet of Rikki taxis (see page 79) that operates in the Hout Bay area, T021-786 2136, rikkis.co.za, Mon-Thu 0630-0200 and Fri-Sun 24 hrs.
Map: Cape Town, B7, p80.

Hout Bay, a historical fishing harbour with an attractive beach, attracts swarms of South African families during peak season. Most come for the seafood restaurants and boat trips, but the best reason for heading here is for spectacular Chapman's Peak Drive (see page 145), which begins just outside town. As the sun sets in the summer months every lay-by along the road is filled with spectators, drink in hand.

Hout Bay itself is fairly attractive, with a busy fishing harbour at the western end of the bay; at the other end is a collection of shops and popular restaurants. By the harbour is a commercial complex known as Mariners Wharf, a popular attraction, although looking a little wind-worn these days. It is based upon Fisherman's Wharf in San Francisco, with a whole string of fish 'n' chip

Below: The Twelve Apostles. Opposite page: Fog rolls into the harbour of Hout Bay.

restaurants, souvenir shops, boats for hire and Snoekies Fresh Fish Market, close to the harbour gates. Even if you're not intending to buy anything it is worth a quick look to see the huge variety of fish that are caught off this coast. Boats run from here to see the seals on Duiker Island (see page 171).

Back in the town, next to the **tourist office** (T021-791 8380, tourismcapetown.co.za, Mon-Fri 0830-1730, Sat and Sun 0900-1300), is the **Hout Bay Museum** (4 Andrews Rd, T021-790 3474, Tue-Sat 1000-1230, 1400-1630, R5), with displays on the history of the area, aimed at visiting school groups.

The Sightseeing bus (Blue Route) stops at the **World of Birds** (Valley Rd, T021-790 2730, worldofbirds.org.za, 0900-1700, R59, under 16s R37), which has over 400 species of bird housed in impressive walk-through aviaries and is popular with families. There's also the Monkey Jungle, populated with squirrel monkeys and another enclosure with meerkats, banded mongooses and ground squirrels. It's a little run down but small children will enjoy getting close up to cranes, owls and the like and the monkeys are known to jump on visitors' heads.

Chapman's Peak Drive

chapmanspeakdrive.co.za.
It's now a toll road costing R24 per car.

It is worth hiring a car for a day just to drive along Chapman's Peak Drive, a breathtaking 9-km route with 114 curves, carved into the cliffs 600 m above the sea. The route was re-opened a few years ago, following extensive repairs and the rigging of giant nets to catch falling rocks. Although the road up to the toll gates is fairly busy with groups pulled over in viewpoints, the Drive itself is remarkably quiet, allowing outstanding and uninhibited views of the craggy coastline and thrashing ocean. The best time to drive along here is close to sunset in the summer, but the views of the crescent of white sand at Hout

Tip...

At the start of the drive just after the Chapman's Peak Hotel, look out for the lifelike bronze statue of a leopard crouching on a boulder, which commemorates the last living leopard sighted in the area in 1935.

Bay on one side and the vast stretch of Noordhoek on the other are recommended at any time. The Drive sometimes closes in bad weather. Check on the website.

Noordhoek

Map: Cape Peninsula, p140.

The greatest attraction here is the 8-km-long deserted beach, backed by a couple of tidal lagoons which offer excellent birdwatching. There's very little to the village itself, but the Noordhoek Farm Village on Beach Road is a pleasant spot for a coffee or light lunch, with restaurants and a couple of shops selling antiques, crafts and organic produce. The beach also offers the Cape's finest setting for horse riding along the shore (see page 172).

Kommetjie

Map: Cape Peninsula, p140.

Driving along the Atlantic side of the peninsula, you could miss Kommetjie altogether. The name means 'little basin', a reference to the natural inlet in the rocks which has been developed into a tidal pool. The settlement is small with a pub, restaurant, caravan park and little else. It is, however, a major surfing spot and Long Beach to the north is always busy with surfers, even in winter. There is also an interesting walk along Long Beach to the wreck of the *Kakapo*, offering a rare opportunity to examine a wreck at close quarters without having to don full scuba equipment. The *Kakapo* is a steamship which was beached here in May 1900 on her maiden voyage when the captain apparently mistook Chapman's Peak for Cape Point during a storm. The boiler and shell are still intact about 100 m above the high tide mark.

Imhoff Farm (on the M65 just before Kommetjie on the right, T021-783 4545, naturefarm.co.za. 0900-1700) is a collection of old whitewashed farm buildings. This is home to a number of gift shops, the Blue Water Café which does good breakfasts, light lunches and afternoon

teas, and a deli selling organic produce and excellent cheese where you can build a picnic. There are also a couple of camels here and some ponies; children will enjoy the short rides and there are a few farmyard animals for them to pet too.

Cape Point Ostrich Farm

Just outside Scarborough, 400 m north of the entrance to the Table Mountain National Park, T021-780 9294, capepointostrichfarm.com. Daily 0930-1730, R30, children R10. Map: Cape Peninsula, p140.

This is worth visiting for its in-depth tours, describing the lifecycle of the ostrich and during breeding season you can watch eggs hatching. The farm is home to 40 pairs of breeding ostriches. There's a pleasant tea garden on site and ostrich leather items and decorated eggs are for sale in the shop.

Nearby **Scarborough** consists of a scattering of weekend and holiday homes on the hillside overlooking the Atlantic. The beach is broad and long but swimming is not a good idea as the water is cold and there are strong currents.

**Above: Horse riding on Noordhoek Beach.
Opposite page: Lighthouse at Kommetjie.**

Table Mountain National Park

It is about 70 km from Cape Town centre to the reserve gate, access is by car or day tours from Cape Town, T021-701 8692, sanparks.org, capepoint.co.za.
Oct-Mar 0600-1800, Apr-Sep 0700-1700, ₨70, children ₨20.
Map: Cape Peninsula, p140.

Formerly the Cape of Good Hope Nature Reserve, this is now part of Table Mountain National Park, and was established in 1939 to protect the unique flora and fauna of this stretch of coast. Today, it is a dramatically wild area of towering cliffs, stupendous ocean views, some excellent hiking and, to top it all off, beautiful, deserted beaches. The area is an integral part of the Cape Floristic Kingdom, the smallest but richest of the world's six floral kingdoms. A frequently quoted statistic is that within the 7750 ha of the reserve there are as many different plant species as there are in the whole of the British Isles. In addition, it's home to several different species of antelope: eland, bontebok, springbok, Cape grysbok, red hartebeest and grey rhebok, as well as the elusive Cape mountain zebra, snakes, tortoises, ostriches and pesky baboons. Over 250 species have been recorded here, of which about 100 are known to breed within the reserve. There are plenty of vantage points where you can watch open-sea birds such as Cape gannet, shy albatross, sooty shearwater, white-chinned petrel, Sabine's gull and Cory's shearwater. In the Strandveld vegetation along the coast you can expect to see many fruit-eating birds such as the southern boubou, Cape robin and bully canary. Around Sirkels Vlei you will find freshwater birds.

Tip...

You can walk between Cape Point and the Cape of Good Hope (or vice versa) on a wooden boardwalk and access the beautiful Diaz Beach between the two via a 253-step staircase, and maps for other hiking routes are available from the information centre at Cape Point.

Cape Point

Cape Point Lighthouse is nothing special in itself, but the climb is well worth it for spectacular views of the peninsula. On a clear day the ocean views stretching all around are incredible – as is the wind, so be sure to hold on to hats and sunglasses. You can take the funicular railway (0800-1700, R40 return, R30 single, children under 16 R15/12) to the top, but the walk allows better views of the coast. It's about 500 m, is fairly steep and takes about 20 minutes, depending on how fit you are. There are plenty of viewpoints, linked by a jumble of footpaths.

The first lighthouse came into service in May 1860, but it quickly became apparent that the most prominent point on a clear day was far from ideal in poor weather. It was quite often shrouded in cloud while at sea level all was clear. After the Portuguese ship, the *Lusitania*, struck Bellows Rock in April 1911, work started on a new lighthouse built just 87 m above sea level, close to Diaz Rock. The current beam can be seen up to 63 km out to sea, and 18 km out there is a red lamp that warns ships that they are in the danger zone.

From the top point of the railway there are still approximately 120 steps to the old lighthouse where you get some of the finest views. If you are reasonably fit and have a good head for heights, there is a spectacular walk to the modern lighthouse at Diaz Point. From the renovated old lighthouse you can see the path running along the left side of the narrow cliff that makes up the point. The round trip takes about 30 minutes, but do not attempt it if it is windy – the winds around the Cape can reach up to 55 knots.

As you look down from the lighthouse at Cape Point it is easy to see how ships could suffer on a dark night in a storm, especially before the lighthouse was built. There are 23 wrecks in the waters around the Cape, but only five can be seen when walking in the reserve: *Thomas T Tucker* (1942); *Nolloth* (1964); *Phyllisia* (1968) and *Shir Yib* (1970), at Diaz Beach, and the *Tania* (1972), the most recent wreck, which can be seen at Buffel's Bay.

Places to eat

At Cape Point the **Two Oceans Restaurant** (T021-780 9200, two-oceans.co.za, 0900-1700) specializes in seafood and in summer it is advisable to book a table. There is also a takeaway cafeteria and a number of *braai* and picnic spots around the reserve.

False Bay

On the eastern side of the peninsula lies False Bay, a popular stretch of coast thanks to the warmer waters – temperatures can be as much as 8°C higher than elsewhere. The area is also more sheltered and better developed for tourism, although some of the landscape seems almost dull after the Atlantic Seaboard. Nevertheless, the area has some excellent beaches and gets busy with domestic tourists in summer. In spring, False Bay is the favoured haunt of calving whales, offering excellent opportunities to see southern right, humpback and Bryde whales. There are also some interesting fishing villages. False Bay is also known for its population of white sharks. A shark watch service operates from Muizenberg, signalling alerts when sharks come in proximity of bathers and surfers.

Across the bay from Cape Point, the clearly defined massif of rock on the eastern headland of the bay near the holiday resort of Pringle Bay is known as Hangklip. The name False Bay was coined by early sailors arriving from the east who confused the bay with Table Bay as, when they rounded Hangklip, they thought they were rounding Cape Point, which is similar in shape.

Constantia

Map: Cape Town, E6, p80.

South of Kirstenbosch National Botanical Gardens and the city's southern suburbs, lies the verdant area of Constantia and its winelands. This historical district was the first site of wine-making in South Africa and today it is an attractive introduction to the country's wines, as well as offering some fine examples of Cape Dutch architecture. There are five estates here, of which Groot Constantia (see below) is the best known and definitely worth a visit.

Groot Constantia

Groot Constantia Rd, T021-794 5128, grootconstantia.co.za.
Mon-Fri 0900-1800, Sat-Sun 1000-1800, free entrance to the main estate and orientation centre, museum R10, under 16s R2.
Map: Cape Town, D7, p80.

This old wine estate has some of the finest Cape Dutch architecture in South Africa, and with its rolling, vineyard setting and wine-tasting centre is a delightful place to spend an hour or two – although it does get swamped with tour buses in high season.

The main Manor House was originally home to Cape Governor Simon van der Stel between 1699 and 1712. He named the estate after Constantia, the daughter of the company official who had granted the land to him. Before his death, van der Stel planted most of the vines, but it was not until 1778 that the estate became famous for its wines. During this period the estate was unable to meet the demand from Europe, especially France. The house is now a museum full of period furniture and a booklet is available giving a brief description of the objects on show. The magnificent wine cellar behind the main house was designed by the renowned French architect, Louis Thibault, and today has displays on brandy and wine-making. There are two impressive giant oak vats each with a capacity of over 4000 litres. The Orientation Centre near the car park has some interesting storyboards on the history of the estate.

Essentials

❷ **Getting around**
By car False Bay is easily accessed from the city centre by the M3, which runs around the mountain and along the coast. There are also two routes across the mountainous spine linking the roads that hug the coast around the peninsula: you can cross from Noordhoek to Fish Hoek via the M65 and Sun Valley or, further south, take the Red Hill road from Scarborough to Simon's Town. Each route is convenient if your time is short, but the most scenic route is to follow the M65 along the coast from the Atlantic seaboard to False Bay (if Chapman's Peak is open).

By train The metro (T0800-656463, capemetrorail.co.za) continues through the southern suburbs to Simon's Town – the stretch following False Bay is spectacular. The line is marketed as a tourist route known as the Southern Line. For R25 (children 4-18 half price, under 4s free) you can travel between Cape Town, Observatory, Newlands, Muizenberg, Kalk Bay and Simon's Town as many times as you like between 0800 and 1630. Buy your ticket at the stations or Cape Town Tourism's head office in the city centre. You will get a map that indicates tourist attractions within walking distance of each station.

Historic manor house at Groot Constantia.

Five of the best

Constantia estates

❶ **Buitenverwachting** (Klein Constantia Rd, T021-794 5190, buitenverwachting.co.za, wine tasting Mon-Fri 0900-1700, Sat 0900-1300). This used to be part of Simon van der Stel's original Constantia estate, and today there are over a quarter of a million vines producing well-regarded reds and whites and a pink Blanc Noir. There is an excellent restaurant (see page 165) that also offers picnic baskets during the summer (Nov-Apr) from 1200-1600.

❷ **Constantia Uitsig** (off Spaanschemat River Rd, T021-794 1810, constantia-uitsig.com, Mon-Fri 0900-1700, Sat 0900-1300). Also part of Simon van der Stel's original Constantia estate, this has fine wines including a Méthode Cap Classique (South Africa's equivalent to champagne), luxury accommodation (see page 162), three excellent restaurants (see page 166), a cricket oval and a new spa.

❸ **Groot Constantia** (see page 151).

❹ **Klein Constantia** (Klein Constantia Rd, T021-794 5188, kleinconstantia.com, Mon-Fri 0900-1700, Sat 0900-1300). This is a beautiful hilly estate that began producing wine in 1689 with a great tasting centre but no restaurant. It is famed for its dessert wine, Vin de Constance, allegedly Napoleon's favourite wine.

❺ **Steenberg** (Steenberg Rd, T021-713 2222, steenberghotel.com, Mon-Fri 0900-1630, Sat-Sun 1000-1600). The first wine was produced here in 1695 and the beautiful H-shaped manor house dates to 1740. There are superb wines as well as luxurious lodgings (see page 162), a good restaurant (see page 166) and a spa and golf course.

The magnificent wine cellar behind the main house was designed by the renowned French architect, Louis Thibault, and today has displays on brandy and wine-making.

There are two restaurants: Jonkershuis has traditional Cape food; Simon's serves burgers, salads and seafood. Wine tastings at the sales centre, R25 for five wines; cheese platters available. Cellar tours are every hour on the hour.

Tokai Forest

Take the M3 out of town towards the southern suburbs. Just before Muizenberg, turn right into Tokai Rd and follow the signs for Tokai Manor House, T021-712 7471.
Open 0730-1700, R5.

Tokai was set up as a forest nursery in 1883 to start a programme of reforestation. Due to this, large parts of the Constantiaberg Mountains are covered in pine trees and as they are non-indigenous there is some debate on whether they should remain. Today, the forest is part of Table Mountain National Park. The arboretum contains 40 tree species – there are two walking trails, and horse riding and mountain biking are possible in the low-lying section (permits from the main gate).

Rondevlei Nature Reserve

From Cape Town take the M5, Prince George Dr, turn left into Victoria Rd in Grassy Park, and then right into Fisherman's Walk, 17 km from the city centre, 6 km from Muizenberg, T021-706 2404, rondevlei.co.za.
Open 0730-1700, on summer weekends 0730-1900, R5, under 13s R2.

This 220-ha reserve was originally established to protect the birdlife and the coastal fynbos vegetation. Today it is an important environmental education centre for local schools and, despite being surrounded by suburban sprawl, it is one of the best birdwatching spots around Cape Town. Only the northern shore of the lake is open to the public. A path follows the vlei's edge, along which there are two lookout towers equipped with telescopes. There are several hides along the water's edge, and cuts within the reeds allow views across the water. The best time to visit the reserve is from January to March when many European migrants can be seen. Over 230 bird species have been recorded; on a good day visitors should be able to see more than 65 species including white pelican, greater flamingo, African spoonbill and Caspian tern. There are a few small, shy mammals in the reserve, plus a small population of hippos. Inside the reserve is a small aquarium showing the freshwater fish that inhabit the area and a snake and amphibian house.

Muizenberg

Map: Cape Peninsula, p140.

Travelling out from the city centre on the M3, Muizenberg is the first settlement you reach on False Bay and as such has long been a popular local bathing spot. The Battle of Muizenberg was a small but significant military affair that began in June 1795 and ended three months later with the (first) British occupation of the Cape. Cecil Rhodes bought a holiday cottage here in 1899 and many other wealthy people followed, building some fine Victorian and Edwardian cottages along the back streets and attracting the likes of Agatha Christie and Rudyard Kipling to its shores. The resort has decayed significantly over the last couple of decades and now, with paint-peeled buildings and pot-holed roads, it's rather faded. Nevertheless the beach certainly remains beautiful: a vast stretch of powdery white sand sloping gently to the water. It is safe for swimming as there is no backwash, and

Below: Tokai Forest. Opposite page: Traditional Cape Dutch homestead in Constantia.

it is very popular with surfers who head out to the bigger breakers. At low tide you can walk into the shallow sea for more than 300 m without having to swim.

Historic Mile The walk along Main Street towards St James is known locally as the Historic Mile, as it takes you past a number of interesting old buildings. The first of note is the Station building, a fine example of art-deco architecture built in 1912. Further along on the right is the thatched **Het Post Huijs** (The Post House, 186 Main Rd, T021-788 7972, Mon-Fri 0800-1530, Sat 0900-1300, Sun 1400-1700, entry by donation), thought to be the oldest building in False Bay, dating back to 1742 and built by the Dutch East India Company as a toll-house to levy taxes on farmers passing by to sell their produce to ships moored in Simon's Bay. Inside are exhibits on the history of Muizenburg, with photos of the resort in its heyday and displays on the Battle of Muizenburg of 1795.

Rhodes Cottage (246 Main St, T021-788 9140, daily 1000-1600, entry by donation) is surprisingly small and austere for someone as wealthy as Cecil

Rhodes. It has been restored and now contains many of his personal items, including his diamond-weighing scales and the chest in which he carried his personal belongings, and there are displays on his life and achievements. This is where he died on 26 March 1902, and his body was transported by train with great ceremony to the Matobo Hills outside Bulawayo in Zimbabwe, where he was buried in a giant rock outcrop.

Not open to the public are Graceland, further along Main Road, with arched balconies and glazed clay roof tiles, which was the home of John Garlick, a well-known merchant at the turn of the 20th century, and Stonehenge, an Italian-style villa that once belonged to HP Rudd of De Beers Consolidated Mines.

St James

Map: Cape Peninsula, p140.

Just beyond Muizenberg lies the more upmarket resort of St James, an appealing village with characteristic brightly coloured bathing huts lining the tidal pool. The village is named after a Roman

Catholic church which was built here in 1854 to save Catholics having to travel as far as Simon's Town to attend services – interestingly, some of the early settlers were Catholic Filipino fishermen. There is a small sheltered beach and reasonable surf off Danger Beach and the tidal pool is a safe place for a swim.

St James is also a suitable starting point for a hike in the excellent Silvermine section of the Table Mountain National Park. A path starts on Boyes Drive and climbs up through the Spes Bona Forest to Tartarus Cave. The views alone are worth the hike (see pages 93 and 148 for further details of hiking in the reserve).

Kalk Bay

Map: Cape Peninsula, p140.

Kalk Bay is one of the most attractive settlements on False Bay, with a bustling fishing harbour and a bohemian vibe. The town is named after the lime kilns that produced kalk from shells in the 17th century, and created the white-walled appearance of many houses in the Cape, especially amongst the Bo-Kaap community. The word kalk is derived from the Dutch word for lime. Today it remains a fishing harbour, worked mainly by a coloured community which somehow escaped the Group Areas Act under Apartheid. It is one of the few coloured settlements on the peninsula.

Main Road is an appealing spot, lined with bric-a-brac and antiques shops – Kalk Bay Gallery, Cape to Cairo and Railway House have the most intriguing offerings – and a handful of arty cafés.

Tip…

Look out for returning deep-sea fishing boats around the middle of the day, as there's a daily impromptu quayside auction. You can buy a variety of fresh fish at the counters and for an extra small fee get them gutted for you too. Between June and July the harbour is busy with the *snoek* season, one of the most plentiful local fish harvests. You can see seals in the harbour who cheekily hop up to try and get to the fish on the counters.

The beach is sandy and safe for swimming, with a couple of tidal pools for children to explore. Another attraction is Seal Island, an important breeding ground for birds and seals, the latter attracting hungry great white sharks. Cruises run from Simon's Town (see page 157). At the harbour, Kalky's (see page 167) serves up great fish and chips in a colourful wooden shed. The Holy Trinity Church on Main Road has a thatched roof, and its windows are considered to be some of the finest in the Cape. On Quarterdeck Road is a tiny mosque built in the 1800s.

High up behind the town is Boyes Drive, a scenic road connecting the bay with Muizenburg. It's a spectacular route offering sweeping views of False Bay and the Atlantic, and takes just 10 minutes to complete – look out for the signs from Main Road as you head out of Kalk Bay towards Simon's Town.

Below: Fishing boats in Kalk Bay harbour.
Opposite page: Colourful beach huts on Muizenberg beach.

Around the region

Clovelly

Map: Cape Peninsula, p140.

Continuing along the main road, the next settlement you reach is Clovelly, tucked between the waters of False Bay and the mountains of the Silvermine reserve. Along the main street are several shops and places to have a snack. Anyone visiting from the West Country in Britain will be interested to know that this community is named after the village in Devon. Golf enthusiasts should head a little way inland for the Clovelly Country Club (clovelly.co.za).

Silvermine Nature Reserve

From Cape Town, follow the M3 from Newlands to its very end and then take a right. After 2 km turn left into Ou Kaapseweg Road, M64. The reserve is clearly signposted after 4 km.
Sunrise-sunset.
Map: Cape Peninsula, p140.

This is a popular local reserve, now part of the Table Mountain National Park, but not often visited by overseas visitors. Table Mountain and Cape Point tend to dominate the open-air attractions, and rightly so, but this reserve is well worth a visit if you enjoy hiking, plus there are great views across False Bay and the Atlantic Ocean.

Like much of the Cape, the reserve encompasses one of the oldest floral kingdoms in the world. Over 900 rare and endangered species have been recorded in the mountains, including many types of proteas, ericas and reeds. In addition to the plants there are a couple of patches of indigenous forest in the Spes Bona and Echo valleys. Ornithologists should look out for black eagles, ground woodpeckers, orange-breasted sunbirds and rock kestrels. If you're extremely lucky, you may also come across small shy mammals such as lynx, porcupine and various species of mongoose.

A tarred road leads from the western sector gates to the Silvermine Reservoir built in 1898 to supply Kalk Bay and Muizenberg with water until 1912. There is a shady picnic site under some pine trees close to the dam. One of the more popular walks from here is to Noordhoek Peak (754 m), a

Below: Silvermine Nature Reserve. Opposite page: Fish Hoek.

Sea Dog

An enormous great dane, Just Nuisance is the only dog in history to ever receive the naval ranking of Able Seaman and, on his death in 1944, he was buried with full military honours. His favourite spot was to lie on the deck at the top of the gangplank. No one could easily get past him and he was loath to move, hence the name. Just Nuisance escorted sailors home after a night on the town, pulling them by the sleeve and guiding them back to their barracks. He also enjoyed commuting between Simon's Town and Cape Town on the train and as a sailor was entitled to a free rail pass. He carried this in his collar.

circuit of about 7 km. The path is marked by stone cairns. At the summit there are spectacular views of the Sentinel and Hout Bay. Another interesting walk is from the car park to Elephant's Eye Cave covered with ferns and hanging plants. En route you pass the Prinz Kasteel waterfall. Allow about three hours for the round trip.

Fish Hoek

Map: Cape Peninsula, p140.

Fish Hoek is one of the most conservative settlements on the coast, not least because the sale of alcohol is prohibited here. It does, however, have a fine beach – perhaps the best for swimming after Muizenberg – which stretches right across the Fish Hoek valley. Swimming is safe at the southern end of the bay, but avoid the northern end where a small river enters the sea, as there is the danger of quicksand. From mid-August to October, there is a good chance of catching a glimpse of whales from here. The valley which stretches behind the town joins with Noordhoek beach on the Atlantic coast. In recent geological times this was flooded and all the lands towards Cape Point were in fact an island.

Glencairn

Map: Cape Peninsula, p140.

It is easy to drive through this coastal resort without realizing you've actually been here,

although it does have one of the best mid-range hotels in False Bay (see page 162). There is a small beach by the railway station but it is exposed to the southeast winds. Be wary of the cross currents close to the inlet where a small river enters the sea. At low tide you can occasionally see the remains of a steamship, the *Clan Stuart*. She was blown aground on 20 November 1914 while the crew drank in the local hotel.

Simon's Town

Tourist office, 111 St George's St,
T021-786 8440, simonstown.com.
Map: Cape Peninsula, p140.

This is the most popular town on False Bay, with a pleasant atmosphere and numerous Victorian buildings lining Main Street. If you want a break from Cape Town, this makes for a good alternative base from which to explore the peninsula. It's also a good place to spot whales in False Bay and notice the statue of a life-size southern right whale on the quayside of the waterfront.

Simon's Town is named after Simon van der Stel, who decided that an alternative bay was needed for securing ships in the winter months as Table Bay suffered from the prevailing northwesterly. However, because of the difficult overland access, the bay was little used in the early years. It was not until 1743 that the Dutch East India Company finally built a wooden pier and some barracks here. In 1768 the town transferred into British hands and, following the end of the Napoleonic Wars in Europe, the British decided to turn Simon's Town into a naval base. It remained as such until 1957 and is now a base for the South African Navy.

Take some time to wander up the hill away from the main road – the quiet, bougainvillea-bedecked houses and cobbled streets with their sea views are a lovely retreat from the bustling beaches. The main swimming spot is Seaforth Beach, not far from Boulders. To get there, turn off St George's Street into Seaforth Road after passing the navy block to the left. The beach is the second on the right, on Kleintuin Road. It has changing and toilet facilities, snack bars, restaurants and a clean stretch of shady lawn bordering the beach with some picnic spots and bench seats. The swimming is safe, as there is no surf due to offshore rocks which protect the beach.

Simon's Town Museum (Old Residency, Court Rd, T021-786 3046, Mon-Fri 0900-1600, Sat 1000-1300, Sun 1100-1500, entry by donation) This has displays related to the town's history as a naval base for the British and South African navies. Several displays are dedicated to a dog, Just Nuisance (see box, page 157), whose image has become Simon's Town's unofficial mascot, and there's a bronze statue of him on Jubilee Square. Also of interest is the Peoples of Simon's Town Exhibit, a collection referring to the forcible removal of coloured families from the area in the 1960s and 1970s. The building itself was built in 1777 as the winter residence of the Governor of the Cape.

South African Naval Museum (Court Rd, T021-787 4686, 1000-1600, entry by donation) This will appeal to anyone who has maritime interests and includes a collection of model ships, gunnery displays, mine-sweeping equipment, old diving suits, naval uniforms, and a modern submarine control room. It's housed in a dockyard storehouse built in 1810.

Warrior Toy Museum (St George's St, T021-786 1395, 1000-1600, entry by donation) This is a tiny museum with an impressive collection of model cars, trains, dolls and toy soldiers. It is a great little place and definitely worth a stop – nostalgic for adults and fun for kids. New and old model cars are also for sale.

Heritage Museum (Amlay House, St George's St, T021-786 2302, Tue-Fri 1100-1600, Sat 1100-1300, entry by donation) The museum faithfully charts the history of the Muslim community in Simon's Town, which was designated a 'white' area during the Group Area Act and over 7000 people classified as coloured were relocated. The Amlay family were the last to be forcibly removed from Simon's Town in 1975 and were the first to return in 1995. Today the Muslim community has all but disappeared here, although there is still an attractive working mosque up behind Main Road. The exhibition consists mainly of pictures and artefacts dating back to the turn of the 20th century. There is a traditional bridal chamber, with wedding clothes and a display in the Hadj room.

Boulders Beach

2 km south of Simon's Town, well signposted off the main road, T021-786 2329, sanparks.org. Apr-Sep 0800-1700, Oct-Mar 0700-1900, R30, children (1-11) R10.
Map: Cape Peninsula, p140.

In a lovely series of little sandy coves surrounded by huge boulders (hence the name), the attraction here is the colony of African penguins that live and nest between the boulders. One of the highlights of a visit to Cape Town is watching them happily go about their business of swimming, waddling and braying (their characteristic braying was the reason they were, until recently, known as Jackass penguins). This is one of two colonies on mainland Africa, the other being in Betty's Bay (see page 188). While visitors used to be able to walk on the beach it is now a protected area (as part of Table Mountain National Park) and from the visitors' centre a (wheelchair accessible) boardwalk leads you down to viewpoints over the beach. Look out for the little concrete half moon huts that have been recently installed for the penguins to nest in and look up from the beach where you're likely to see a single penguin contemplating life from the top of a boulder. Every visitor gets a leaflet telling the story of the colony – it started from just two breeding pairs in 1985 and now numbers some 3000 penguins – and the shop sells all things 'penguiney'.

If you want to swim, go to the adjoining Seaforth Beach, which is a lovely sandy cove with a picnic lawn; you may bump into a stray penguin in the water.

Miller's Point

Map: Cape Peninsula, p140.

This is the last easy access to the sea on this side of the peninsula. Beyond Partridge Point the main road cuts into the hillside, and access to the beach is via steep footpaths. Miller's Point has two sandy coves and a tidal pool. There is a large caravan site here plus a picnic area and a good restaurant, the Black Marlin (see page 168), which is a popular lunch stop for coach tours of the Cape Peninsula. The beach itself is mainly used for speedboat launches;

there are a few scuba-dive sites off shore and the Cape Boat and Ski-Boat Club is located here.

The road then climbs before rounding the mountains by Smitswinkel Bay. On a clear day you can look back to a perfect view of the cliffs plunging into the sea. A short distance from the shore is the Table Mountain National Park entrance to Cape Point and the Cape of Good Hope.

Beyond Miller's Point be on the lookout for baboons. They are not shy and will approach cars. Wind windows up and remember they can be vicious.

Tip...

A number of boat trips to the Cape of Good Hope originate from Simon's Town harbour. Taking a trip from here allows views of the spectacular coastline and its hinterland from a different angle. In addition to straightforward sightseeing tours, there are several options for viewing bird life, seals and whales during the right season. For tour operators, see page 172.

African penguin, Boulders Beach.

Sleeping

Camps Bay & the Twelve Apostles

The Bay ℝℝℝℝ
Victoria Rd, Camps Bay, T021-438 4444, thebay.co.za.
Map: Cape Town, C3, p80.
Set just across the road from the beach, with 78 modern deluxe air- rooms all with views across the bay, pleasant contemporary feel, large pool with deck, wellness spa that also offers cosmetic procedures and beach-facing restaurant with a good reputation. Excellent service, a well known place for the rich and famous, and has a jovial holiday atmosphere in summer.

Twelve Apostles ℝℝℝℝ
Victoria Rd, Twelve Apostles, T021-437 9000, 12apostleshotel.com.
Map: Cape Town, B4, p80.
In a gloriously scenic spot just to the south of Camps Bay beneath the Twelve Apostles, this 70-room five-star hotel, has a commanding position overlooking the ocean and features an award-winning spa, pool, excellent restaurant, bar that also offers afternoon tea and a small cinema. Spacious rooms have a luxurious cream and white decor, and have air conditioning, satellite TV and DVD players.

The Bay Atlantic Guest House ℝℝℝ
3 Berkley Rd, T021-438 4341, thebayatlantic.com.
Map: Cape Town, C3, p80.
Family-run guesthouse with some of the best views in Cape Town, with six individually decorated rooms, satellite TV, light and airy with terracotta tiles and white linen, some with private balcony and the penthouse has a jacuzzi. Quiet garden with good-sized pool, breakfast served on balcony overlooking the bay, relaxed atmosphere and 150 m walk to the beach.

Whale Cottage Guest House ℝℝℝ
57 Camps Bay Dr, T021-438 3840, whalecottage.com.
Map: Cape Town, C4, p80.
Small tasteful place with marine decor, 11 sunny air-conditioned double rooms and one self-catering apartment with separate entrance, breakfast deck overlooking the beach, good views of the Twelve Apostles, satellite TV and internet access, 500-m walk to the restaurants and beach. Also has properties in Hermanus, Franschhoek and Plettenberg Bay.

Hout Bay

Hout Bay Manor ℝℝℝℝ
Baviaanskloof, off Main Rd, T021-790 0116, houtbaymanor.com.
Map: Popout, Cape Town, B7.
A beautifully restored manor house built in 1871, with 20 air-conditioned individually decorated rooms, with polished wooden floors, chandeliers, plasma satellite TV, Wi-Fi, some with free-standing baths. The decor throughout is stunning and best described as Afro-chic, with bright splashes of colour, African antiques and modern items like a giant lamp made from enamel pots. There's a pool, gorgeous bar and lounge and celebrated Pure restaurant (see page 164).

Tintswalo Atlantic ℝℝℝℝ
2 km south of Hout Bay, off Chapman's Peak Dr, reservations T011-300 8888, tintswalo.com.
Map: Cape Town, B7, p80.
Luxury option right by the waves beneath Chapman's Peak Drive, with 10 themed suites named after islands – Zanzibar is decorated with Swahili antiques

Above: The bar at Hout Bay Manor.
Opposite page: Chapman's Peak Hotel.

and Antigua has a colourful Caribbean feel. The highlight is the long wooden deck with jaw-dropping views with pool and jacuzzi, and there's a restaurant, bar and open kitchen where guests can interact with the chefs.

Chapman's Peak Hotel ℞℞℞-℞℞
Chapman's Peak Dr, T021-790 1036, chapmanspeakhotel.co.za.
Map: Popout, Cape Town, B7.
This traditional hotel has 10 double rooms in the original historical building and 21 stylish more expensive rooms in a new block, with simple, contemporary decor, large windows, underfloor heating, baths for two, some with sea views. Pool, good restaurant (see page 165), popular bar with seating on veranda, great location just across from the beach and at the start of Chapman's Peak Drive.

Noordhoek
De Noordhoek Hotel ℞℞℞
At the Noordhoek Farm Village, at the junction of Chapman's Peak Dr and Village Lane, T021-789 2760, denoordhoek.co.za.
Map: Cape Peninsula, p140.
Newly built but in traditional Cape Dutch-style architecture, this has 21 sleekly modern air-conditioned rooms with satellite TV and internet, a comfortable lounge with bar and fireplace. Restaurants are in the farm village. Strong on environmental policies – water is heated by solar energy, everything is recycled, the gardens have been designed in a water-wise way and staff all live within a 10-km radius.

Monkey Valley Resort ℞℞℞
Mountain Rd, T021-789 1391, monkeyvalleyresort.com.
Map: Cape Peninsula, p140.
Resort with attractive self-catering thatched log cottages set in woodland overlooking Noordhoek Beach. Each sleeps four to eight, with two or three bedrooms, kitchen, lounge and bathroom, log fires, plus secluded veranda with superb views. There's also a good restaurant specializing in pizzas and seafood and serving breakfast all day.

Goose Green Lodge ℞℞
Briony Close, T021-789 2933, goosegreen.co.za.
Map: Cape Peninsula, p140.
B&B accommodation in main house, also has five self-catering cottages in converted family homes dotted around pretty gardens, sleeping up to eight, very comfortably furnished, close to Chapman's Peak and the beach. Pool, *braai*, children's playground and excellent farm breakfasts, which are also available to self-catering guests.

Kommetjie
The Long Beach ℞℞℞℞
1 Kirsten Av, T021-799 6561, thelongbeach.com.
Map: Cape Peninsula, p140.
Six modern luxury suites with views over Long Beach, spacious airy decor in pale blues and pinks, internet access, air conditioning and satellite TV, lunch and dinner on request, stunning swimming pool right on the sand dunes, bar, rates include all drinks. Special touches include fresh flowers, mobile phone with useful numbers punched in, and a chauffeur service is available to take guests to restaurants on the peninsula.

Listings

Tip...

Constantia is one of Cape Town's most exclusive suburbs dotted with luxury hotels. All are superb in lovely settings but are firmly in the upper price category.

False Bay

Constantia
Alphen Hotel ℞℞℞℞
Alphen Dr, T021-794 5011, alphen.co.za.
Map: Cape Town, F6, p80.
21 spacious rooms on an elegant 18th-century Cape Dutch estate, which is a National Monument. Suites and rooms are decorated with fine antiques and have polished floors and log fires. Lunch and supper in the Boer & Brit pub with its roaring fires or in the gardens during the summer, or gourmet dinners in the formal restaurant in the manor house, swimming pool.

The Cellars-Hohenhort Hotel ℞℞℞℞
93 Brommersvlei Rd, T021-794 2137, cellars-hohenort.com.
Map: Cape Town, E6, p80.
Part of the Relais & Chateaux group and one of the most luxurious hotels in Cape Town, set in two converted manor houses on a wine estate, with 13 spacious suites and 33 individually decorated double rooms, plus the Madiba Presidential Suite, a two-storey house with private pool. Two excellent restaurants

(see page 166). Two swimming pools, tennis court, golf course, set in 3½ ha of mature gardens which overlook False Bay, impeccable service.

Constantia Uitsig ℞℞℞℞
Spaanschemat, River Rd, T021-794 6500, constantia-uitsig.com.
Map: Popout, Cape Town, D7.
On the well-known wine estate, with 16 luxurious and spacious cottages set in neat gardens with views across vineyards to the mountain. Plush furnishings, private verandas, activities include horse riding and vineyard walks and there's a stunning spa, and two excellent restaurants of which La Colombe (see page 166) is considered one of the best in South Africa.

Steenberg Hotel ℞℞℞℞
Steenberg Rd, T021-713 2222, steenberghotel.com.
Map: Popout, Cape Town, D7.
Luxurious country hotel with 30 elegant, traditional rooms furnished with beautiful antiques, in converted farm buildings overlooking manicured gardens and working vineyards. Swimming pool, gym, spa and steam room, horse riding and 18-hole golf course. The award-winning Catharina Restaurant (see page 166) has an excellent reputation. Relaxed and friendly atmosphere.

Muizenburg
Bluebottle Guest House ℞℞
18 Mount Rd, T021-788 6100, blue-bottle.co.za.
Map: Cape Peninsula, p140.
There are outstanding views over False Bay and the Cape Flats from the six neat rooms with floor-to-ceiling glass windows and balconies. A mixture of modern decor with bright colours and antiques, wooden floors, self-catering kitchen, TV lounge, bar, lovely gardens carefully planted with indigenous plants. You need to be fit to get here though, as there are 131 steps to climb.

Kalk Bay
The Inn at Castle Hill ℞℞
37 Gatesville Rd, T021-788 2554, castlehill.co.za.
Map: Cape Peninsula, p140.
Elegant restored Edwardian house with wrought-iron balconies and veranda offering fine sea views. Six comfortable rooms with white linen and fresh flowers, guest lounge and breakfast room. The veranda is the most pleasant part of the house and perfect for whale watching during the season. Secure parking, well run.

Fish Hoek
Tranquillity Guest House ℞℞℞
25 Peak Rd, T021-782 2060, tranquil.co.za.
Map: Cape Peninsula, p140.
A peaceful family-run option, again reached by stairs, 600 m

above the town with jaw-dropping views, and four stylish rooms with huge showers, balconies, percale linen, satellite TV, Wi-Fi, nice touches include fruit platters and fresh roses. Generous home-cooked breakfasts. Watching the sunrise over the mountains on the other side of False Bay is quite special.

Sunny Cove Manor ℞℞
72 Simon's Town Rd, T021-7822274, sunnycovemanor.com.
Map: Cape Peninsula, p140.
Friendly, efficient family-run B&B in a solid old manor house overlooking False Bay and just a short walk from the beach, with four rooms with microwave, fridge, kettle and binoculars for whale-watching, some have wide ocean views, breakfast room and lounge. Rather fussy floral decor but recommended for families as affordable rooms sleep four.

Glencairn
Southern Right Hotel ℞℞
12-14 Glen Rd, T021-782 0314, southernright.info.
Map: Cape Peninsula, p140.
Delightful hotel in turn-of-the-20th-century building set a short walk from the sea. Eight double and twin rooms with high ceilings, dark polished wood floors, subtle decor, some with four-poster beds and baths only, others with shower and bath. Stylish bar and restaurant serving pub meals, seafood and grills and three boules pistes in front

of the hotel with regular matches on Friday and Sunday afternoons (guests can join in). A fashionable place but family friendly.

Simon's Town
British Hotel Apartments ℞℞℞℞
90 St George's St, T021-786 2214, britishhotelapartments.co.za.
Map: Cape Peninsula, p140.
Despite the unpromising name, this is one of the best places to stay in False Bay, with six elegant self-catering apartments in a Victorian building. Each is enormous, stretching over two open-plan floors, with three bedrooms, all with delightful Victorian bathrooms. Polished wood floors throughout, attractive mix of maritime antiques, art deco and stylish modern furnishings, open-plan kitchen and lounge, separate TV room, great views of the bay from magnificent balconies, breakfasts available on request.

Quayside Hotel ℞℞℞
Jubilee Centre, St George's St, on the seafront, T021-786 3838, relaishotels.com/quayside.
Map: Cape Peninsula, p140.
A smart, modern development in a great central location overlooking the harbour, with 26 spacious, air-conditioned double rooms with satellite TV and comfortable marine blue and white decor, bright and sunny with good views. Book well in advance during local holidays.

No restaurant but within walking distance of restaurants in Jubilee Square for which you get a voucher for breakfast.

Simon's Town Backpackers ℞
66 St George's St, T021-786 1964, capepax.co.za.
Map: Cape Peninsula, p140.
38-bed backpacker joint spread across cramped dorms and fairly pleasant doubles, some en suite, brightly painted walls and bush-camp-style furniture, small kitchen, honesty bar, TV lounge, *braai* on balcony overlooking the main street and harbour, bikes for hire and can organize sea kayaking. Fairly simple but spotlessly clean and within walking distance of shops and restaurants.

Boulders Beach
Boulders Beach Lodge ℞℞℞
4 Boulders Pl, T021-786 1758, bouldersbeachlodge.com.
Map: Cape Peninsula, p140.
One of the most relaxing places you could stay in the area. This friendly, well-run beachside guesthouse is a firm favourite, with nine double rooms and two family rooms with bathrooms, most arranged around a paved yard without sea view, good-sized beds and baths, simple, refreshing design. At night you're likely to see penguins exploring the grounds after everyone has gone home. Good restaurant and souvenir shop.

Eating

Clifton
Salt ℝℝℝ
34 Victoria Rd, Bantry Bay,
T021-439 7258,
saltrestaurant.co.za.
Open 1200-1500, 1830-2200.
Map: Cape Town, B2, p80.
Sophisticated formal restaurant
with contemporary decor and
magnificent ocean views from
the floor to ceiling windows,
especially at sunset. The menu
changes regularly but expect
the likes of slow-roasted pork,
braised duck leg or rib eye steak.
Free valet parking.

Camps Bay &
the Twelve Apostles
Blues ℝℝℝ
Victoria Rd, Camps Bay,
T021-438 2040, blues.co.za.
Open 1200-late.
Map: Cape Town, C3, p80.
Popular and well-known
restaurant and lounge/bar
with superb views and
Californian-style seafood menu
served to a beautiful crowd,
but you pay for the restaurant's
reputation. The newly revamped
interiors are luxurious and the

Tip...

Parking is always a problem in
Camps Bay on busy evenings and
the police regularly monitor the
road on the lookout for drunk
driving. Rather than drive, get
a regular or Rikki taxi.

long cocktail menu features
the signature Blues Bellini.

The Codfather ℝℝℝ
Corner of Geneva Dr and The
Drive, Camps Bay, T021-438 0782.
Open 1200-2300.
Map: Cape Town, C3, p80.
One of the best seafood
restaurants in Cape Town and a
stylish laid-back place offering a
range of superbly fresh seafood
with good views over the bay.
No menu – the waiter takes you
to a chilled counter and you pick
and choose whatever you like
the look of to make up a platter.
Also has an excellent sushi bar.

Ocean Blue ℝℝ
Victoria Rd, Camps Bay,
T021-438 9838.
Open 1000-late.
Map: Cape Town, C3, p80.
A friendly seafood restaurant on
Camps Bay trendy strip
overlooking the beach with
tavern-style decor, and less
pretentious than many of the
restaurants in the area. Good
fresh seafood, including superb
grilled prawns, butterfish kebabs,
seafood curries and a legendary
paella. Also has a breakfast menu.

Tuscany Beach ℝℝ
41 Victoria Rd, T021-438 1213,
tuscanybeachrestaurant.com.
Open 0700-2300.
Map: Cape Town, C3, p80.
Italian seafood place overlooking
the beach, open all day from
breakfast. Delicious seafood

specials – don't miss the
kingklip *espetadas* or the paella.
Also serves wood-fired pizzas,
salads, burgers and steaks.
Trendy place which gets very
busy for sundowners and
there's a long list of cocktails.

Cafés
Dizzy Jazz Café
41 The Drive, Camps Bay,
T021-438 2686, dizzys.co.za.
Open 1130-late.
Map: Cape Town, C3, p80.
Busy bar and music venue with a
pub-like atmosphere, popular at
the weekend, regular live music,
mostly jazz but has everything
from funk to rock and is a
platform for local bands,
comfortable couches, low tables,
food includes sushi and pizza.

Hout Bay
Pure ℝℝℝ
Hout Bay Manor, Baviaanskloof,
off Main Rd, T021-790 0116,
houtbaymanor.com.
Tue-Sat 1900-2130,
Sun 1200-1500.
Map: Popout, Cape Town, B7.
A beautifully decorated restaurant
almost entirely in silver, with lovely
chandeliers and neatly dressed
tables, run by a celebrated
German chef. There are three-,
five- and seven-course tasting
menus, which are paired with
wine, or an à la carte menu of
gourmet dishes including veal,
scallops, lobster, tuna and game
meat. Each is fabulously presented
with jus, foams and jellies.

Chapman's Restaurant ℞℞
Chapman's Peak Hotel, Chapman's Peak Dr, T021-790 1036, chapmanspeakhotel.co.za.
Open 1100-2200.
Map: Popout, Cape Town, B7.
A lively restaurant and bar with wood-panelled interior, serving good seafood dishes in frying pans, also grills and pub fare. They are famous locally for their grilled calamari and have Stella Artois beer on tap. The outside terrace gets packed in summer so arrive early to get a table.

Dunes ℞℞
Hout Bay Beach, T021-790 1876.
Open 0900-late.
Map: Cape Town, A7, p80.
Sprawling restaurant overlooking the dunes behind the beach, very popular with families, large menu, quick service but the food can disappoint – stick to the tasty fish and chips. Book ahead at weekends or you'll be stuck in the hot courtyard instead of the breezy balcony tables.

Cafés
Fish on the Rocks
Harbour Rd (beyond Snoekies Market), T021-790 1153.
Open 1000-1900.
Map: Cape Town, B7, p80.
Simple and delicious fresh fish and chips, deep-fried calamari and prawns, eaten from cardboard boxes at wooden tables overlooking the fishing boats in the harbour. You can try the popular local fish *snoek* here.

Noordhoek
The Foodbarn ℞℞℞
Noordhoek Farm Village, Chapman's Peak Dr, T021-789 1390, thefoodbarn.co.za.
Daily 1200-1500, Wed-Sat 1830-2100.
Map: Cape Peninsula, p140.
A French restaurant with lovely white linen-clad tables in an old barn and outside on the farm *stoep*. The short menu features well-thought-out dishes like leek and truffle risotto, crusted rack of lamb in garlic jus or beef sirloin with horseradish. There's also a deli (0800-1700) which is well known locally for its homemade bread.

Cafés
Café Roux
Noordhoek Farm Village, Chapman's Peak Dr, T021-789 2538, caferoux.co.za.
Tue-Sun 0830-1630.
Map: Cape Peninsula, p140.
A family-friendly restaurant with outside tables on crunchy gravel, this serves gourmet breakfasts like eggs Benedict or French toast with berries and syrup, plus salads and sandwiches, and more substantial meals like grilled line-fish and calamari, prawn curry and chicken pie.

False Bay

Constantia
Buitenverwachting ℞℞℞
Klein Constantia Rd, T021-794 5190, buitenverwachting.co.za.
Mon-Sat 1200-1500, 1830-2200.
Map: Popout, Cape Town, D7.
Fine dining with a cosmopolitan menu of flawless Italian, French and South African dishes from an award-winning chef and expect the likes of quail or scallops. Good service, upmarket, prices reflect the quality of the food, though the set three-, four- or five-course menus represent good value.

Chapman's Peak Hotel Restaurant.

What the locals say

A must-do in the winter months is to go to Catharina's at Steenberg in Constantia for their lunchtime buffet. The long table is laden with irresistible gourmet dishes from salads, pâtés, giant prawns, and savoury tartlets, to a full roast with all the trimmings. But my favourite are the to-die-for desserts like brulées, parfaits, mousses and an excellent Cape Brandy pudding.

Trevor Jordaan, Cape Town resident.

Catharina's ℝℝℝ
Steenberg Hotel, Steenberg Rd, T021-713 2222, steenberghotel.com.
Open 1200-1500, 1900-2130.
Map: Popout, Cape Town, D7.
One of the finest restaurants in the area, where meals are served outside under the oaks or in the contemporarily decorated dining room next to log fires. The menu features gourmet South African fare such as West Coast mussels, Knysna oysters and springbok loin, and there's a fine wine list.

The Greenhouse at Cellars ℝℝℝ
The Cellars-Hohenort Hotel, 93 Brommersulei Rd, T021-794 2137, cellars-hohenort.com.
Open 0730-2200.
Map: Cape Town, E5, p80.
One of two highly rated restaurants at this five-star hotel, set in a pretty conservatory with white wicker furniture. The Michelin-trained chef produces top-quality fare – mostly modern South African, so expect fresh

fish and game, and divine desserts. Excellent wine list to match.

La Colombe ℝℝℝ
Constantia Uitsig, Spaanschemat, River Rd, T021-794 6500, constantia-uitsig.com.
Mon-Sat 1230-1430, 1930-2130.
Map: Popout, Cape Town, D7.
This is a foodie shrine and was 2009 winner in *Eat Out* magazine as South Africa's best restaurant. Excellent French menu with strong Provençal flavours and some Asian influences, and you can expect the likes of rabbit, duck, fish and game dishes, with emphasis on rich sauces, jus and foams. The fine food is paired with wine on the seven-course tasting menus. Also here is the **Constantia Uitsig Restaurant** and the **River Café**.

Muizenburg
Empire Café ℝ
11 York Rd, T021-788 1250, empirecafe.co.za.
Tue-Sat 0700-2100,
Sun and Mon 0700-1600.
Map: Cape Peninsula, p140.
A little tatty but popular with local surfers, this serves eclectic breakfasts and lunch-time fare, including interesting salads and omelettes (try the famous bacon, banana and honey) and some specials like line-fish, rump of lamb or saucy pastas.

Kalk Bay
Harbour House ℝℝℝ
Kalk Bay Harbour, T021-788 4133, harbourhouse.co.za.
Open 1200-1600, 1800-2200.
Map: Cape Peninsula, p140.
Perched right on the rocks overlooking the ocean with great views of the jaunty fishing boats, with bright white decor and wooden decks, this is well known for its seafood including grilled crayfish, but also has rich meat dishes and vegetarian specials.

Cape to Cuba ℝℝ
Main Rd, T021-788 1566, capetocuba.com.
Open 1100-2300.
Map: Cape Peninsula, p140.
Atmospheric Cuban restaurant and cocktail bar serving good-value seafood with Caribbean flavours. Great setting on water's edge with tables overlooking the harbour, funky decor, Cuban music, good

cocktails and cigars for sale. The bar stays open till 0200 if there is the demand and cocktails include mojitos and daiquiris.

Brass Bell ℝℝ-ℝ
By the railway station, T021-788 5455, brassbell.co.za.
Open 1000-late.
Map: Cape Peninsula, p140.
A well-known and very popular pub and restaurant in a great location. The downstairs pub serves pizzas and burgers and gets packed with a young crowd around sunset, and is great for a cool beer outside close to the waves. The more expensive restaurant upstairs serves fresh fish and steak.

The Timeless Way ℝ
106 Main Rd, T021-788 5619.
Open 1200-2200.
Map: Cape Peninsula, p140.
An excellent, old-fashioned restaurant with polished wooden floors serving Cape cuisine, steaks and seafood. The *bobotie* is good, as is the pasta, gourmet burgers and Sunday roast lunch. The bar is popular with locals and has beer on tap.

Cafés
Kalky's
Kalk Bay Harbour, T021-788 1726.
Open 1000-2000.
Map: Cape Peninsula, p140.
Simple seafood and chips at plastic tables, very popular and freshly cooked, counter service and then listen for your number

to be called out. You'll rub shoulders with Kalk Bay's characterful fishermen here; look out for seals in the harbour.

Olympia Café & Deli
134 Main Rd, T021-788 6396.
Open 0700-2100.
Map: Cape Peninsula, p140.
Another Kalk Bay institution, this laid-back café serves some of the freshest bread on the peninsula, plus light lunches, fabulous cakes and fresh daily specials. Great atmosphere and good service, but expect to chalk your name on the blackboard and queue for a table at weekends.

Simon's Town
Bon Appetit ℝℝℝ
90 St George's St, T021-786 2412.
Tue-Sat 1200-1400, 1830-2200.
Map: Cape Peninsula, p140.
One of the finest restaurants on the peninsula specializing in top-notch French cuisine – the chef is Michelin-trained. Excellent set menus and imaginative main meals such as ravioli of rabbit plus French staples like confit de canard. Popular but quite small. Book ahead.

Bertha's ℝℝ-ℝ
Jubilee Sq, Wharf Rd, T021-786 2138, berthas.co.za.
Open 0700-2200, sushi only served at lunch and dinner.
Map: Cape Peninsula, p140.
During the day the outside terrace is a good place to enjoy

good fresh seafood and watch the goings on in the harbour. Inside is a dining area perfect for large family meals and there's a kiddies' menu. There's also a good range of breakfasts served until 1130.

The Two and Sixpence Tavern and Captain's Table ℝℝ-ℝ
88 St George's St, next to the British Hotel, T021-786 5735, captains-table.co.za.
Open 1100-0200.
Map: Cape Peninsula, p140.
Local British-style pub serving standard bar food such as burgers, bangers and mash, ploughman's, plus Yorkshire pudding specials, Sunday roasts and curry nights. Also has pool tables and occasional live music. The Captain's Table upstairs is the formal restaurant serving game and seafood dishes.

Quarterdeck ℝ
Jubilee Sq, T021-786 3825.
Sat-Thu 0800-1900,
Fri 0800-2300.
Map: Cape Peninsula, p140.
Simple café with great views over the harbour from the outside tables under shady trees, serving sandwiches, burgers and interesting salads like avocado with smoked chicken and biltong. Also has a Cape Malay buffet on Fri evenings. Just Nuisance (see page 157) watches diners from the square.

Entertainment

Cafés

Salty Sea Dog
Next to Quayside Centre,
T021-786 1918.
Mon-Sat 1000-2100,
Sun 1000-1630.
Map: Cape Peninsula, p140.
Cheap and cheerful place
serving fresh grilled or battered
fish and calamari and chips on
trestle tables in the little shack or
on outside tables overlooking
the harbour. Friendly and swift
service and sells wine. Popular
with tour groups.

Tibetan Teahouse
2 Harrington Rd, Seaforth,
T021-786 1544,
sopheagallery.com.
Open 1000-1700.
Map: Cape Peninsula, p140.
At the Sophea Art Gallery, this
offers wholesome vegetarian
fare and some vegan dishes, like
vegetable stews and soups, lentil
burgers, and dairy-free desserts.
Decor is bright red with Tibetan
prayer flags on the walls.

Boulders Beach

Boulders Beach Restaurant ℝℝ
Boulders Beach Lodge,
4 Boulders Place, T021-786 1758,
bouldersbeachlodge.com.
Open 0800-1115, 1200-1500,
1800-2130.
Map: Cape Peninsula, p140.
Homely place with wooden
floors and fireplace and broad
outside deck, serving good
English breakfasts, cocktails
(including Pickled Penguins),

delicious seafood platters and
daily specials like lamb rump in
soy sauce or prawn ravioli, plus
salads for a light meal. Dishes are
beautifully presented.

Miller's Point

Black Marlin ℝℝℝ
2 km south of Simon's Town,
T021-786 1621, blackmarlin.co.za.
Open 1200-1600, 1800-2100.
Map: Cape Peninsula, p140.
Set in an old whaling station, this
place is well known for its
excellent seafood and is a good
lunch stop on the way to or from
Cape Point. Fabulous sea views
and wide range of fresh seafood
– try the delicious crayfish and
oysters or the signature kingklip
skewers. Great wine list. It can get
busy with tour buses in summer
so reservations are essential.

Atlantic Seaboard

Bars & clubs
La Med
Glen Country Club, Victoria Rd,
Clifton, T021-438 5600,
lamed.co.za.
Open 1100-late.
Something of a Cape Town
institution, hugely popular
meeting place for locals, busy
bar overlooking the sea, good
pub food, great for a sundowner
when you'll be hard pressed to
find a seat, turns into a raucous
club later on. Also a venue for
watching rugby matches on
giant TVs and well known for its
New Year's Eve party.

Bars & clubs
Baraza
Victoria Rd, Camps Bay,
T021-438 1758, baraza.co.za.
Tue-Fri 1700-0200,
Sat-Sun 1200-0200.
Stylish lounge-bar with ocean
and sunset views, popular for
sundowners and livens up later
when the DJs start, glamorous
decor in muted earthy colours
with African touches, long list
of cocktails and imported
bottled beers and you can
order food from Blues (see
page 164) next door.

Café Caprice
Victoria Rd, Camps Bay, T021-438
8315, cafecaprice.co.za.
Open 0900-late.
Popular café and bar throughout
the day with outdoor seats, great

Shopping

fresh fruit cocktails. Then it gets packed and very noisy around sunset, and loud house music is played until late by a DJ every night in season and at the weekends in winter.

Theatre
Theatre on the Bay
Link St, Camps Bay, T021-483 3301, theatreonthebay.co.za.
Slightly alternative shows, and an interesting mix of plays, comedy and musicals. Licensed so you can take your drinks in. The restaurant here is good and there's the option of a pre-show dinner and then dessert in the interval. Alternatively eat at one of the nearby restaurants on Victoria Road.

False Bay

Theatre
Kalk Bay Theatre
52 Main Rd, Kalk Bay, T073-220 5430, kbt.co.za.
Delightful community theatre in a converted church built in 1876 with an upstairs bar, showing light plays like *Shirley Valentine* or *Educating Rita*, and visiting comedy acts.

Atlantic Seaboard

Markets
Hout Bay Craft Market
Hout Bay Common, Main Rd.
Sunday 1000-1600.
Held by the local Lions Club, this weekly craft market offers locally made crafts, clothes, garden ornaments, homemade jams and pickles, olives and cheese and there are pony rides for kids.

False Bay

Markets
Noordhoek Farm Village
Chapman's Peak Dr, Noordhoek, T021-789 2812, noordhoekvillage.co.za.
Open 0900-1700.
This is a collection of restored thatched farm buildings, which are home to a number of specialist shops, some selling African art and curios and clothes, as well as a wine boutique, a deli and restaurants. Children will enjoy the ducks and rabbits wandering around.

Porter Estate Produce Market
Chrysalis Academy Grounds, Tokai Rd, T021-781 0144, pepmarket.co.za.
Sat 0900-1300, R5 per car.
Weekly farmers' market selling organic fresh produce, free range meat and eggs, cheese, bread,

Tip...
There are several informal roadside craft and curio markets around the peninsula including on the road between Camps Bay and Hout Bay and outside the entrance to the Table Mountain National Park. Prices aren't fixed so expect to haggle.

jams and pickles, gifts and farm-style breakfasts, plus activities for kids like face-painting and a sandpit.

Art & antiques
Railway House
23 Main Rd, Kalk Bay, T021-788 4761.
Mon-Sat 0900-1700,
Sun 1000-1700.
A treasure trove of collectibles from vintage Irish linens and weather-beaten tables, to nautical items and Victorian kitchen sinks and a good selection of characterful antique pieces.

Cape to Cairo
100 Main Rd, Kalk Bay, T021-788 4571.
0900-1700.
Wacky and unusual decor and gift items sourced from unusual places like Manila and Cuba, including gilt mirrors, chandeliers and religious statues, all displayed in the vibrantly painted shop.

Activities & tours

Books

Kalk Bay Books
124 Main Rd, Kalk Bay, T021-788 2266, kalkbaybooks.co.za.
Open 0900-1700, Oct-Apr 1800.
Housed in a historic building and run by an ex-women's magazine editor, this has an interesting selection of books, leather couches for browsing and literary magazines to pick up and read through.

Quagga Art & Books
86 Main Rd, Kalk Bay, T021-788 2752, quaggabooks.co.za.
Mon-Sat 0930-1700,
Sun 1000-1700.
An antiquarian bookshop specializing in Africana books as well as military, maritime, natural history and biographies, and also sells some contemporary books, maps, watercolours and paintings.

Souvenirs

Mineral World
Dido Valley Rd, Simon's Town, T021-786 2020, scratchpatch.co.za.
Mon-Fri 0830-1645, Sat and Sun 0900-1730.
This is an important gemstone factory where you can watch the different stages of polishing and buy the finished product. There is also the 'Scratch Patch', a large landscaped yard covered with a deep layer of polished stones, which is ideal for children to explore.

Tip...

For a list of tour operators which run day tours around the Cape Peninsula, see page 133.

Atlantic Seaboard

Boat tours

Drumbeat Charters
Hout Bay Harbour, T021-791 4441, drumbeatcharters.co.za.
₨50, children (under 12) ₨25.
Daily boat trips from Hout Bay Harbour to see the seals on Duiker Island. Boats leave at 0830, 0915, 1000 and 1045 and the round trip takes about 30 minutes.

Hooked on Africa
Hout Bay Harbour, T021-790 5332, hookedonafrica.co.za.
Deep-sea fishing is popular around the peninsula and the most common catches are mako shark, long-fin tuna and yellowtail, but there are strict rules governing all types of fishing. The simplest way of dealing with permits and regulations is through a charter company. This operator runs deep-sea tuna trips, in-shore light tackle and fly fishing and crayfish charters. There are four boats to choose from, and all gear is supplied.

Nauticat
Hout Bay Harbour, T021-790 7278, nauticatcharters.co.za.
₨60, children (under 12) ₨30.
Again 30-minute trips to see the seals on Duiker Island but in a glass-bottomed boat. Boats leave 0845, 0945, 1100, 1230, 1430, 1530. Can also arrange game fishing.

Below: Boats in Hoat Bay. Opposite page: Handicraft vendors in Hout Bay.

The Hoerikwagga Trail

South African National Parks (SANParks), T021-422 2816, sanparks.org.

There are numerous opportunities for hiking in the reserves and in the sections of the Table Mountain National Park already mentioned. However, for those wanting to spend more time on the mountain, a 100-km overnight trail – the Hoerikwagga Trail (meaning 'sea mountain' in Khoi) – has recently been introduced. The six-day trek involves sleeping in tented camps and renovated forester houses dotted along the top of the mountain; food and overnight gear is carried by porters. The trail starts in central Cape Town and ascends Platteklip Gorge and then follows the spine of the peninsula down to Cape Point. The full trail will be fully operational by mid-2010 but for now hikers can hike sections of it from ₨420 for two days and one night. There is a maximum of 12 on the trail so advance booking is essential.

Tip...

The whale-watching season in False Bay is July to November. Rules surrounding trips to see the whales are very stringent, and only one boat a year is given a permit to run whale-watching cruises. This is presently held by the Simon's Town Boat Company.

Horse riding
Sleepy Hollow Horse Riding
Sleepy Hollow Lane, Noordhoek, T021-789 2341, sleepyhollowhorseriding.co.za.
The 8-km beach at Noordhoek is very popular for horse riding, and this offers two-hour beach rides for ₨350 with great views looking up to Chapman's Peak. They have horses suitable for novices, but children under 14 are not catered for.

Diving
Scuba Shack
Lekkerwater Rd, Sunnydale, T021-785 6742, scuba-shack.co.za.
Not far from Kommetjie, this is a well-run local scuba-diving school with practice pool. Dives go out to both the Atlantic and False Bay sides of the peninsula. Full range of PADI instruction and equipment hire and also arranges snorkelling with the seals for non-divers for ₨455, including boats and wetsuits.

False Bay

Boat tours
Simon's Town Boat Company
Simon's Town Harbour, T082-257 7760 (mob), boatcompany.co.za.
In whale-watching season, trips go out daily at 0900, 1200 and 1430, ₨650, children (under 12), ₨400, booking essential. Weather permitting, they also offer fast speed-boat rides to Cape Point for ₨350, children (under 12) ₨200, and the round 2½-hour trip includes a stop on the seaward side of Boulders Beach (see page 158) to watch the penguins in the water. There are also short boat tours around the harbour area for ₨40, children (under 12) ₨20, on the *Spirit of Just Nuisance*, which include entertaining stories about the famous dog and the history of Simon's Town and a visit to the naval dockyard.

Transport

The metro route from the city to Simon's Town (one hour 10 mins) on the Cape Peninsula is marketed as a tourist route known as the Southern Line. For ₨25 (children 4-18 half price, under 4s free) you can travel between Cape Town, the southern suburbs, and on the peninsula, Muizenberg, St James, Kalk Bay, Fish Hoek, Glencairn and Simon's Town as many times as you like between 0800 and 1630. Buy your ticket at the stations or Cape Town Tourism's head office in the city centre. You will get a map that indicates tourist attractions within walking distance of each station. Trains run approximately every 30 minutes.

African penguins at Boulders Beach Simon's Town.

Contents

Winelands

Fertile vineyards in the Stellenbosch region.

Introduction

The first vines were grown by van Riebeeck in Constantia, Company's Garden and in the area known today as Wynberg, and the first wine was produced in 1652. There was soon a great demand from the crews of ships when they arrived in Table Bay as red wine was drunk to fight off scurvy and it kept better than water. But the Cape's wine industry was started in earnest in 1679 by Simon van der Stel, who produced the first quality wines at Constantia. These were mostly sweet wines made from a blend of white and red Muscadel grapes, known locally as Hanepoot grapes. Then, as the early settlers moved inland and farms were opened up in the sheltered valleys, more vines were planted. Every farmer had a few plants growing alongside the homestead, and by chance the soils and climate proved to be ideal. Today, South Africa has 120,000 ha of vineyards and produces some 800 million litres of wine each year. Many of the beautiful historic estates are open to visitors for wine-tasting and sales, most of them have restaurants or offer picnic baskets, and some provide luxury accommodation and additional features like spas.

What to see in…

…one day
On a day trip from Cape Town, visit estates around Stellenbosch such as **Spier** and **Simonsig** before heading to the **Franschhoek wine route** for lunch on a historic estate like **Boschendal** or at one of the gourmet restaurants in the village.

…a weekend or more
Explore Stellenbosch on foot and visit the **Village Museum**, see the grand manor house at **Vergelegen** and learn the history of the Huguenots in Franschhoek's **Huguenot Memorial Museum**. Take in more wine estates around Paarl including **Fairview**, **Nederburg** and **KWV**, or follow the scenic **Four Passes** route for great views of the Winelands and False Bay.

Leafy vines in spring.

Around the region

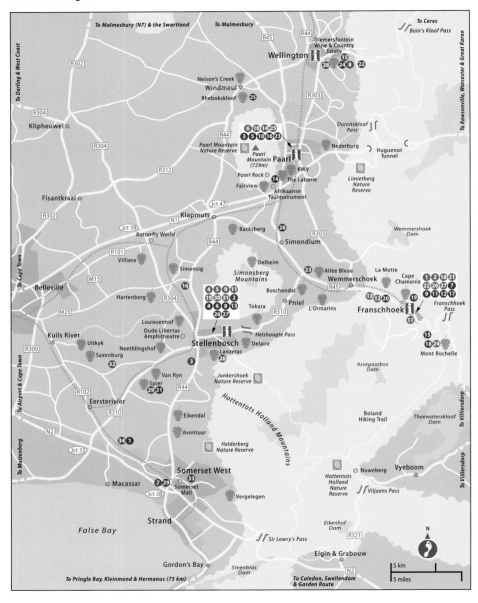

The vineyards of Stellenbosch.

Winelands listings

Sleeping

1 Auberge Bligny (in Franschhoek)
2 Auberge La Dauphine (in Franschhoek)
3 Bellevue Manor
4 Bonne Esperance (in Stellenbosch)
5 D'Ouwe Werf Country Inn (in Stellenbosch)
6 De Oude Paarl (in Paarl)
7 Die Ou Pastorie
8 Diemersfontein Wine and Country Estate
9 Dorpshuis & Spa (in Stellenbosch)
10 Eben-Haëzer Country House (in Paarl)
11 Eendracht (in Stellenbosch)
12 Franschhoek Country House
13 Grande Provence
14 Grande Roche (in Paarl)
15 Klein Rhebokskloof
16 L'Avenir Country Lodge
17 La Cabrière Country House
18 La Fontaine (in Franschhoek)
19 Labri Manor (in Stellenbosch)
20 Lanzerac Manor
21 Le Ballon Rouge (in Franschhoek)
22 Le Quartier Français (in Franschhoek)
23 Lekkerwijn
24 Mont Rochelle
25 Pontac Manor Hotel (in Paarl)
26 Protea Hotel Franschhoek (in Franschhoek)
27 Résidence Klein Oliphants Hoek (in Franschhoek)
28 Roggeland Country House
29 Spier Hotel
30 Stellenbosch Hotel (in Stellenbosch)
31 Stumble Inn (in Stellenbosch)
32 Wedgeview Country House & Spa
33 Willowbrook Lodge
34 Zandberg Guest House

Eating & drinking

1 96 Winery Road
2 Blue Orange (in Stellenbosch)
3 Bosman's (in Paarl)
4 Brazen Head (in Stellenbosch)
5 Café Cuba (in Paarl)
6 Café Nouveau (in Stellenbosch)
7 Essence (in Franschhoek)
8 Fishmonger (in Stellenbosch)
9 French Connection Bistro (in Franschhoek)
10 Goatshed (in Paarl)
11 Grapevine (in Franschhoek)
12 Ici at Le Quartier Français (in Franschhoek)
13 Jan Cats (in Stellenbosch)
14 Laborie
15 La Petite Ferme
16 La Vita e Bella @ Perfect Place (in Paarl)
17 Le Bon Vivant (in Franschhoek)
18 Mange Tout
19 Mon Plaisir
20 Monneaux
21 Moyo
22 Oude Wellington
23 Pontac (in Paarl)
24 Seasons
25 Victorian Restaurant and Terrace
26 Volkskombuis (in Stellenbosch)
27 Wijnhuis (in Stellenbosch)
28 Wilderer's
29 XO Modern Bistro & Wine Bar

Stellenbosch

Stellenbosch, the centre of the Winelands, was named after the governor of Cape Town, Simon van der Stel, and dates to 1679; it is the oldest and most attractive town in the region. The centre has a pleasing mix of architectural styles: Cape Dutch, Georgian, Regency and Victorian houses line broad streets, dappled with shade from centuries-old oak trees, and furrowed with water ditches which still carry water to the gardens. However, like Swellendam (see page 223), many of the earliest buildings were lost to fires in the 18th and 19th centuries; what you see today is a collection of perfectly restored buildings. Following each fire, the destroyed buildings were recreated with the help of photographs, original plans and sketches, although the technology and materials of the day were used. This is perhaps why they appear to have survived in such good condition. Stellenbosch offers two approaches to sightseeing: walking around the town centre viewing public buildings, oak-lined streets and stately homes; or going on a wine tour, visiting any number of the roughly 130 wineries and private cellars. Spend a couple of days in Stellenbosch and you'll get to do both.

This was the first wine route to open in South Africa, in April 1971. It has been hugely successful, attracting tens of thousands of visitors every year, and today the membership comprises around 130 private cellars. It's possible to taste and buy wines at all of them, and the cellars can arrange for wine to be delivered internationally. Many of the estates have excellent restaurants as well as providing very popular picnic lunches – at weekends it is advisable to book in advance.

Delaire

R310, T021-885 1756, delairewinery.co.za.
Sales and tastings: Mon-Fri 0900-1700, Sat 1000-1700, Sun 1000-1600.
Map: Winelands, p178.

This small estate has some of the best views in the valley, and has produced some very high-standard wines. Their flagship Merlot is very popular, while the Chardonnay remains a favourite export label.

L'Avenir Estate, Stellenbosch Valley.

The Green Door restaurant serves lunch Tuesday to Sunday; picnic hampers are available. On a clear day visitors are rewarded with views of the Simonsberg Mountains.

Essentials

❷ Getting around
By car With a designated driver, the easiest and most leisurely way to explore the Winelands is by car. The N2 highway goes past Cape Town International airport, 22 km east of the city, and then continues along the northern fringes of the Cape Flats, home to the sprawling townships of Mitchells Plain, Nyanga and Khayelitsha. Beyond these the R310 left turning is the quickest route to Stellenbosch, the heart of the Winelands, 16 km from the N2. The N2 continues east splitting the towns of Strand and Somerset West before climbing over the Hottentots Holland Mountains. The R44 is an alternative route from Somerset West and Strand to Stellenbosch. Paarl and Wellington are best accessed by the N1 from Cape Town, and Franschhoek by either route. The wine estates in the region are far too numerous to list in full, but on an organized tour (for operators, see page 214) or a self-drive trip, there is ample opportunity to visit several estates in one day.

By train The **Cape Metrorail** (capemetrorail.co.za) does have services from Cape Town to Stellenbosch, Wellington and Strand, but these are not recommended because of safety concerns as they travel through the townships on the Cape Flats.

❻ ATM
These are found in all the towns and shopping malls. All the wine estates take credit cards.

⊕ Hospital
Stellenbosch Medi-Clinic, corner of Saffraan and Rokewood avenues, T021-883 8571, stellenboschmc.co.za.

❶ Tourist information
Tourist offices in Cape Town (see page 78) can provide brochures and maps, as can the tourist offices in the Winelands towns listed later on; also visit tourismcapewinelands.co.za. **Stellenbosch Tourism** (36 Market St, T021-883 3584, stellenboschtourism.co.za, Mon-Fri 0800-1800, Sat 0900-1700, Sun 1000-1600, in Jun and Aug the office opens 1 hr later and closes 1 hr earlier) can provide information for the whole region and there are other tourist offices listed under the towns.

A stroll through Stellenbosch

A walk around central Stellenbosch takes you through the oldest parts of town and past some of the best-preserved old buildings concentrated in a small area along Dorp, Church and Drostdy streets. Dorp Street itself, which runs east-west in the southern part of town, has all the classic features – an avenue of oak trees, running water in open furrows and carefully restored white-walled buildings.

At the western end of Dorp Street, and now an art gallery, Libertas Parva (No 31) is a beautifully restored classic H-shaped manor house built in 1783, though the present front gable and twin front doors date from the late Georgian period. Walking east along Dorp Street, you'll pass Oom Samie se Winkel (No 82), a Victorian-style general store that is still functioning as a shop today. Of particular note, the town houses just past the junction with Helderberg Street, Hauptfleisch House (No 153), Bakker House (No 155), Loubser House (No 157), and Saxenhof (No 159), are regarded as the best-preserved street façades in old Stellenbosch.

Branching off from Dorp Street on Drostdy Street, is the town church, the Moederkerk. The steeple church was designed by Carl Otto Hagen and built in 1862. Inside, it's worth admiring the pulpit and the unusually thick stained-glass windows. Turn right at the top of Drostdy Street into Van Riebeeck Street, then left into Neethling

Tip...

Stellenbosch itself is perfect for exploring on foot. **Stellenbosch On Foot** (T021-887 9150, or book at the tourist office, R80 per person, min 3 people) offers 90-minute guided walks that leave from the tourist office every day at 1100 and 1500.

Street to reach the Botanical Gardens. These were established in the 1920s and are part of the University of Stellenbosch, they have a fine collection of ferns, orchids and bonsai trees.

Heading west back along Van Riebeeck Street brings you to Ryneveld Street, where you'll find the engaging Village Museum, which spreads over two blocks in the oldest part of town. If you follow the guide numbers you will be taken through four houses, each representing a different period of the town's history. The oldest of these is Schreuderhuis (1709), one of the earliest houses to be built in Stellenbosch by Sebastian Schreuder, a German. The simple furniture and collection of household objects are from the same period. Blettermanhuis (1789) is a perfect example of a typical H-shaped Cape Dutch home. The furnishings are those of a wealthy household between 1750 and 1780. The house was built by Hendrik Lodewyk Bletterman, the last *landdrost* to be appointed by the Dutch East India Company. Notice the contrast in furnishings between Schreuder the messenger and Bletterman the magistrate. The third building is Grosvenor House (1803), in Drostdy Street, an excellent example of the two-storeyed town houses that once dominated Cape Town. The home was built by Christian Ludolph Neethling, a successful farmer, in 1782. The fourth and final house is the fussy OM Bergh House (1870), which once had a thatched roof. In all four houses, guides dressed in period clothes answer any questions and point out interesting details.

Much of the town's activity today takes place around the Braak, at the western end of Church Street, the original village green and one-time military parade ground. On the western edge by Market Street is the VOC Kruithuis or Powder House, built in 1777 as a weapons store, and now a military museum. A short distance north, on the corner of Alexander Street, is the Burgerhuis, a classic H-shaped Cape Dutch homestead built by Antonie Fick in 1797, which is now decorated to represent the house of a well-to-do Stellenboscher in the Victorian era. Two churches overlook the Braak: Rhenish Church, built in 1832 as a training school for coloured people and slaves, which has a very fine pulpit, and St Mary's-on-the-Braak, an

Museums

Botanical Gardens (0800-1700, tea room 1000-1700, free).

Burgerhuis (T021-887 0339, museums.org.za/burgerhuisstel, Mon-Fri 0800-1630, Sat 1000-1300, 1400-1600, free).

Rembrandt van Rijn Art Museum (Libertas Parva, T021-886 4340. Mon-Fri 0900-1245, 1400-1700, Sat 1000-1300, 1400-1700, free).

Toy and Miniature Museum (T021-887 2948, Mon-Sat 0930-1700, Sun 1400-1700, ₽5, children under 14 ₽1).

Village Museum (T021-887 2902, museums.org.za/stellmus, Mon-Sat 0930-1700, Sun 1400-1700, ₽20, children under 14 ₽5).

VOC Kruithuis (T021-887 2902, Sep-May, Mon-Fri 0930-1300, ₽2).

Anglican church completed in 1852. A little to the west, on Market Street just behind the tourist office, is the Toy and Miniature Museum, a small but fairly diverting collection of antique toys.

Oom Samie Se Winkel store, Stellenbosch.

Delheim

Knorhoek Rd, off the R44, T021-888 4600, delheim.com.
Sales and tastings: Mon-Fri 0900-1700, Sat 0900-1600, Sun 1030-1600 (Oct-Apr only); cellar tours: Mon-Fri 1030 and 1430, Sat 1030; restaurant: Mon-Sat 0930-16300, Sun (Oct-Apr only) 0930-1630.
Map: Winelands, p178.

This is one of the more commercially oriented estates and may seem a little too impersonal. However, the restaurant has a beautiful setting with views towards Cape Town and Table Mountain, and serves breakfasts, lunches and teas. Tastings are conducted in a cool downstairs cellar.

Eikendal

R44, T021-855 1422, eikendal.com.
Sales and tastings: Oct-Apr, Mon-Sat 0900-1630, Sun 1000-1600, May-Sep, 1000-1600; cellar tours: Oct-Apr, Mon-Fri, 1000 and 1430, May-Sep, on request.
Map: Winelands, p178.

The microclimate on the western slopes of the mountain is ideal for viticulture, and there is a wide selection of both whites and reds. Lunch is served in the wine-tasting room or the gardens; Swiss owned so expect unusual European dishes on the menu.

Hartenberg

Bottelary Rd, T021-865 2541, hartenbergestate.com.
Sales and tastings: Mon-Fri 0900-1715, Sat 0900-1500; lunches: 1200-1400.
Map: Winelands, p178.

This privately owned estate, founded in 1692, is off the Bottelary Road, 10 km north of Stellenbosch. During the summer, lunches are served in the shade and peace of the gardens; come winter the tasting room doubles up as a restaurant with warming log fires. A number of red and white wines are produced, but their reds seem the most successful – past award winners include their 2003 Shiraz and Pinotage.

Neethlingshof

R310, T021-883 8988, neethlingshof.co.za.
Sales and tastings: Mon-Fri 0900-1700, Sat-Sun 1000-1600; cellar and vineyard tours: by appointment; meals are served in 2 restaurants, Lord Neethling and Palm Terrace, 0900-2100.
Map: Winelands, p178.

With its fine restaurants, Cape Dutch buildings and grand pine avenue (which now features on the labels of the estate wines), this estate is a very pleasant one to visit. The first vines were planted here in 1692 by a German, Barend Lubbe, and the manor house was built in 1814 in traditional Cape Dutch H-style. Today the house has been converted into the Lord Neethling restaurant renowned for its venison and veal. Neethlingshof has won a clutch of awards – the Lord Neethling Pinotage is a consistent trophy winner.

Saxenburg

Polkadraai Rd, T021-903 6113, saxenburg.co.za.
Sales and tastings: Mon-Fri 0900-1700, Sat 1000-1700, Sun 1000-1600 (Sep-May only). The Guinea Fowl restaurant is open Wed-Mon for lunch and Wed-Sat for dinner.
Map: Winelands, p178.

Saxenburg has a long history, starting in 1693 when Simon van der Stel granted land to a freeburgher, Jochem Sax. Sax planted the first vines and built the manor house in 1701, and the estate has been producing ever since. It produces a small number of cases each year; its Private Collection of red wines is very good. The restaurant attracts most of the visitors.

Tip...

Wine estates charge a small tasting fee of about R15-30, which often includes a free wine glass.

Eikendal Cellar and dam.

Spier

R310, T021-809 1100, spier.co.za.
Sales and tastings: daily 1000-1630.
Meals are available throughout the day and evening at Moyo restaurant (book several days ahead) or from the deli which also makes up picnics. Accommodation is at the Spier Hotel (see page 202).
Map: Winelands, p178.

This is the Winelands' most commercial wine estate, offering a vast array of activities and wine tastings – of both Spier's own wines and those of other Stellenbosch estates. Spier wines are well regarded, and their Private Collection Chenin Blanc and Chardonnay are especially good and frequently win awards. As well as wine tasting, there is a cheetah outreach programme (although the creatures seem rather lacklustre) and a birds of prey area, plus horse riding, fishing, an 18-hole golf course and the Camelot spa. There is a superb onsite restaurant, the outdoor 'African' Moyo BBQ, which is hugely popular with tourists, see page 208. An annual music and arts festival is held at the open-air amphitheatre during the summer months.

Simonsig

Kromme Rhee Rd, M23, T021-888 4900, simonsig.co.za.
Sales and tastings: Mon-Fri 0830-1700, Sat 0830-1600, cellar tours: Mon-Fri 1000 and 1500, Sat 1000.
Map: Winelands, p178.

This large estate has been in the Malan family for 10 generations, and in recent years has produced some exceptionally fine wines. There is an attractive outdoor tasting area with beautiful views out over the mountains. One wine worth looking out for is the Kaapse Vonkel, a sparkling white considered the best of its kind in South Africa. Their Chardonnay is consistently very good too and not badly priced.

Villiera

T021-865 2002/3, villiera.co.za.
Sales and tastings: Mon-Fri 0830-1700, Sat 0830-1500.
Map: Winelands, p178.

Villiera is highly regarded and produces some of the best wines in the Cape. There are plenty of classic wines to choose from, including their Merlot and Sauvignon Blanc. They don't conduct cellar tours, but allow self-guided tours.

It's a fact...

All major wine grape varieties are grown in South Africa, plus the fruity red Pinotage, a variety produced in Stellenbosch in 1925 by crossing Pinot Noir and Cinsault, which is unique to South Africa.

Five of the best

Brandy estates

❶ Avontuur (R44, 3 km from Somerset West, T021-855 3450, avontuurestate.com, Mon-Fri 0830-1700, Sat-Sun 0900-1600), produces a five-year-old copper-distilled brandy and a 10-year-old limited edition made from Chenin Blanc grapes.

❷ Backsberg (R44 towards Paarl, T021-875 5141, backsberg.co.za, Mon-Fri 0800-1700, Sat 0930-1400, Sun 1030-1630), produces brandies in a state-of-the-art still imported from the Cognac region of France.

❸ Louiesenhof (R304, 4 km outside Stellenbosch towards the N1, T021-865 2630, louiesenhof.co.za, Mon-Fri 0900-1700, Sat-Sun 1000-1700), produces 16-year-old blend brandies using an antique distilling kettle that was built in Stuttgart in 1930.

❹ Uitkyk (R44 towards Paarl from Stellenbosch, T021-8844 416, Mon-Fri 0900-1700, Sat-Sun 1000-1600), produces one of South Africa's finest 10-year-old estate brandies in a lovely setting on the slopes of the Simonsberg Mountain.

❺ Van Ryn (R310, 8 km from Stellenbosch, T021-881 3875, vanryn.co.za, tours Mon-Fri 1000, 1130 and 1500, Sat 1000, 1130), is the oldest working cellar in the Cape, where you can view the distillation process and the workshop where the coopers make the maturation barrels from French oak.

Somerset West & Strand

Map: Winelands, p178.

South of Stellenbosch, and roughly 50 km from Cape Town along the N2, are the adjoining suburbs of Somerset West and Strand. Although principally an industrial area, Strand is a popular seaside resort and commuter town with an excellent 5-km white-sand beach. It mainly caters for domestic tourists and, despite its proximity to Cape Town, the Winelands and the Whale Coast, it holds little appeal. Further inland, Somerset West is a prosperous town and again a major commuter centre. It has a beautiful location on the slopes of the Helderberg Mountains, with unimpeded views of False Bay and, occasionally, Cape Point. However, again there's not much of interest for visitors, though it has a large shopping mall, Somerset Mall, accessed from the N2, with the usual facilities.

Vergelegen Estate

From Somerset West, take the R44, turn right at the traffic lights into Main Rd, and after 2 km, turn left into Lourensford Rd. Vergelegen estate is approximately 3 km on the right,
T021-847 1334, vergelegen.co.za.
Open 0930-1600, R10, under 16s R5. There is a gift shop, displays on the history of the estate, a smart wine-tasting room and 2 restaurants: Lady Phillips Restaurant is à la carte, teas and coffees are served 1000-1145 and 1430-1600, lunch 1200-1430, booking essential for lunch T021-847 1346; the Rose Terrace is an open-air light lunch spot, Nov-Apr 1000-1600. There is also a picnic hamper service (Nov-Apr) - bookings essential through Lady Phillips Restaurant.
Map: Winelands, p178.

This is one of the Cape's finest estates and the highlight is a visit to the magnificent manor house filled with beautiful period furniture and historical paintings, similar to the collection at Groot Constantia. At the front of the house are five Chinese camphor trees that were planted by

Willem van der Stel between 1700 and 1706. They are the oldest living documented trees in South Africa and are now a national monument. Behind the house is a walled octagonal garden – many of the plants were planted here by Lady Phillips (wife of Sir Lionel Phillips, owner for 25 years from 1917), who wished to recreate a typical English garden, complete with herbaceous border. Look out for the collection of roses next to the main house. The surrounding parkland, much of it similar to an English country estate, is also open for exploration.

Below: Vergelegen Estate. Opposite page: Simonsig wine label.

The Whale Coast

Between Somerset West and Hermanus is an exhilarating coastline, where mountains plunge into the ocean forming steep cliffs, sandy coves, dangerous headlands and natural harbours. This is the evocatively named Whale Coast, which lives up to its title from July to November, when large numbers of southern right whales seek out the sheltered bays for breeding. Whales can be seen close to the shore from False Bay all the way to Mossel Bay, but by far the best place for whale watching is Hermanus where they favour the sheltered Walker Bay.

Somerset West to Hermanus

The R44 leaves the N2 at Somerset West and follows the headland through the villages of Gordon's Bay, Rooiels and Pringle Bay, which are set in the lee of the Hottentots Holland Mountains at the eastern end of False Bay. Next, Betty's Bay is known for its small breeding colony of African penguins that can be seen at Stoney Point. Kleinmond is a popular summer resort where the Bot River meets the sea, where there is a large marsh that is home to thousands of waterfowl. After Kleinmond the R44 joins the R43, which then continues along the coast through the suburbs of Vermont and Onrus, before arriving in Hermanus proper.

Hermanus

Hermanus has grown from a rustic fishing village to a much-visited tourist resort famed for its superb land-based whale-watching. The town's advantage is that whales can come very close to the shore, and the combination of low cliffs and deep water means that you are able to look down from above into clear water and see the outlines of whales from as close as 10 m. To add to the excitement there is a whale crier, who, during season, strolls around the town centre blowing a kelp horn to announce the arrival of each whale in Walker Bay. An excellent cliff path starts at the new harbour in Westcliff in the west and follows the shore all the way round Walker Bay to the mouth of the Klein River in the east, a distance of just over 10 km. Between cliffs the path goes through stands of milkwood trees and takes you around the sandy

Tip...

Hermanus is 142 km from Cape Town via the scenic R44, or 120 km via the N2, and makes a pleasant day trip from Cape Town by car.

jetty and a group of restored fishermen's cottages. Outside is a collection of small restored fishing boats, the earliest dating from 1855, and inside displays include models of fish, a whale skeleton, some shark jaws, fish tanks and early fishing equipment. One of the most interesting features is the sound recordings of calls between whales. There are also telescopes to watch the whales further out.

beaches. The best of these is **Grotto Beach** and is one of South Africa's 20 Blue Flag beaches. The fine white sands stretch beyond the Klein River Lagoon, and there are changing facilities, a restaurant and a beach shop.

Old Harbour Museum

Marine Dr, T028-312 1475,
old-harbour-museum.co.za.
Mon-Sat 0900-1300, 1400-1700, ₹15,
children (under 16) ₹5.

The old harbour is a national monument and a ramp leads down the cliff to the attractive old

Festivals & events

The **Hermanus Food and Wine Festival** (hermanuswineandfood.co.za) in August offers wine tasting from over 70 vineyards, plus cheese, olives and sushi in the gourmet food tent. The **Hermanus Whale Festival** (whalefestival.co.za) in September hosts lots of festivities and entertainment along the cliff-tops, while visitors watch the whales.

Below: Derelict boats in Hermanus Harbour. Oppposite page: Tourists watching a southern right whale at Hermanus.

Franschhoek

Although the first Huguenots arrived at the Cape in 1688, the village of Franschhoek only took shape in 1837 after the church and the manse had been built. The first immigrants settled on farms granted to them by Simon van der Stel along the Drakenstein Valley at Oliphantshoek in 1694. Franschhoek was built on parts of La Motte and Cabrière farms. The village became the focal point of the valley but the oldest and most interesting buildings are to be found on the original Huguenot farms and estates.

This is the most pleasant of the Wineland's villages, with a compact centre of Victorian whitewashed houses backed by rolling vineyards and the soaring slopes of the Franschhoek Mountains. It does, however, have an artificial feel to it as most of the attractions here have been created to serve the tourist industry. The outlying wine estates all have their individual appeal, but the village itself is made up of restaurants and touristy craft shops. Nevertheless, Franschhoek is famed for its cuisine and dubs itself the 'gastronomical capital of the Western Cape', so a visit here should guarantee an excellent meal accompanied by a fine glass of wine.

Huguenot Memorial Museum

T021-876 2532, museum.co.za.
Mon-Sat 0900-1700, Sun 1400-1700, R10,
children (under 16) R5.
Map: Winelands, p178.

This is housed in two buildings either side of
Lambrecht Street. The main building, to the left of
the Huguenot Monument, is modelled on a house
designed by the French architect, Louis Michel
Thibault, built in 1791 at Kloof Street, Cape Town.
The displays inside trace the history of the
Huguenots in South Africa. There are some fine
collections of furniture, silverware and family
bibles, but the most interesting displays are the
family trees providing a record of families over the
past 250 years. One of the roles of the museum
today is to maintain an up-to-date register of
families, so that future generations will be able
to trace their ancestors.

Huguenot Memorial Monument

Map: Winelands, p178.

A highly symbolic memorial built to mark 250 years
since the first Huguenots settled in the Cape, this is
set in a peaceful rose garden with the rugged
Franschhoek Mountains providing a contrasting
background. The three arches represent the Trinity,
and the golden sun and cross on top are the Sun of
Righteousness and the Cross of Christian Faith. In
front of the arches, a statue of a woman with a
bible in her right hand and a broken chain in her
left symbolizes freedom from religious oppression.
If you look closely at the globe you can see objects
carved into the southern tip of Africa: a bible, harp,
spinning wheel, sheaf of corn and a vine. These
represent different aspects of the Huguenots' life,
respectively their faith, their art and culture, their
industry and their agriculture. The final piece of
the memorial, the curved colonnade, represents
tranquillity and spiritual peace after the problems
they had faced in France.

Essentials

❷ Getting around Franschhoek is 71 km from Cape
Town (via the N1), 26 km from Paarl and 31 km from
Stellenbosch. There is no regular public transport so
you will need a car. Most of the tour operators offering
Winelands tours don't usually include Franschhoek.

❶ Tourist information The tourist office,
70 Huguenot Rd, T021-876 3603, franschhoek.org.za,
Mon-Fri 0900-1800, Sat 1000-1700, Sun 1000-1600,
has helpful staff with a good knowledge of
accommodation and restaurants. The office also
has the Franschhoek Wine Route desk and a wine-
and cheese-tasting area, and there's a plant nursery
at the back.

Right: Huguenot Memorial, Franschhoek.

Around the region

All the vineyards lie along the Franschhoek Valley, making it one of the most compact wine routes in the region. What makes this such a rewarding route is that many estates have opened their own excellent restaurants and several also offer luxury accommodation. There are now 43 wine estates on the route, with more being added every year. All the valley's wine can be tasted at the Vignerons de Franschhoek at the tourist office (70 Huguenot Rd, T021-876 2086, franschhoek.org.za/drink.co.za, Mon-Fri 0930-1700, Sat 1000-1600, Sun 1100-1500), on the right just before you enter the village when approaching from Stellenbosch. Maps and information on all the estates are available here.

Allée Bleue

R45, T021-874 1021, alleebleue.com.
Sales and tastings: daily 0900-1700.
Map: Winelands, p178.

This estate is a good place to drop in for some quick wine-tasting if you haven't the time to see a whole vineyard. There is a small, fashionable restaurant and deli set just off the R45 towards Franschhoek at the entrance, serving light meals 0830-1730. Tastings include four wines accompanied by four cheeses to offset the flavours.

Boschendal

R310, T021-870 4272, boschendal.com.
Sales and tastings: daily 0830-1830, vineyard tours: 1030 and 1130, by appointment. The restaurant serves an excellent buffet lunch; between Nov-Apr Le Pique Nique offers picnic hampers in the gardens. Le Café is open daily for snacks and afternoon teas.
Map: Winelands, p178.

Boschendal estate has been producing wine for 300 years and is today one of the most popular estates in the region, not least for its excellent food and pleasant wine-tasting area underneath a giant oak. The estate started life as two farms in 1687, and was bought in 1715 by Abraham de Villiers. The restored H-shaped manor house (1812) is one of the finest in South Africa, and is open as a museum

Wine sales at Boshendal in the Franschhoek Valley.

to the public. Interestingly, a third of the estate is now owned by a black empowerment consortium. Most of the wine produced on the estate is white; their sparkling wines are highly regarded.

Cape Chamonix

Uitkyk St, T021-876 2494, chamonix.co.za.
Sales and tastings: daily 0930-1630;
cellar tours: by appointment.
Map: Winelands, p178.

This is one of the largest farms in the valley, with an underground cellar providing pleasantly cool tours at the height of summer. Wine tastings are held in the Blacksmith's Cottage; you can also try their fruit schnapps or the Chamonix mineral water. The Mon Plaisir restaurant (see page 209) is family friendly and highly rated. Food is prepared on a stove built in Paris in 1908. Accommodation is also available in seven comfortable whitewashed self-catering cottages (ℝℝ).

Mont Rochelle

Dassenberg Rd, T021-876 2770, montrochelle.co.za.
Sales and tastings: daily 0930-1800;
cellar tours: Mon-Fri 1100, 1230, 1500.
Map: Winelands, p178.

This estate has one of the most attractive settings in the region with beautiful views of the valley and it produces some good full-bodied red wines and a couple of whites. Tastings are informal and friendly and picnic baskets are available. The estate is also home to a hotel and restaurant (see page 205).

La Motte

R45, T021-876 3119, la-motte.co.za.
Sales and tastings: Mon-Fri 0900-1630,
Sat 1000-1500; cellar tours: by appointment;
light lunches served in summer.
Map: Winelands, p178.

The original manor house was built in 1752 and the grand old cellars, worth a visit in themselves, are now used as a classical concert venue once a

Tip...

Remember the drink-drive laws in South Africa: when wine-tasting, you may be offered up to 15 different wines to sample at each estate, so make sure the driver stays sober. Alternatively, book on a tour.

month. Wine-tasting takes place in a smart tasting centre overlooking the cellars. As a relatively small producer, only 15,000 cases a year, the estate has managed to create some excellent wines. The La Motte Millennium Claret blend remains their most popular wine.

Anthonij Rupert Wines (L'Ormarins)

R45, T021-874 9000, rupertwines.com.
Sales and tastings: Mon-Fri 0900-1630,
Sat 1000-1430; cellar tours by appointment.
Map: Winelands, p178.

This vineyard has a beautiful setting on the slopes of the Drakensteinberge, above the Bellingham estate (excellent, but no longer open to visitors). In 1694 the original land was granted to the Huguenot, Jean Roi, who named the farm after his village in the South of France. The present homestead was built in 1811 – from its grand marble halls and staircases you look out across an ornamental pond and neat gardens. The other notable attraction is the original wine cellar; this has been carefully restored and now houses a set of giant wine vats. On offer is the classic range of wines, plus the Italian varietal range, Terra del Capo. Cheeseboards are available during summer.

The original manor house was built in 1752 and the grand old cellars, worth a visit in themselves, are now used as a classical concert venue once a month.

Four Passes

One of the popular recommended day drives from Cape Town is known as the Four Passes route. This takes you through the heart of the Winelands, and, as the name suggests, over four mountain passes. It is a wonderful day out from Cape Town, especially if combined with fine wine and gourmet food in Franschhoek.

From Cape Town, drive to Stellenbosch via the N2 and then follow the R310 towards Franschhoek. Driving up out of Stellenbosch you cross the first pass – **Helshoogte (Hell Heights) Pass**, which winds up to the saddle between the Simonsberg and the Jonkershoek Mountains and was built in 1854. After 17 km you reach a T-junction with the R45: a left turn would take you to Paarl, 12 km, but the route continues to the right. This is a pleasant drive up into the Franschhoek Valley. The road follows a railway line and part of the Berg River. After passing through Franschhoek – and perhaps stopping for lunch – take a left in front of the Huguenot Monument and climb out of the valley via the **Franschhoek Pass**. From the 750-m-high summit, there are splendid views back over the Franschhoek Valley. This pass was built in 1823 along the tracks formed by migrating herds of game centuries earlier, and was originally known as the Olifantspad (elephant's path).

One of the more surprising aspects of this drive is the change in vegetation once you cross the lip of the pass, 520 m above the level of Franschhoek. As the road winds down towards Theewaterskloof Dam, you pass through a dry valley full of scrub vegetation and fynbos – gone are the fertile vineyards. The Theewaterskloof Dam was built in the 1970s, primarily for irrigation, but also to provide water for Cape Town, Stellenbosch and Paarl. Covering an area of approximately 52 sq km, it is the seventh largest dam in South Africa. Take a right across the dam on the R321 towards Grabouw and Elgin. To the right lies the Hottentots Holland Nature Reserve. This covers 42,000 ha and provides protection to some 1300 species of mountain fynbos and is a popular hiking region.

The road climbs higher into an important apple-growing region, which is also a major producer of pears, plums and nectarines. After driving through orchards the route reaches **Viljoen's Pass**, the third of the four passes. Built in the 1900s, the name honours local apple pioneer Sir Antonie Viljoen. Beyond the pass are the villages of Grabouw and Elgin, from where apples are packed for distribution, and several local farm stalls tempt travellers to buy fresh fruit, as well as homemade farm produce. At the N2 highway turn right and follow the road 60 km back into Cape Town. The fourth and most spectacular pass is **Sir Lowry's Pass**, which crosses the Hottentots Holland Mountains. It was built in 1828 and named in honour of Sir Lowry Cole, the Cape Governor at the time. From the viewpoint at the top you will be rewarded with fine views of False Bay and the Cape Flats with the brooding Cape Peninsula beyond.

Below: Dead trees on the banks of the Theewaterskloof.
Opposite page: Driving through the Hottentots Holland mountains.

Paarl

All of the attractions and restaurants are strung out along Main Street at the base of Paarl Mountain. When the first European arrival, Abraham Gabbema, saw this mountain in October 1657 it had just rained; the granite domes sparkled in the sunlight and he named the mountains *paarl* (pearl) and *diamandt* (diamond). The first settlers arrived in 'Paarlvallei' in 1687 and, shortly afterwards, the French Huguenots settled on four farms: Laborie, Goede Hoop, La Concorde and Picardie. The town grew in a random fashion along an important wagon route to Cape Town. Several old buildings survive, but they are spread out over about a kilometre on the main road rather than being concentrated in a few blocks as in Stellenbosch. Paarl is home to two of South Africa's better-known wine estates; KWV and Nederburg (see page 200). Paarl is today also well known for education and some of the schools are rated as the best in the Western Cape.

Pretty vineyard in the Paarl Valley.

Paarl Museum

303 Main St, T021-876 2651,
museums.org.za/paarlmuseum.
Mon-Fri 0900-1700, Sat 0900-1300, ₨5, children
(under 16) donation.
Map: Winelands, p178.

This 18th-century U-shaped Cape Dutch former
parsonage is one of the oldest buildings in Paarl
and stands on a former farm that stretched from
the Paarl Mountain to the Berg River. It houses a
reasonably diverting collection of Cape Dutch
furniture and kitchen copperware plus some
more delicate silver. There is also a small section
outlining Paarl during Apartheid.

Afrikaans Language Museum

Gideon Malherbe House, Pastorie St,
T021-872 3441, taalmuseum.co.za.
Mon-Fri 0900-1600, Sat 0900-1300, ₨12,
children (under 16) ₨5.
Map: Winelands, p178.

This gives a detailed chronicle of the development
of the Afrikaans language and the people involved.
Afrikaans is essentially a modification of Dutch
influenced by the languages of the early slave
populations and the Huguenots. The house itself
was built in 1860 by a wealthy wine farmer of the
same name and the downstairs rooms have been
decorated with period furniture donated by his
descendants. The museum was opened in 1975 on
the centenary of the establishment in Paarl of the
Genootskap van Regte Afrikaners (GRA), meaning
'Company of True Afrikaners'. It was the Company's
intent to promote the Afrikaans language – which
at that time already was the spoken language of
thousands of people – to a written language.
Ironically, it opened just one year before the tragic
events of the Soweto Uprising, when school
children were killed while demonstrating against
the use of Afrikaans in schools.

Tip...

The helpful tourist office is at 216 Main St, T021-877
0860, paarlonline.com, Mon-Fri 0800-1700, Sat 0900-
1400, Sun 1000-1400.

It's a fact...

Nelson Mandela spent the last three years of his
incarceration in Paarl's Victor Verster Prison (now the
Drakenstein Correctional Centre), 9 km south of town
on the road to Franschhoek. His first steps to freedom
were on 11 February 1990, when he walked out of the
prison; an event broadcast live all over the world.

Paarl Arboretum

On the east bank of the Berg River, from the tourist
office, go down Market St and cross the river; the
arboretum is on the right.
Open daylight hours, free.
Map: Winelands, p178.

The 31-ha arboretum was created in 1957 to mark
the tercentenary of the discovery of the Berg River
Valley. To help establish the parkland the town
treasurer asked other municipalities in South Africa
to contribute trees and shrubs from their region.
The response was excellent and when the
arboretum was inaugurated there were trees
from 61 different regions. Today there are over
700 different species and around 4000 trees.

Paarl Mountain Nature Reserve

Jan Phillips Mountain Drive, T021-872 3658.
Nov-May 0700-1900, Apr-Oct 0700-1800, free.
The tourist office should be able to give you a
clear colour map which has details of access roads
and footpaths. There are several car parks with
toilets and *braai* spots. To fish in one of the dams
you need to go to the municipality for a permit.
Map: Winelands, p178.

Paarl runs along the eastern base of Paarl
Mountain, a giant granite massif, which in 1970
was declared the Paarl Mountain Nature Reserve.

Around the region

Within the 1900-ha reserve is a network of footpaths, a circular drive and a couple of dams. The vegetation differs from the surrounding countryside because of the bedrock – the granite mass is not as susceptible to veld fires and many of the fynbos species grow exceptionally tall.

The domed summit is easy to climb, and near the top is an old cannon dating from the early days of the Cape Colony. On the summit are three giant granite rocks. The highest point is 729 m and there is a chain to help you up the last steep incline. Just below the summit a mountain stream flows through the Meulwater Wild Flower Reserve. This garden was created in 1931, and contains specimens of the majority of flowers found around Paarl Mountain including 15 species of proteas.

Afrikaanse Taalmonument

T021-872 3441, museums.org.za/Taal.
0800-1700, free.
Map: Winelands, p178.

Set high on the slopes of Paarl Mountain amongst granite boulders and indigenous trees stands the controversial monument with its three concrete columns linked by a low curved wall. This is the Afrikaans Language Monument, inaugurated in October 1975 and designed by Jan van Wijk. Built to celebrate 100 years of Afrikaans being declared as a different language from Dutch, it is thought to be the only monument in the world dedicated to a language. Each column represents different influences in the language. The phrase 'Dit is ons

Afrikaanse Taalmonument, Paarl.

erns', roughly meaning 'this is our earnestness' is inscribed on the pathway leading up to the monument. There are excellent views across the Berg River Valley from here, and on a clear day you can see False Bay, Table Mountain and all the vineyards.

Butterfly World

Klapmuts, T021-875 5628, butterflyworld.co.za.
0900-1700, ℝ35, children (3-16) ℝ20, family of 4 ticket ℝ90.
Map: Winelands, p178.

Those with little children in tow may wish to visit the largest such park in South Africa, with butterflies flying freely in colourful landscaped gardens. They are at their most active on sunny days. There are also spiders, scorpions and meerkats to see and you can buy packets of seeds for children to feed the ducks and chickens in the garden. There is a craft shop and the Jungle Leaf Café on site.

Paarl Wine Route

The route was set up in 1984 by local producers to help promote their wines and attract tourists into the area. The programme has been a great success and some of the estates have opened their own restaurants. All of the estates have tastings and wine sales on a daily basis. Today there are 35 members, but only the largest estates conduct regular cellar tours. Below is a short selection.

Fairview

Suid-Agter-Paarl Rd, off the R101, T021-863 2450, fairview. co.za.
Wine and cheese sales and tastings: Mon-Fri 0830-1700, Sat 0830-1600, Sun 0930-1600; restaurant daily 0900-1700.
Map: Winelands, p178.

This popular estate has a rather unusual attraction in the form of a goat tower, a spiral structure which is home to two pairs of goats. In addition to a

Tip...
The wine route information office can be found at Paarl Vintners at 86 Main Rd, Paarl, T021-863 4886, winecountry.co.za.

variety of good wines (look out for the popular Goats do Roam and Bored Doe blends – a humorous dig at French wines), visitors can taste delicious goat cheeses, which are now produced from a herd of 600 goats and sold in South African supermarkets. Their camembert has won awards as the best in the world at the World Cheese Awards held in London. A new addition is the Goatshed restaurant (see page 212).

The Laborie

Taillefer St, T021-807 3390, laborie.co.za.
Sales and tastings: Oct-Mar 0900-1700, Apr-Sep, Mon-Sat 0900-1700, Sun 1100-1500; restaurant from 1000, cellar tours by appointment.
Map: Winelands, p178.

Part of KWV (see below), this is a beautifully restored original Cape Dutch homestead – in many ways the archetypal wine estate – developed with tourism firmly in mind. It's an attractive spot, with a tasting area overlooking rolling lawns and vineyards, and a highly rated restaurant. As well as a good range of wines they produce an award-winning brandy.

KWV

57 Main St, T021-807 3007, kwv.co.za.
Sales and tastings: Mon-Sat 0900-1600, Sun 1100-1600; cellar tours: Mon-Sat 1000, 1015 (in German), 1030, 1415.
Map: Winelands, p178.

A short distance from the Laborie estate is the famous KWV Cellar Complex which contains the five largest vats in the world. The Ko-operative Wijnbouwers Vereniging van Zuid-Afrika (Cooperative Wine Growers' Association) was established in Paarl in 1918 and is responsible for

Around the region

exporting many of South Africa's best- known wines. They are also well known for their brandy and tastings are served with Belgian chocolates.

Nederburg

Sonstraal Rd; to get there from the centre of Paarl, cross the Berg River towards Wellington, the estate is signposted to the right, T021-862 3104, nederburg.co.za.
Sales and tastings: Mon-Fri 0830-1700, Sat 1000-1600, Sun 1100-1600; cellar tours are available in English, German and French but must be booked in advance; picnic lunches are available (vegetarian and children's menu available) or enjoy a 2-hr 3-course lunch where the food is matched to a selection of 6 wines. Map: Winelands, p178.

This is one of the largest and best-known estates in South Africa. Their annual production is in excess of 650,000 cases. As such a large concern they are involved in much of the research in South Africa to improve the quality of the grape and vine. Every April the annual Nederburg Auction attracts buyers from all over the world and is considered one of the top five wine auctions in the world.

The homestead was built in 1800, but throughout the 19th century the wines were not considered to be anything special. This all changed in 1937 when Johann George Graue bought the estate. Riesling and Cabernet Sauvignon vines were planted, and the cellars completely modernized. Today their wines win countless annual awards.

Nelson's Creek

R44, T021-869 8453, nelsonscreek.co.za.
Sales and tastings: Mon-Fri 0800-1800, Sat 0900-1400; restaurant is open during the summer months; picnic baskets also available for lunches on the estate. Map: Winelands, p178.

This is a very pleasant estate to spend the afternoon exploring. Its most recent owner, Alan Nelson, has been successfully producing wines since 1987. In 1996, he donated part of his estate to his farm labourers who now produce wines under the 'New Beginnings' label. A farmers' market is held here on Saturday morning (see page 214), and a mountain bike challenge is held on the estate in September.

Rhebokskloof

Northern Agter-Paarl Rd, off the R44, T021-869 8386, rhebokskloof.co.za.
Sales and tastings: daily 0900-1700; the Victorian Restaurant serves breakfast, lunch and tea daily, and dinner Fri-Sun.
Map: Winelands, p178.

This old estate is now a thoroughly modern outfit informal tastings are accompanied by cheese and biscuits, or pre-booked formal guided tastings by a variety of snacks to bring out the flavours of the wines and a cellar tour. The terrace café is popular with tour groups and on Sundays they offer a family buffet lunch with children's entertainment.

Wellington

Map: Winelands, p178.

A short drive north of Paarl reveals steep hills where all the farmland is given over to vines. Wellington, like the other Winelands towns, is surrounded by beautiful countryside and has a number of fine historic buildings, with the added bonus of far fewer tourists thronging the streets. Nevertheless, there is little in the town to keep visitors for long, and though there are a few wine estates in the surrounding area, Wellington is best known for its dried fruit. The Murray Jubilee Hall and Samuel House were once an institute for training Dutch Reformed Church missionaries; they are now part of Huguenot College. The shady Victoria Park in Church Street is notable for its roses. Look out for the archway which was built to commemorate the coronation of King Edward VII in 1902. The fountain in Joubert Square was unveiled in 1939 as a memorial to the Huguenot settlers in the valley. To the north of the town, the countryside opens up into the rolling Swartland, an important wheat region.

Tip...

The staff at Wellington Tourism Bureau (104 Main St, housed in the Old Market Building next to the Dutch Reformed Church, T021-873 4604, wellington.co.za, Mon-Fri 0800-1700, Sat 0900-1400, Sun 1000-1300) are helpful and well organized and there is a good selection of local wines on sale.

The Rhebokskloof Estate.

Sleeping

Lanzerac Manor ℝℝℝℝ

2 km from town centre towards Jonkershoek Reserve, Jonkershoek Rd, T021-887 1132, lanzerac.co.za.
Map: Winelands, p178.
Very expensive but fittingly luxurious hotel set around an 18th-century Cape Dutch manor house on a wine estate, tastings and cellar tours on offer. 48 suites, some around a patio and swimming pool, spacious and plush with all mod cons, two restaurants, the formal Governor's Hall, and the more relaxed Lanzerac Terrace for al fresco dining during summer. There's an extensive wellbeing centre and beauty spa with a separate pool overlooking the vines.

Spier Hotel ℝℝℝℝ

Spier Wine Estate on the R44, T021-809 1100, spier.co.za.
Map: Winelands, p178.
Accommodation is in village-style buildings set around courtyards with private pools for each section. The 155 rooms are enormous and very comfortable, with neutral, stylish decor, trendy polished concrete floors, huge beds, lots of windows, TV, minibar, beautiful bathrooms stocked with aromatherapy products, and a restaurant (though Moyo, see page 208, on the estate is better). See page 185 for details of the wines and all the activities on offer.

Wedgeview Country House & Spa ℝℝℝℝ

The Bonniemile, 5 km south of town, T021-881 3525, wedgeview.co.za.
Map: Winelands, p178.
Attractive thatched farmhouse with 11 garden thatched luxury suites and one family cottage with Wi-Fi and satellite TV, main house has snooker room, bar, drawing room, breakfast room, all set in 1½ ha of attractive gardens surrounded by vineyards, two swimming pools, jacuzzi and wellness and beauty spa. Light lunches and snacks available but dinner on request.

Bellevue Manor ℝℝℝ

5 km south of Stellenbosch on the R44, T021-880 1086, bellevuestellenbosch.co.za.
Map: Winelands, p178.
Purpose-built air-conditioned cottages in Cape Dutch style with thatched roofs, pleasant country-style furnishings, TV, fireplace, bathroom, honesty bar fridge, private terrace, good-sized pool with *braai* area, close to two golf courses. Rates drop in winter. Debi, the on-site therapist, offers de-stress treatments such as reiki and reflexology.

Die Ou Pastorie ℝℝℝ

41 Lourens St, Somerset West, T021-850 1660, die-ou-pastorie.com.
Map: Winelands, p178.
Restored parsonage originally built in 1819 and one of the oldest buildings in Somerset West and a National Monument, with 16 luxurious rooms in the mature gardens with comfortable, traditional furnishings, satellite TV, some with balconies or patios, and there's a swimming pool. The restaurant is popular and has won national awards for its food and wine list (see page 208).

Dorpshuis & Spa ℞℞℞
22 Dorp St, T021-883 9881,
proteahotels.com.
Map: Winelands, p178.
A very smart Victorian townhouse with 27 air-conditioned rooms, some of which are suites, all have TV, marble-clad bathrooms, heavy fabrics and dark furniture, private patios, antiques, large breakfasts with plenty of choice, neat gardens, heated swimming pool and the Oak Leaf à la carte restaurant. The spa is also open to day visitors and they provide transport from other hotels.

D'Ouwe Werf Country Inn ℞℞℞
30 Church St, T021-887 4608,
ouwewerf.com.
Map: Winelands, p178.
Converted Georgian house with 32 air-conditioned rooms and six apartments with kitchenettes, all individually decorated with antique furnishings and polished floors with internet and satellite TV. There's off-street parking, a good-sized heated pool, wooden sunbathing deck, beauty salon and vine-shaded terrace where meals are served. The 1802 Restaurant has an excellent reputation.

Labri Manor ℞℞℞
71 Victoria St, T021-886 5652,
labrimanor.co.za.
Map: Winelands, p178.
A fine Victorian house with 10 luxury rooms with satellite TV, beautiful decor, polished wooden floors, huge four-poster beds,

Above: Spier Hotel. Opposite page: L'Avenir Country Lodge.

subtle yellow walls and dark wood antiques, and spacious Victorian-style bathrooms. Spa room, cobbled courtyard, dinner and picnic baskets on request, extras include fresh flowers and a glass of port.

L'Avenir Country Lodge ℞℞℞
5 km north of Stellenbosch off the R44 towards the N1 and Paarl, T021-889 5001, lavenir.co.za.
Map: Winelands, p178.
A peaceful setting on a smart wine farm with nine luxury bedrooms with contemporary African decor, flat-screen TVs, air conditioning, Wi-Fi, honeymoon suite has private heated splash pool. Price includes breakfast and wine tasting, meals arranged on request. Substantial discounts are available off season. A well-run, peaceful and elegant place to experience the Winelands.

Stellenbosch Hotel ℞℞℞
162 Dorp St, T021- 887 3644,
stellenboschhotel.co.za.
Map: Winelands, p178.
Central hotel with 27 air-conditioned rooms and two apartments in a neat whitewashed Cape Dutch building which is a National Monument. Each room has TV, minibar and pleasant bathroom, and country style decor. Friendly bar popular with locals, bright dining room with tables on terrace overlooking the street, serving game and seafood (see page 208).

Willowbrook Lodge ℞℞℞
Morgenster Av, Somerset West, T021-851 3759, willowbrook.co.za.
Map: Winelands, p178.
Homely country lodge set in a beautiful garden, in a pleasant setting on the outskirts of Somerset West, with 12 large,

well-appointed rooms with air conditioning, TV, private patio and crisp white linen. The D'Vine restaurant serves beautifully presented gourmet food and a good choice of wine in a sunny dining room or on the terrace, and there's a swimming pool.

Zandberg Guest House ℞℞℞
96 Winery Rd, just out of Somerset West towards Stellenbosch, T021-842 2945, zandberg.co.za.
Map: Winelands, p178.
Guesthouse on a working wine estate, with 18 luxury rooms set in thatched cottages in immaculate gardens dotted with impressive oak trees, some have fireplaces, all have private terraces and contemporary decor. Swimming pool, *braai*, fine restaurant (see page 208) and a full range of treatments in the spa. Rates drop considerably in winter.

Bonne Esperance ℞℞
17 Van Riebeeck St, T021-887 0225, bonneesperance.com.
Map: Winelands, p178.
An appealingly rambling Victorian townhouse built in 1901 with a wrap-around veranda and a corner turret opposite the botanical gardens. 15 comfortable rooms with high ceilings and an English feel to the decor, satellite TV, Wi-Fi, sunny and spacious breakfast room, lounge with fireplace, and lovely garden with plunge pool.

Eendracht ℞℞
161 Dorp St, T021-883 8843, eendracht-hotel.com.
Map: Winelands, p178.
Housed in a reconstruction of what was one of Stelllenbosch's oldest houses, this boutique hotel has 12 rooms, with modern understated decor and luxuries like silk-filled duvets, air conditioning, satellite TV and Wi-Fi. The teen room has a bunk-bed and X-Box games console. There's a pool, bar, lounge, and the small restaurant serves traditional South African dishes such as *water-blommetjiebredie*.

Stumble Inn ℞
12 Market St, T021-887 4049, stumbleinnstellenbosch. hostel.com.
Map: Winelands, p178.
Popular hostel in two separate Victorian bungalows, with spacious double rooms, cramped dorms and camping. Original house has attractive garden, bar, TV room, kitchen, hammocks, shady cushion banks; the other house next door has a small pool and kitchen. Very relaxed and friendly place. Excellent value. Easy Rider Wine Tours (see page 215), bicycles to hire, remains by far the best (and only) budget option in town.

Franschhoek Country House ℞℞℞℞
A few kilometres to the west of town on the Paarl road, T021-876 3386, fch.co.za.
Map: Winelands, p178.
Very elegant boutique hotel with 14 rooms and 12 suites, some with fireplace, underfloor heating, private verandas, the new suites are 100 sq m and very luxurious, French-style furniture, dramatic drapes and candelabras, two swimming pools, spa treatment room, lovely fountains in the grounds, excellent and elegant restaurant in the original manor house's dining room.

Grande Provence ℞℞℞℞
Next door to the above on the Paarl road, T021-876 8600, grandeprovence.co.za.
Map: Winelands, p178.
With just five private suites in the converted estate farmhouse, with contemporary decor in plums, greys and cream, elegant spacious bathrooms, unique TVs that flip-up from ostrich leather cabinets, and a lovely swimming pool with rooftop jacuzzi, and views across the vines. The restaurant and the award-winning wine are highly rated, and there's an upmarket art gallery with new exhibitions every six weeks. A favourite of the Earl and Countess of Wessex.

La Cabrière
Country House ℞℞℞℞
Middagkrans Rd, T021-876 4780,
lacabriere.co.za.
Map: Winelands, p178.
Small luxurious and stylish
guesthouse set just outside town
in formal lavender and herb
gardens on a wine estate, with
six en suite, air-conditioned
rooms with Provençal decor,
antique furniture, satellite TV,
Wi-Fi, some rooms have
fireplaces, all have views of
vineyards and mountains,
swimming pool. Personal and
friendly service and within
walking distance of restaurants.

Le Quartier Français ℞℞℞℞
16 Huguenot Rd, T021-876 2151,
lequartier.co.za.
Map: Winelands, p178.
An elegant country house with
15 enormous en suite rooms all
with fireplaces, beautiful
bathrooms, plush furnishings
and views over the gardens, plus
two family suites in private
walled gardens with their own
pools. Small central swimming
pool and peaceful, shady
courtyard, and the attached
restaurant (see page 209) is
rated as one of the best in
Franschhoek. A superb hotel
with impeccable service, and
child-friendly.

Mont Rochelle ℞℞℞℞
Dassenberg Rd, T021-876 2770,
montrochelle.co.za.
Map: Winelands, p178.
24 luxury suites and rooms set in
the main manor house or in
garden units, elegantly
decorated in colonial or
contemporary themes with
enormous bathrooms, superb
award-winning restaurant (see
page 209) cigar bar, swimming
pool, gym and sauna, attentive
service, good mountain views
and pleasant rolling gardens.
Rates vary considerably
depending on room and season.

Auberge Bligny ℞℞℞
28 Van Wijk St, T021- 876 3767,
bligny.co.za.
Map: Winelands, p178.
A beautifully restored house
dating from 1861, with nine
double rooms, some with brass
beds, patchwork quilts, and
Victorian claw-foot baths; apart
from the TVs, attention to detail
includes furniture specifically
from the period. A special
honeymoon suite opens on to a
shaded veranda, and one room is
wheelchair-friendly. Lounge with
a small library and open fire in
winter, neat gardens, swimming
pool, friendly management,
German spoken.

Tip...

Most of the hotels in the Winelands will collect and drop off guests at Cape Town International Airport.

La Fontaine ℝℝℝ

21 Dirkie Uys St, T021-876 2112, lafontainefranschhoek.co.za.
Map: Winelands, p178.
One of the finest guesthouses in Franschhoek, with 14 rooms set in two Victorian houses near the village centre, elegant decor with antiques, polished wooden floors and Persian carpets, some rooms are set in the garden around pool with tasteful ethnic decor, and the stables have been converted into a family unit. Friendly, efficient and a beautiful place to stay.

Le Ballon Rouge ℝℝℝ

7 Reservoir St, T021- 876 2651, ballon-rouge.co.za.
Map: Winelands, p178.
Eight double rooms set in a converted Victorian bungalow with wrap-around shady veranda offering private entrances to the rooms, which are small but nicely

La Fontaine.

and individually decorated, swimming pool, no children under 12. The large loft room is the best and has a Victorian bath. There's a bright breakfast room and other light meals can be arranged.

Lekkerwijn ℝℝℝ

10 mins' drive from the centre of Franschhoek, heading towards Paarl, just before the junction with the R310 to Stellenbosch, T021-874 1122, lekkerwijn.com.
Map: Winelands, p178.
A fine B&B in an old Cape Dutch homestead close to Boschendal wine estate, in fine park-like gardens with peacocks and guinea fowl. Three double rooms and one single, plus a cottage suitable for a family of four. The bedroom wing was designed by Herbert Baker and is arranged around a private pillared courtyard, tastefully furnished lounge and swimming pool.

Protea Hotel Franschhoek ℝℝℝ

34 Huguenot Rd, T021-876 3012, proteahotels.co.za.
Map: Winelands, p178.
A quality offering from the Protea Hotel group and in an excellent location right in the village centre, though there are more atmospheric places to stay. The 30 spacious rooms are individually decorated, have Wi-Fi, DSTV and air conditioning, and are arranged in a double-storey block around the

swimming pool, and there's a decent restaurant and bar.

Auberge La Dauphine ℝℝℝ-ℝℝ

At La Dauphine Wine Estate off Excelsior Rd, T021-876 2606, ladauphine.co.za.
Map: Winelands, p178.
One of the most peaceful locations in the valley, with six luxury air-conditioned rooms each with a spacious lounge and patio in a carefully restored and converted wine store, surrounded by beautiful gardens and vineyards. There is a large swimming pool, guided tours of the farm available, plus mountain bike trails and horse riding in the nearby mountains.

Résidence Klein Oliphants Hoek ℝℝℝ-ℝℝ

14 Akademie St, T021-876 2566, kleinoliphantshoek.com.
Map: Winelands, p178.
A very fine guesthouse close to the centre of Franschhoek which was built originally as a missionary hall in 1888, with six comfortable and old-fashioned air-conditioned double rooms with TV, some have their own plunge pools. The vast, high-ceilinged lounge, once the original meeting hall, is filled with antiques, big sofas and has a fireplace. Good-sized pool, small restaurant and cigar bar.

Grande Roche ℝℝℝℝ
Plantasie St, T021-863 5100, granderoche.co.za.
Map: Winelands, p178.
An 18th-century manor which has established itself as one of the top hotels in South Africa. The 34 luxury air-conditioned suites are set in a collection of restored farm buildings that stand in peaceful gardens, surrounded by vineyards, two floodlit tennis courts, two swimming pools, gym. Bosman's restaurant is regarded as one of the best in the country (see page 211).

Roggeland Country House ℝℝℝℝ
Roggeland Rd, Dal Josafat, 7 km southwest of Wellington towards Paarl, follow the signs off the R301, T021-868 2501, roggeland.co.za.
Map: Winelands, p178.
A fine Cape Dutch farmhouse (declared a national monument) with 10 spacious luxury rooms, with shuttered windows and reed ceilings, large en suite bathrooms, Cape-style furnishings, mature gardens, swimming pool. Highlight of a stay here is the excellent cuisine: lodging prices include four-course dinner, bed and breakfast.

De Oude Paarl ℝℝℝ
132 Main St, T021-872 1002, deoudepaarl.com.
Map: Winelands, p178.
Swanky hotel in a set of national monument buildings dating back to 1700, with 26 air-conditioned, individually designed rooms, with a nod at 'boutique' hotel style, a swimming pool, off-street parking, two excellent restaurants (see page 211) and friendly, efficient service.

Diemersfontein Wine and Country Estate ℝℝℝ
Van Riebeeck Dr, Wellington, off the R301, T021-864 5050, diemersfontein.co.za.
Map: Winelands, p178.
A classic luxury country house set in beautifully tended gardens on a wine estate, with 17 rooms, either in the main house or in garden annexe, and three self-catering cottages on the estate, traditional, plush furnishings, elegant teak-panelled lounge, grand veranda, swimming pool, very good restaurant (see page 211), horse riding. Wine tasting daily 1000-1700.

Pontac Manor Hotel ℝℝℝ
16 Zion St, T021-872 0445, pontac.com.
Map: Winelands, p178.
Elegant fully restored Victorian manor house with gardens full of oak trees that are home to an army of squirrels. 22 spacious individually decorated rooms (one is wheelchair accessible),

TV and air conditioning, a mix of African and antique decor, the five rooms in the pool annexe also have microwave and fridge and there's a five-bed cottage with kitchenette. Smart bar, lounges and very good restaurant (see page 211).

Eben-Haëzer Country House ℝℝ
Sonstraal Rd, T021-862 7420, eben-haezer.co.za.
Map: Winelands, p178.
Original Cape Dutch homestead, seven large and very comfortable double rooms, individually decorated with antiques and with Victorian-style bathrooms, one self-catering cottage, swimming pool, breakfast served under oak trees in the tea garden or in the 18th-century dining room, beautiful whitewashed chapel for weddings. Friendly management, also offers fishing in the dam.

Klein Rhebokskloof ℝℝ
4 km out of Wellington, off Berg St, T021-873 4115, wine-estate-hildenbrand.co.za.
Map: Winelands, p178.
Old country guesthouse set on an olive and wine farm, with four double rooms, simple and comfortable with TV, ceiling fans, private terrace, mountain or dam views, good farm breakfasts, plus two self-catering apartments, swimming pool with sun deck and beautiful garden; children will enjoy the farm animals.

Eating

Moyo ℞℞℞
Spier Estate, on the R44,
T021-8091133, moyo.co.za.
Open 1200-1600, 1800-2300.
Map: Winelands, p178.
Consistently fully booked so make a reservation at least a week ahead. Superb restaurant in a beautiful location and a highlight of a trip to South Africa. Arranged in Bedouin tents with outside tables in delightful tree houses or wrought-iron gazebos lit by candles. The vast buffet has just about everything imaginable from hot mussels to fine cheese and pan-African food. Each table is entertained by women who decorate your face with traditional Xhosa white paint, Zimbabwean musicians, jazz bands and township opera singers.

Volkskombuis ℞℞℞
Aan de Wagen Rd, T021-887 2121,
volkskombuis.co.za.
Daily 1200-1430, 1830-2130, closed Sun during winter.
Map: Winelands, p178.
High standards of food and service, with a focus on

Tip...
As well as the restaurants in town, most of the wine estates on the Stellenbosch wine route also have restaurants that are especially nice for lazy lunches in a picturesque setting.

traditional Cape cooking; try the home-made oxtail or springbok pies. Housed in a characterful building – a restored Herbert Baker Cape Dutch homestead, with views across the Eerste River. A sensibly priced treat.

XO Modern Bistro & Wine Bar ℞℞℞
Die Ou Pastorie, 41 Lourens St,
Somerset West, T021-852 2120,
dieoupastorie.com.
Thu-Mon 1200-1400,
Wed-Mon 1900-2130.
Map: Winelands, p178.
Bistro-style restaurant in a lodge in a gracious Victorian parsonage, serves plenty of wine by the glass, and there are lime green loungers on the terrace. Expect hearty dishes like duck with red cabbage or lamb cutlets with sweet potato and there are traditional desserts like crème brûlée or crêpes suzette.

96 Winery Road ℞℞
Zandberg Wine Estate, 96 Winery Rd, just out of Somerset West on the Stellenbosch road, T021-842 2020, zandberg.co.za, 96wineryroad.co.za.
Open 1200-1500, 1900-late,
Sun closed in the evening.
Map: Winelands, p178.
An excellent award-winning restaurant in an informal farmhouse setting. Very good grills, and some fish such as Norwegian salmon, and specials like guinea fowl or duck and cherry pie. Also has luxury

overnight cottages on the estate (see page 204).

Brazen Head ℞℞
62 Andringa St, T021-882 9672.
Open 1100-late.
Map: Winelands, p178.
Friendly, informal Irish-themed pub and restaurant with beer garden, Guinness and Kilkenny on tap, Irish whiskies, long varied menu including a 1-kg steak, seafood platter and traditional Irish stew, children's menu and a roast at Sunday lunch.

Fishmonger ℞℞
Corner of Plein and Ryneveld streets, T021-887 7835, fishmonger.co.za.
Open 1200-2200.
Map: Winelands, p178.
Portuguese-style seafood restaurant serving a great choice of fresh Cape seafood – kingklip, calamari, tiger prawns, oysters and the like – including taster platters for those who can't decide. Also has a sushi chef, and a choice of vegetarian dishes.

Jan Cats ℞℞
162 Dorp St, T021-887 3644.
0700-2200.
Map: Winelands, p178.
Part of the Stellenbosch Hotel and well known for its game dishes, and just about everything from the African bush is served up, from crocodile kebabs to kudu steaks. Also has specials like ostrich cottage pie or warthog ribs, plus some

seafood including excellent fresh crayfish. Cheaper pub lunches are available.

Wijnhuis ℞℞
Andringa St, T021-887 5844, wijnhuis.co.za.
Open 0800-late.
Map: Winelands, p178.
Bustling wine bar and wine shop in an historical building, pretty outside eating in a courtyard, the Mediterranean-influenced menu offers steak, some seafood and venison, delicately presented, and over 20 wines available by the glass.

Cafés
Blue Orange
77-79 Dorp St, T021-887 2052.
Mon-Sat 0700-1800,
Sun 0830-1700.
Map: Winelands, p178.
Delicious range of breakfasts, good-value snacks and sandwiches plus light lunches such as quiche and pasta. Interesting mix of students, well-coiffed locals and backpackers. Also has an attached deli selling local produce such as jams, bread, fruit and veg.

Café Nouveau
Corner of Plein and Ryneveld streets, T021-887 5627.
Open 0700-1700.
Map: Winelands, p178.
Lovely old-fashioned café with gilt mirrors and tightly packed tables serving good breakfasts

– vegetarians will like the three-egg omelette with peppers and feta – sandwiches, light meals, and coffee and cakes throughout the day.

Franschhoek

iCi at Le Quartier Français ℞℞℞
16 Huguenot Rd, T021-876 2151, lequartier.co.za.
Open 0730-1030, 1200-1530, 1800-late.
Map: Winelands, p178.
Rated as one of the best restaurants in the Western Cape with a chef trained in New York, with French and South African dishes, best known for their lamb burgers and slow-roasted pork with sage mash, plus seared tuna and salmon. Nice decor with bright orange walls, expensive but a place for a treat.

La Petite Ferme ℞℞℞
On Franschhoek Pass Rd, T021-876 3016, lapetiteferme.co.za.
Open 1200-1600.
Map: Winelands, p178.
Spectacular views over the Franschhoek Valley from this smart 'boutique' winery. The lunchtime restaurant is known for its wholesome country fare as well as delicate fusion dishes like gourmet pork and fig burgers with beetroot chutney, or hearty braised rabbit with parsnips. Good desserts and wine list, too.

Mange Tout ℞℞℞
Mont Rochelle, Dassenberg Rd, T021-876 2770, montrochelle.co.za.
Open 1200-1500, 1900-2130.
Map: Winelands, p178.
Small, formal restaurant based at the ultra-smart Mont Rochelle Hotel and wine estate. Perfect setting overlooking the vineyards, excellent gourmet menu with separate vegetarian section, also arranges picnics and offers five-course dinners, long wine list. A pianist plays a white baby grand piano.

Monneaux ℞℞℞
Franschhoek Country House, Main Rd, T021-876 3386, fch.co.za.
Open 0800-1000, 1200-1430, 1900-2100.
Map: Winelands, p178.
Highly rated restaurant serving contemporary fusion cuisine, and more up-to-date than many restaurants in Franschhoek. Lots of game and fish with strong spicing; to whet your appetite consider confit of guinea fowl and beef in vanilla bean béarnaise or smoked duck breast with watermelon and feta salad.

Mon Plaisir ℞℞℞
Cape Chamonix,1 Uitkyk St, T021-876 2393, monplaisir.co.za.
Tue-Sat 1200-1430, 1900-2100.
Map: Winelands, p178.
Highly rated upmarket country-style restaurant set on a wine estate (see page 193), which is ideal for a long lazy lunch with

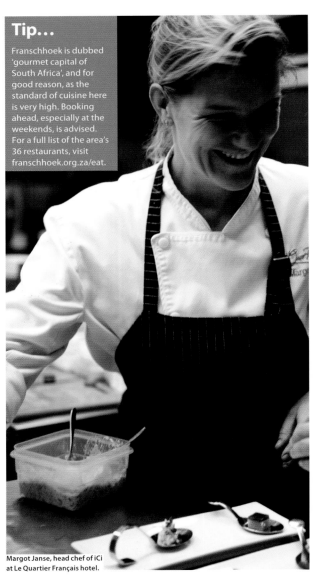

Margot Janse, head chef of iCi
at Le Quartier Français hotel.

Tip...

Franschhoek is dubbed 'gourmet capital of South Africa', and for good reason, as the standard of cuisine here is very high. Booking ahead, especially at the weekends, is advised. For a full list of the area's 36 restaurants, visit franschhoek.org.za/eat.

a fine selection of South African and French dishes, so expect the likes of frogs' legs, foie gras and snails, and it's well known for its whole roasted duck with potatoes to share.

Le Bon Vivant ℞℞℞-℞℞
22 Dirkie Uys St, T021-876 2717, lebonvivant.co.za.
Thu-Tue 1200-1500, 1830-2100.
Map: Winelands, p178.
Small garden restaurant with tables set in dappled shade, serving delicious light lunches (don't miss the local smoked trout sandwich) and a five-course dinner which is paired with wine. The chef creates some interesting combinations; crayfish tails with slow roasted pork belly for example.

The French Connection Bistro ℞℞
48 Huguenot Rd, T021-876 4056, frenchconnection.co.za.
Open 1200-1530, 1830-2145.
Map: Winelands, p178.
French bistro serving refreshingly unfussy food such as steamed mussels, steak-frites or Toulouse sausages and mash. Good food at sensible prices and generous portions. Pleasant bustling atmosphere and you can watch the chef at work in the kitchen behind glass.

The Grapevine ℝℝ
Huguenot Rd, T021-876 2520.
Daily 0800-2100,
closed Sun evening.
Map: Winelands, p178.
Family restaurant serving big breakfasts, light lunches (try the tasty butternut soup) and steaks and pizzas in the evening. Also some good Cape Malay dishes like the ever-popular *bobotie*, and warming hot chocolate with a shot of brandy in it.

Cafés
Essence
7 Huguenot Sq, T021-876 4135.
Open 0700-1800.
Map: Winelands, p178.
Sunny tables are in a courtyard, and there's a broad menu of breakfasts like scrambled eggs and smoked trout or bacon, brie and fig waffles, lunches of salads, filled bagels and paninis, *bobotie* or lamb curry, and carrot cake or scones with jam and cream in the afternoon.

Paarl

Bosman's ℝℝℝ
Grande Roche Hotel, Plantasie St, T021-863 2727, granderoche.co.za.
Aug-May 0700-1030,
1200-1400, 1900-2100.
Map: Winelands, p178.
International cuisine of the highest standard in a grand vineyard-fringed setting, the real treat is the celebrated five-course 'Flavours of the Cape' menu

(℞620), offering superbly created examples of Cape cuisine. Good choice of vegetarian dishes, award-winning wine list. Africa's only Relais Gourmands (Relais & Chateax) establishment.

Laborie ℝℝℝ
The Laborie,Taillefer St, T021-807 3095, laborierestaurant.co.za.
Daily 1000-1700, Wed-Sun 1830-2200. Closed in Jul.
Map: Winelands, p178.
Gourmet restaurant on wine estate with pleasant seating under giant oak trees. Delicious Cape and Mediterranean dishes, lots of contemporary choices such as lamb cutlets with wasabi mash, as well as Cape specialities like *bobotie* and some vegetarian options. Smart but relaxed atmosphere and good service.

Pontac ℝℝℝ
Pontac Manor Hotel, 16 Zion St, T021-872 0445, pontac.com.
Open 1200-1400, 1900-2200.
Map: Winelands, p178.
Informal and friendly restaurant with good service in a cosy setting in a 17th-century manor house, serving traditional and beautifully presented dishes (lots of game), weekly specials and imaginative vegetarian options; everything on the menu is available in full or half portions.

Café Cuba ℝℝ
De Oude Paarl Hotel, 132 Main St, T021-872 1002, deoudepaarl.com.
Mon-Sat 1200-2300.
Map: Winelands, p178.
Fashionable, moodily lit restaurant with a Cuban-decorated interior. The menu offers small tapas-sized dishes, which are ideal to share, of chicken or beef skewers, chorizo sausage, prawns and calamari. Also here is the Butcher's Steakhouse (ℝℝ).

Oude Wellington ℝℝ
R301, Bain's Kloof Pass, 5 km north of Wellington, T021-873 1008, kapwein.com.
Open 1200-late.
Map: Winelands, p178.
Lovely spot in an old whitewashed farmstead with two fireplaces, outside seating in the grounds with dogs, peacocks and ostriches roaming around, good country-style cooking, home-made bread, pasta and ice cream, daily specials are chalked up on a blackboard, also a wine and brandy estate.

Seasons ℝℝ
Diemersfontein Wine and Country Estate, Van Riebeeck Dr, off the R301, Wellington, T021-864 5050, diemersfontein.co.za.
Open 0800-1100, 1215-1530, 1830-2100.
Map: Winelands, p178.
Contemporary restaurant with tables overlooking the farm dam and mountains, open for gourmet breakfasts like eggs

Entertainment

Benedict, light lunches like tomato and goat's cheese tart or warm trout salad, and heavier dishes for dinner such as oxtail or lamb knuckles.

Victorian Restaurant and Terrace RR
Rhebokskloof Estate, T021-869 8606, rhebokskloof.co.za.
Daily 0800-1700, also open for dinner Sep-May, Thu-Mon.
Map: Winelands, p178.
Wonderful views from the terrace over farmland and giant oaks, where light lunches are served. The club sandwiches and salads are good, as is the Sunday starter buffet. Old-fashioned interior is the setting for a heavier international evening menu.

Wilderer's RR
Wilderer's distillery, 3 km outside Paarl on R45, T021-863 3555, wilderer.co.za.
Tue-Sun 1100-1700.
Map: Winelands, p178.
Relaxed lunchtime Continental restaurant in a schnapps distillery, speciality is *lammkuchen*, a type of pizza from Strasbourg, and also has pasta, veal and fish dishes. Finish off with a shot of their pear or fynbos schnapps. Live jazz on the first Sunday of the month.

The Goatshed RR-R
Fairview, Suid-Agter-Paarl Rd, off the R101, T021-863 3609, fairview.co.za.
Open 0900-l700.
Map: Winelands, p178.
Sometimes overrun with tour groups but don't let that put you off as the food is excellent. Cheese platters with freshly baked bread are the highlight, but the mains of duck, lamb, veal and trout will appeal to the hungrier. Naturally the baked cheesecake is superb.

Cafés
La Vita e Bella @ Perfect Place
66 Church St, T021-873 6620.
Mon-Fri 0800-1700,
Sat 0800-1500.
Map: Winelands, p178.
Charming old-world coffee shop in a Victorian house with corrugated-tin roof and decorated with lace, with outside tables under oaks, serving all-day breakfasts, sandwiches and sweet and savoury stuffed pancakes, try the pear, nuts and caramel one, also serves wine and sells antiques.

Stellenbosch

Bars & clubs
Bohemia Pub
Corner of Andringa and Victoria streets, Stellenbosch, T021-882 8375, bohemia.co.za.
Open 1000-late.
One of the main student haunts with an eccentric brightly coloured interior and attractive wrap-around veranda. This popular bar gets very busy with a young clientele who come for the cold beers, relaxed atmosphere and occasional live music.

Fandango
Shop 11, Drostdy Centre, Stellenbosch, T021-887 7506, fandango.co.za.
Open 0900-0100.
Café and bar offering internet access with tables outside on the square, popular for after-work cocktails, occasional live music. Also rents out bicycles.

Theatre
Dorp Street Theatre
59 Dorp St, T021-886 6107, dorpstraat.co.za.
This hosts local productions, including plays in Afrikaans, and occasionally jazz or live Afrikaans rock music, which usually start around 2100 with supper beforehand at 1900.

Shopping

Endler & Fismer Hall
At Stellenbosch University, Victoria St, T021-8082340, sun.ac.za/music.
As part of the university music faculty, this shows classical, choral and chamber music productions by the students and staff, as well as visiting performers, both at lunchtime and in the evening.

Oude Libertas Amphitheatre
Corner of Adam Tas and Oude Libertas Rd, on a wine estate just west of the centre of Stellenbosch off the R310, T021-808 7473, oudelibertasamphitheatre.co.za.
This holds contemporary and classical music events from November to March in an attractive outdoor amphitheatre surrounded by lawns where patrons can have a picnic and bottle of wine before the shows. It also shows occasional children's theatre. There's also a farmers' market here every Saturday morning.

Stellenbosch

Art & antiques
Stellenbosch Antiques
17 Andringa St, T021-883 3917, stellenboschantiques.co.za.
Mon-Fri 0900-1700, Sat 0900-1300.
A 30-year-old shop and a veritable treasure trove of antiques and collectables, including oriental carpets, jewellery, silver and copper ware, ceramics and Victorian and art deco furniture.

Food & drink
Simonsberg Cheese Shop
Stoffel Smit St, Plankenbrug Industria, T021-809 1017, simonsbergcheese.co.za.
Mon-Fri 0900-1700, 0900-1300.
This popular brand of cheese is found in all South African supermarkets and in this shop you can sample and buy; other products like preserves to complement the cheese are also available.

Franschhoek

Art & antiques
Bordeaux Street Gallery
42 Huguenot Rd, T021-876 2165.
Open 0900-1700.
There's a series of rooms on two storeys selling local arts and crafts, including antique furniture, Maasai jewellery, woven baskets, fabrics and batiks, and paintings and sculptures by local artists are on display.

The Old Corkscrew
11 Main Rd, T021-876 3671, theoldcorkscrew.com.
Open 0930-1730.
Reputedly this has the largest collection of corkscrews in Africa, both modern and antique devices. It also sells wine-related antiques including porcelain, ceramics, silver and copper.

Oom Samie se Winkel
84 Dorp St, Stellenbosch, T021-887 0797, Mon-Fri 0830-1730, Sat-Sun 0900-1700.

Uncle Sammy's Shop has been trading since 1791. The first owner, Pieter Gerhard Wium, traded in meat, but the shop became famous between 1904 and 1944 when the store was owned and run by Samuel Johannes Volsteedt. He stocked virtually everything you could need, and was known throughout the town. Today the shop still sells a wide range of goods and it has retained its pre-war character with items hanging from all corners, and old cabinets full of bits and pieces. It has all the makings of a tourist trap, but unlike many others it is genuine.

Tip...
The largest shopping mall serving the Winelands is the Somerset Mall (somersetmall.co.za) on the N2 in Somerset West, which has all the usual facilities; Mon-Sat 0900-1800, Sun 0900-1600.

Vineyard Gallery
21 Huguenot St, T021-876 3301,
fineartportfolio.co.za.
Open 0900-1700.
Art for sale includes South
African landscapes and

seascapes, wildlife and township
art, abstract and impressionist art
as well as unique African
sculptures. International
shipping can be arranged.

Books
The Treasure House
3 Bordeaux St, T021-876 2167,
treasurehouse.co.za.
With over 10,000 rare, antiquated,
out-of-print, and contemporary
books, as well as paintings and
vinyl records, this is worth a
browse and they can organize
international shipping.

Food & drink
Huguenot Chocolates
62, Huguenot St, T021-876 4096,
huguenotchocolates.com.
Mon-Fri 0800-1730, Sat-Sun
0930-1700.
A chocolaterie making fine
Belgian chocolates and sold in
elegant boxes tied up with
ribbon. You can watch them
being made and the aromas are
irresistible.

La Fromagerie at La Grange
13 Daniel Hugo, T021-876 3420,
lagrange.co.za.
Open 1200-1600.
Excellent deli specializing in
cheese with 40 varieties for sale,
set up in a 200-year-old barn,
salads and quiches, soups and all
things cheesy such as soufflé
and pasta, recommended is the
Camembert with caramelized
pears.

Paarl

Food & drink
**Nelson's Creek Farmers'
Market**
R44, T021-869 8453,
nelsonscreek.co.za.
Sat 0800-1300.
Popular market with over 50 stalls
selling home-made produce like
bread and pastries, olives and
cheese, and organic fruit and
vegetables. There's wine on tap
from barrels and entertainment
for kids like pony and tractor rides.

Activities & tours

Stellenbosch

Cycling
Adventure Centre
*36 Market St, next to the tourist
office, T021-882 8112,*
adventureshop.co.za.
Will drop off bikes at hotels or
you can arrange to pick them
up at the office. **Stumble Inn**
(see page 204) and **Fandango**
(see page 212) also rent out
bicycles in Stellenbosch.
Cycling between the wine
estates is a pleasurable way of
exploring the Winelands. Expect
to pay about R120 per day for
bike and helmet hire.

Horse riding
Spier Horse Trails
Spier wine estate on the R130, T021-881 3683, spier.co.za.
Open 1200-1600.
Horse trails go through the vines on the estate; expect to pay R160 per hour. The horses are well trained and can take complete novices. Pony rides for children and carriage rides for non-riders are also on offer.

Wine tours
Easy Rider Wine Tours
Stumble Inn (see page 204), T021-886 4651, stumbleinn stellenbosch.hostel.com.
Good value tours aimed at backpackers. They take in five estates, with several tastings in each, and include lunch in a farm restaurant and cheese tasting. Things can get a little messy towards the end of the day.

Vine Hopper
T021-882 8112, vinehopper.co.za, or book through the tourist office.
Pick-ups between 0900 and 1630, R170, children (under 16) R85.
A useful hop-on, hop-off bus that tours between some estates and the tourist office in town. There are two routes – one to the north of town and one to the

south – and six estates on each are visited. Allow for around an additional R80 for wine-tasting per route.

Franschhoek

Cycling
Manic Cycles
Franschhoek Centre, Huguenot St, T021-876 4956, maniccycles.co.za.
Has a range of bikes for hire for self tours around Franschhoek including mountain bikes, hybrids, a tandem, children's bikes and bikes with baby seats.

Horse riding
Paradise Stables
Outside the village on the Robertsvlei Rd, T021-876 2160, paradisestables.co.za.
Guided trails through the vineyards with stops at two estates for wine-tasting for R450 (including tastings) or hourly rides for R150. Beginners welcome, children over 12.

Paarl

Wine tours
Vintage Cape Tours
T082-656 3994, vintagecape.co.za.
Specialist tailor-made wine tours, which can also take in historical walks around Stellenbosch, Paarl and Franschhoek and pick-ups at all hotels in the region. More suited to the older client with a passion for wine.

Transport

Stellenbosch

Somerset West is 50 km from central Cape Town and 31 km from Cape Town International Airport along the N2. The only public transport is the Metrorail, which is not advised for visitors as it runs through the townships on this route and theft is a problem.

Paarl

The Cape Town–Johannesburg train stops in Paarl on Sunday, Monday, Wednesday and Friday. It departs Paarl 1125 for Cape Town (75 mins), and departs Cape Town at 1230.

The Cape Town–Johannesburg train stops in Wellington on Sunday, Monday, Wednesday and Friday. It departs Wellington 1110 for Cape Town (90 mins), and departs Cape Town at 1230.

Contents

Garden Route

Tsitsikamma Coast.

Introduction

The Garden Route is a 200-km stretch of coast separated from the arid interior by the Tsitsikamma and Outeniqua mountains. These mountains provide a watershed for the region, which is no more than about 20 km wide, feeding dense forests, extensive wetlands and fertile valleys – hence the name. It's undeniably a beautiful part of South Africa and, with a generously warm climate, is a popular holiday destination; few tourists to Cape Town miss it. The larger towns, such as Plettenberg Bay and Knysna, are highly developed tourist resorts, while other areas offer untouched wilderness and wonderful hikes, including one of the most famous in the country, the Otter Trail. This runs along the coast in Tsitsikamma National Park, one of the most popular national parks in South Africa. There is a second national park, Wilderness, which is also very popular. If hiking isn't your scene, the beaches are stunning, offering a mix of peaceful seaside villages and livelier surfer spots, and there are various attractions hugging the N2 to distract the motorist. Finally, the Garden Route is coming into its own as an adventure destination and there are numerous activities on offer from bungee jumping to mountain biking.

What to see in…

…one day
With **Knysna** or **Plettenberg Bay** as a base, explore the seaside towns and attractions along the N2 highway including **Monkeyland**, **Birds of Eden** and the **Knysna Elephant Park**. Take a cruise on the **Knysna Lagoon** or ride the **Outeniqua Choo-Tjoe** steam train between **George** and **Mossel Bay**.

…a weekend or more
Spend some time in the national parks; both **Wilderness** and **Tsitsikamma** offer scenic hiking and unrivalled views, or the five-day **Otter Trail** is South Africa's most popular hiking trail. Take part in adventure activities from mountain biking in the **Knysna Forest** to bungee jumping from the **Bloukrans Bridge**.

Knysna turaco.

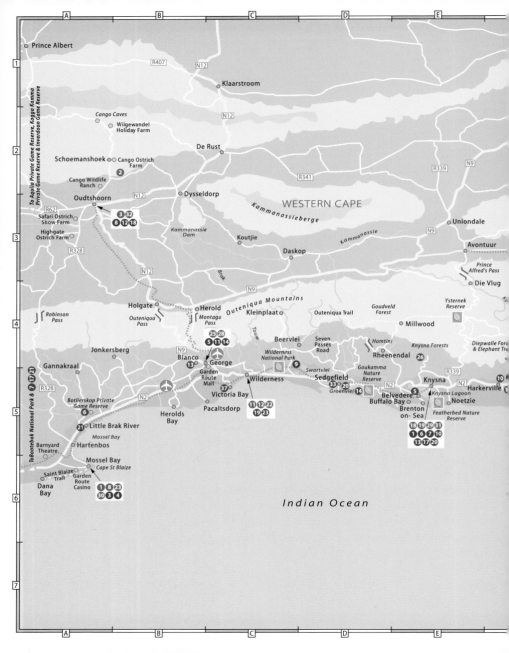

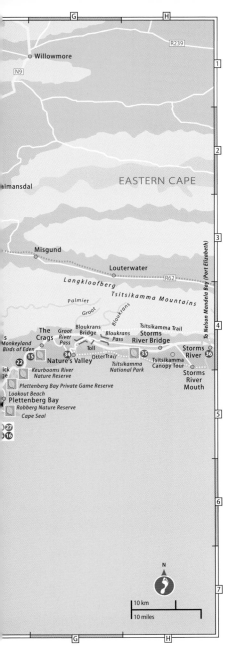

Garden Route listings

● Sleeping

1 1 Point Village Guest House (in Mossel Bay) A6
2 Altes Landhaus B2
3 Backpacker's Paradise (in Oudtshoorn) A3
4 Beacon Island (in Plettenberg Bay) F5
5 Belvedere Manor E5
6 Botlierskop Private Game Reserve A5
7 Caledon Hotel, Spa & Casino A6
8 Diaz Strand (in Mossel Bay) A6
9 Ebb & Flow Rest Camps C5
10 Elephant Lodge F5
11 Fairy Knowe Backpackers (in Wilderness) C5
12 Fairy Knowe Hotel (in Wilderness) C5
13 Fancourt Hotel & Country Club A6
14 Goukamma Nature Reserve D5
15 Hog Hollow Country House F4
16 Hunter's Country House F5
17 Klippe Rivier Country House A6
18 Knysna Backpackers (in Knysna) E5
19 Knysna Belle (in Knysna) E5
20 Lake Pleasant D5
21 Lang Elsie's Rest Camp A6
22 Moontide Guest Lodge (in Wilderness) C5
23 Mossel Bay Backpackers A6
24 Nothando Backpackers (in Plettenberg Bay) F5
25 Outeniqua Backpackers (in George) B5
26 Phantom Forest Eco-Reserve E4
27 Plettenberg (in Plettenberg Bay) F5
28 Protea Hotel King George (in George) B4
29 Protea Hotel Knysna Quays (in Knysna) E5
30 Protea Hotel Mossel Bay (in Mossel Bay) A6
31 Rex Hotel (in Knysna) E5
32 Rosenhof Country House (in Oudtshoorn) A3
33 Sedgefield Arms D5
34 Tranquility Lodge G4
35 Tsitsikamma National Park H4
36 Tube 'n Axe H4
37 Waves C5

● Eating & drinking

1 34' South (in Knysna) E5
2 57 Kloof (in Plettenberg Bay) F5
3 Bahia Dos Vaqueiros (in Mossel Bay) A6
4 Café Gannet (in Mossel Bay) A6
5 Conservatory at Meade House (in George) B4
6 Cruise Café (in Knysna) E5
7 Drydock Food Co. (in Knysna) E5
8 Headlines (in Oudtshoorn) A3
9 Hunter's Country House F5
10 Ile de Pain Bread & Café (in Knysna) E5
11 Kafé Serefé (in George) B4
12 Kalinka (in Oudtshoorn) A3
13 Knysna Oyster Co. (in Knysna) E5
14 La Locanda (in George) B4
15 Lookout Deck (in Plettenberg Bay) F5
16 Med Seafood and Grill (in Plettenberg Bay) F5
17 O'Pescador (in Knysna) E5
18 Paljas (in Oudtshoorn) A3
19 Palms (in Wilderness) C5
20 Paquitas (in Knysna) E5
21 Stonehill A5
22 Thyme and Again F4
23 Wilderness Grille (in Wilderness) C5

Overberg

Having climbed the spectacular Sir Lowry's Pass from Somerset West into the Hottentots Holland Mountains, the N2 highway cuts east across the interior of the Overberg towards Mossel Bay and George. The landscape is immediately very different on this side of the mountains – the road passes through forested hills before opening on to the endless dry, orange plains of the Overberg. To the north lie the Langeberg Mountains, their smooth foothills and sharp peaks providing a serene backdrop to the route. Most of the towns en route are quiet farming centres, and were some of the first areas settled by white farmers as they ventured east of Cape Town in search of new farmlands. If you are keen to get straight to the Garden Route, Mossel Bay can be reached in three hours, but there are several sights worth lingering over on the way. One centre that deserves a stopover is Swellendam, the third-oldest town in the Cape, which has some well-preserved examples of early Cape architecture.

Below: Harvested farmland in the Overberg. Opposite page: Rustic farm in the wheat-growing Caledon district.

Caledon

The regional capital of the Overberg, 120 km from Cape Town, lies just off the N2 at the foot of the Swartberg Mountains. It is a typical rural town – small and quiet. Mill Street has a collection of historic buildings which have been declared national monuments, but the town is famous for its six naturally occurring hot springs, which produce over 800,000 litres per day. The water has a high ferrous carbonate content. Today the hot springs are within the Caledon Spa (see page 252) and day visitors can use the facilities, which include a waterfall and a series of pools. There are additional saunas, gym, cold pool and steam room, and treatments such as massages and facials are available.

Swellendam

Founded in 1745, Swellendam is the third oldest town in South Africa after Cape Town and Stellenbosch, and it is also one of its most picturesque. The main centre has an avenue of mature oak trees and whitewashed Cape Dutch homesteads, and has an appealing, quiet atmosphere. It makes a very pleasant spot on the way to the Garden Route and is roughly halfway between Cape Town and George. Swellendam started as a trading agriculture outpost for the Dutch East India Company, and was named after Governor Hendrik Swellengrebel and his wife, Ten Damme. Today the town is a prosperous community, and many of the old buildings are still standing, or have been restored.

Drostdy Museum (18 Swellengrebel St, T028-514 1138, drostdymuseum.com, Mon-Fri 0900-1645, Sat-Sun 1000-1545, R15, under 16s R2) is often described as one of the country's great architectural treasures, the main building dates from 1747, and was built as the official residence and seat for the local magistrate or *landdrost*.

Tip...

75% of South Africa's blue cranes, the national bird, are found in the Overberg, so look out for them on open farmland.

Essentials

❷ Getting there
By air The Garden Route is served by **George Airport** (see page 271) at the western end and **Port Elizabeth Airport** (see page 271) at the eastern end. Flights link both these with Cape Town and Johannesburg. The options here are to fly into one, hire a car to explore the Garden Route and return the car to the other. Alternatively drive there from Cape Town and drop off a car in Port Elizabeth and fly back or onwards from there.

By car The most direct route from Cape Town to the Garden Route is along the N2; it's an easy 365-km drive to Mossel Bay and you may break your journey in the attractive town of Swellendam for at least lunch. Driving is ideal as many of the attractions are in between the major resorts so it's good to have the flexibility to stop when you want.

By bus As the N2 links Cape Town with Durban via the Garden Route and Eastern Cape, the three mainline bus companies (see page 273) serve all the towns. However, some travel overnight so arrive at inconvenient times. The Baz Bus (see page 273) drops off at backpacker hostels along the Garden Route.

For information on touring the Garden Route, see page 227.

Originally built in the shape of a T, the addition of two wings changed the form to an H. Inside, some of the floors have been preserved: what was the lounge has a lime-sand floor, while the kitchen floor is made from cow dung, which helps keep the room cool. The museum concentrates on local history, with a well-preserved collection of 18th- and 19th-century furniture.

Five of the best

Swellendam historical buildings

❶ The **Old Gaol** (1755) housed both prisoners and the jailer who was also the postmaster. In the middle is a cell without windows, known as the 'black hole'. Today it's an art gallery and café.

❷ The **Oefeningshuis** (1838) first served as a place for the religious instruction of freed slaves; it now houses the tourist office. Note the painted plaster clock face, which reads 1215, set above a working clock. This was designed for illiterate churchgoers – if the painted face was the same as the clocks, it was time for service.

❸ The **Dutch Reformed Church** (1901) is a large whitewashed building with a mix of architectural styles including baroque gables, gothic windows, and a tall steeple in Renaissance style.

❹ **Auld House** (1802) for many years was the family home of the trader, Joseph Barry, who dominated trade across the Overberg for more than 50 years. Inside is some furniture originally fitted on a steamer which used to sail between Cape Town and Port Beaufort.

❺ **Mayville** (1853), within the grounds of the Drostdy Museum, is a restored Victorian cottage with an antique rose garden plus the original gazebo and is today home to a coffee shop with a vine-covered *stoep*.

Tip...

The tourist office produces a leaflet called *Swellendam Treasures*, which outlines the interesting Cape Dutch buildings (Oefeningshuis, Voortrek St, T028-514 2770, swellendamtourism.co.za, Mon-Fri 0900-1300, 1400-1700, Sat 0900-1200).

Bontebok National Park

The turn-off is 6 km from Swellendam on the George side then 5 km on a gravel track, T028-514 2735, sanparks.org. Oct-Apr 0700-1900, May-Sep 0700-1800, R40, children (3-12) R20.

At the beginning of the 20th century the bontebok was the rarest species of antelope in Africa. It had been hunted and driven off its natural habitat by the settler farmers in the Overberg. Fortunately in 1931 the first reserve was established, and by the 1960s, numbers started to recover significantly, and although no longer endangered, there are

The Langeberg Mountains reflected in a farm dam in Heidelberg.

still not many places where bontebok can be seen in the wild. Today, other antelope indigenous to the Overberg have been introduced to the reserve including red hartebeest, steenbok, duiker plus the rare Cape mountain zebra. There are two gravel game driving tracks taking one and two hours respectively.

Heidelberg to Albertinia

Continuing east from Swellendam along the N2 highway, the road passes several small agricultural towns which have little of interest to detain tourists. Heidelberg is dominated by its Dutch Reformed church on the banks of the Duivenhoks River. Riversdale is a small farming centre based around wheat, wool and potatoes, with no fewer than 15 stone churches, the oldest being the St Matthew's Anglican Church, built in 1856. Albertinia is another important centre for wheat and, more unusually, aloe plants. You can visit the Alcare Aloe Factory (T028-735 1454, alcare.co.za, 0900-1700), just outside town, which sells a variety of aloe skincare products and there's a coffee shop. The Garden Route Game Lodge (see page 72) is 7 km east of Albertinia off the N2, and Mossel Bay is 50 km from Albertinia.

Mossel Bay & George

Built along a rocky peninsula which provides sheltered swimming and mooring in the bay, Mossel Bay is one of the larger and less appealing seaside towns along the Garden Route. During the school holidays the town is packed with domestic visitors. A fact often overlooked in promotional literature is that since the discovery of offshore oil deposits, Mossel Bay is also the home of the ugly Mossgas natural gas refinery and a multitude of oil storage tanks. George owes its status to the fact that it has an airport. It is also an important junction between the N2 coastal highway and the N9 passing through the Outeniqua Pass into the Karoo. It lies in the shadow of the Outeniqua Mountains but, unlike the majority of towns along the Garden Route, it is not by the sea. While it is pleasant enough, it has little appeal compared to other towns along the coast; the main reason overseas visitors come here is to play golf. George has several outstanding golf courses and received worldwide attention in November 2003 when it hosted the President's Cup Golf Tournament.

Mossel Bay

Mossel Bay Tourism Bureau, corner of Church and Market streets, T044-691 1067, visitmosselbay.co.za.
Mon-Fri 0800-1800, Sat-Sun 0900-1700.
Map: Garden Route, A6, p220.

The town has a number of Portuguese flags and names dotted around, thanks to the first European to anchor in the bay – Bartolomeu Dias, who landed in February 1488, followed by Vasco da Gama, who moored in the bay in 1497. The bay's safe anchorage and freshwater spring ensured that it became a regular stopping-off point for other seafarers. The town was named by a Dutch trader, Cornelis de Houtman, who in 1595 found a pile of mussel shells in a cave below the present lighthouse. Many of the local attractions relate to the sea and reflect the bay's importance to early Portuguese navigators and Dutch explorers.

Bartolomeu Dias Museum Complex (1 Market St, T044-691 1067, diasmuseum.co.za, Mon-Fri 0900-1645, Sat-Sun 0900-1545, R25, under 12s R8) Here you'll find the Culture Museum, the Shell Museum, an Aquarium, the Maritime Museum, some Malay graves, and the original freshwater spring that attracted the early sailors and which still flows into a small dam. There's also a tea shop on site in a restored 1830s cottage. The displays in the Maritime Museum are arranged around a full-size replica of Bartolomeu Dias's caravel. Also here is a tree with a fascinating past: the Post Office Tree is a giant milkwood situated close to the freshwater spring. History relates that in 1500 a letter was left under the tree by a ship's captain. A year later it was retrieved by the commander of the Third East India Fleet en route to India. Messages were also left carved in rocks and in old boots tied to the branches. The tree has been declared a national monument and it is still possible to send a postcard home from here – all mail dispatched from the Post Office Tree is franked with a special commemorative stamp and makes a great souvenir. The Outeniqua Choo-Tjoe steam train now stops at the station (see page 231).

Touring the Garden Route

If you don't want to self drive, there are a number of options for exploring the Garden Route. Baz Bus (T021-439 2323, bazbus.com) offers a very adequate service and drops and picks up at Garden Route hostels every day. Mainline buses operate a daily service, but most departures and arrivals are in the middle of the night and it's not as economical as the Baz Bus. For those on a budget and short of time, the Bok Bus (T082-320 1979, bokbus.com) is a comprehensive award-winning five-day tour of all the major attractions along the Garden Route starting and finishing in Cape Town. The tour visits most of the adventure activities (optional extras) and accommodation is in hostels or you can upgrade to guesthouses. Prices start at R4450 and include breakfasts, most dinners and entrance fees. There are numerous other coach and minibus operators running short tours from Cape Town along the Garden Route that appeal to a wide range of age groups and offer a variety of accommodation alternatives. These include: African Eagle (T021-464 4266, daytours.co.za); Cape Rainbow (T021-551 5465, caperainbow.com); Eco-Tours (T021-788 5741, ecotourssa.co.za); and Springbok Atlas (T021-460 4700, springbokatlas.co.za).

Essentials

$ ATM These are found in all the towns and shopping malls.

⊕ Hospital Bayview Private Hospital, corner Alhof and Ryk Tulbach streets, Mossel Bay, T044-691 3718, bayviewprivatehospital.com; George Medi-Clinic Clinic, corner Gloucester and York streets, T044-803 2000, georgemc.co.za; Knysna Private Hospital, Hunters Dr, T044-384 1083, lifehealthcare.co.za.

❶ Tourist information There are several tourist offices in the region, listed under the relevant headings below. For more information about the Garden Route visit gardenroute.co.za or gardenroute.org.za.

Above: Seals on a rock near Mossel Bay. Opposite page: Botlierskop Private Game Reserve.

Seal Island

In the middle of the bay, Seal Island can be visited by cruises departing from the harbour. It is inhabited by colonies of African penguins and Cape fur seals (the best month to see seal pups is November). It's also possible to see great white sharks and small hammerhead sharks which prey upon the seals. Between September and November the warm waters of the bay are often visited by southern right, humpback and Bryde's whales while calving. Another vantage point for viewing whales and dolphins is The Point at the end of Marsh Street.

Cape St Blaize Lighthouse

Montague St, The Point.
Mon-Fri 1000-1500, R14, children (under 12) R7.

The 20-m-high Cape St Blaize lighthouse was erected in 1864, and although it is now fully automated, the lighthouse keeper can give guided tours and you can climb to the top.

St Blaize Trail

The St Blaize Trail is a perfect introduction to the stunning coastline that you are likely to encounter along the Garden Route. This is a 13½-km walk along the cliffs and rocky coast west from Mossel Bay. The official trail starts from Bats Cave, just below the lighthouse; the path is marked by the white image of a bird in flight. As you walk further from the town the scenery becomes more and more spectacular. You can leave the coast at Pinnacle Point, and follow a path inland to Essenhout Street. This cuts about 5 km off the walk. The path ends by a group of houses in Dana Bay. From here you will have to organize your own transport back into town, so it helps to have a mobile phone to call a taxi from Mossel Bay. A helpful map is available from the tourism office. You are rightly warned to be careful in places during strong winds, as there are some precipitous and unprotected drops from the cliff tops. Some years ago Khoi-San articles dating back 80,000 years were discovered in Cape St Blaize Cave, also known as Bats Cave; they are now in the museum.

Tip...

The Garden Route's popularity means that accommodation needs to be booked in advance, especially during peak season, which is the two weeks over Christmas and the New Year, and at Easter.

Botlierskop Private Game Reserve

T044-696 6055, botlierskop.co.za.
Turn off the N2 on to the R401 to the northeast of Mossel Bay, the Klein Brakrivier turn-off, and follow signs for 25 km.
Map: Garden Route, A5, p220.

This private reserve is situated on a 2400-ha game farm, which is home to 24 different species of animal and a wide variety of birds. A former farm, Botlierskop was bought in 1996, and the new owners saw the opportunity to reintroduce wildlife in this area. After four years of recovering from domestic farming, it was opened in 2000. The land has been restocked and wildlife includes the rare black impala, rhino, elephant, lion, buffalo, giraffe, mountain zebra and eland. Activities include game drives, nature walks, picnics and helicopter flips (rides). The most exciting activity is elephant riding and expect to pay in the region of R550; no children under six. The three elephants are orphans who survived a culling program in the Zambezi Valley in Zimbabwe. There is luxurious accommodation available (see page 253) or you can visit for the day, though booking is essential. Check out the website for prices and programmes.

George

George Tourism Bureau: 124 York St,
T044-801 9295, tourismgeorge.co.za.
Mon-Fri 0800-1700, Sat 0900-1300.
Map: Garden Route, C5, p220.

The first settlement appeared here in 1778 as a forestry post to process wood from the surrounding forests. In 1811 it was formally declared a town, and named after King George III. It was at this time that its wide tree-lined streets – Courtenay, York and Meade – were laid out. For the next 80 years the town remained the centre for a voracious timber industry. Much of the indigenous forest was destroyed supplying wood for wagons, railway sleepers and mine props. Today, the town itself is a mostly modern grid of streets interspersed with some attractive old buildings and churches.

On the corner of Cathedral and York streets, St Mark's Cathedral, consecrated in 1850, has an unusually large number of stained-glass windows for its size; many were designed by overseas artists of limited fame. In 1911 a bible and royal prayer book were given to the church by King George V. The interior of the Dutch Reformed Mother Church at the north end of Meade Street reflects the town's early history as a centre for the timber industry. The pulpit is carved out of stinkwood and took over a year to create. The ceiling was built from yellowwood, and six yellowwood trunks were used as pillars. The mountains create an impressive backdrop to the church when viewed from the corner of Courtenay and Meade streets.

George Museum (Courtenay St, T044-702 3523. Mon-Fri 0900-1630, Sat 0900-1230, ₨5), housed in the old Drostdy (magistrate's house), this has grown from the private collection of Charles Sayer, the owner/editor of the *George & Knysna Herald* newspaper in the 1960s, and has displays on the timber industry as well as musical instruments and a collection of old printing presses. There is also an exhibition devoted to former President PW Botha, who was a member of parliament for George for 38 years.

Slave Tree

In front of the tourist office, housed in the King Edward VII library, is an ancient oak tree known as the Slave Tree. The tree acquired its name because of the chain embedded in the trunk with a lock attached to it. However, the true story of the chain can be traced back to when a public tennis court was in use next to the library (now the information office), and the court roller was secured to the tree to prevent playful children from rolling it down the street.

Outeniqua Choo-Tjoe

Until 2006, the most enjoyable way to travel between George and Knysna was on the Outeniqua Choo-Tjoe, a historic steam train. This picturesque branch line was opened in 1928 and the 67-km journey gave passengers an extraordinary view of some spectacular coastal scenery and forests, passing through Wilderness National Park and along the Goukamma Valley. The journey ended by crossing Knysna Lagoon via a long bridge. Unfortunately, landslides caused by bad weather in August 2006, damaged the line beyond repair and it is now closed. However, it now runs on an alternative line between George and the Dias Museum Complex in Mossel Bay and follows a scenic route traversing the farmlands outside George with the Outeniqua Mountain in the background, before descending to the Indian Ocean. It runs every day except Sunday from 1 April and 30 September, and on Friday only between 1 May and 31 August. The train departs from the Railway Museum in George at 1000, gets to Mossel Bay at 1200, leaves again at 1415 and arrives back in George at 1615; return ₹140, children (3-12) ₹70, children under 3 free; one-way ₹110, children (3-12) ₹60, children under 3 free. Reservations and information, George Railway Museum (T044-801 8288).

Outeniqua Transport Museum (2 Mission Rd, just off Knysna Rd, T044-801 8288, Mon-Sat 0800-1700, ₹20, children 3-12 ₹10) has an interesting display outlining the history of steam train travel, including 13 steam locomotives, a 1947 Royal Mail coach, and a room dedicated to model railways. There's also a collection of vintage cars and flight memorabilia. It is adjacent to the platform from which the Outeniqua steam train departs (see box).

Victoria Bay

9 km south of George, 2 km off the N2.
Map: Garden Route, C5, p220.

If you are based in George and wish to spend a quiet day by the sea, this small resort is only 15 minutes' drive away. It has a narrow cove with a broad sandy beach, a grassy sunbathing area, and a safe tidal pool for children. There's one row of houses with some of the best-positioned guesthouses in the region. It's also a great place to surf during winter.

Oudtshoorn

North of George, the region around Oudtshoorn is a series of parallel fertile valleys, enclosed by the Swartberg Mountains to the north and the Langeberg and Outeniqua Mountains to the south. Oudtshoorn, the pleasant administrative centre, still retains much of the calm of its early days, with broad streets and smart sandstone Victorian houses. It was named after Baron Van Rheede van Oudtshoorn, who died there on his way to the Cape to take up the post of governor in 1773. It was the advent of two ostrich-feather booms (1865-1870 and 1900-1914) that truly established the town, and led to the erection of the fine mansions or 'ostrich palaces' that now line Oudtshoorn's streets. For a period of almost 40 years it was the most important settlement east of Cape Town, and at its peak ostrich feathers were selling for more than their weight in gold. While ostrich farming no longer brings in as much wealth, it remains an important business in the region today. Most people make a detour from the Garden Route, 60 km on the N12 from George, to visit an ostrich farm and the Cango Caves.

Below: A farmhouse in Cape Dutch style. Opposite page: Cango Caves near Oudtshoorn.

CP Nel Museum

3 Baron van Rheede St, T044-272 7306,
cpnelmuseum.co.za.
Mon-Fri 0800-1700, Sat-Sun 0900-1700, ₱12,
children (7-18) ₱3, under 7s free.
Map: Garden Route, A3, p220.

This fine sandstone building with its prominent
clock tower was originally built as a boys' high
school. The masons who designed the building
had been brought to Oudtshoorn by the 'feather
barons' to build their grand mansions. The displays
include a reconstructed trading store, synagogue
and chemist, plus an interesting section on the
history of the ostrich boom and the characters
involved. The rest of the collection of historic
objects was bequeathed to the town by CP Nel,
a local businessman. A short walk away is Le Roux
Town House, at 146 High Street, which is part of the
CP Nel Museum. This classic town house was built
in 1908 and provides a real feel for how the wealthy
lived in the fine ostrich palaces of Oudtshoorn. The
interior and furnishings are in art nouveau style

Essentials

The Oudtshoorn Tourist Bureau is on Baron van
Rheede St, T044-2792532, oudtshoorn.com,
Mon-Fri 0800-1800, Sat 0830-1300.

and the furniture was shipped from Europe
between 1900 and 1920. During the summer,
teas are served in the garden.

Cango Caves

28 km north of Oudtshoorn on the R328,
T044-2727410, cangocaves.co.za.
Open 0900-1700, there are 2 tour options: the
standard tour starting every hour on the hour
from 0900, with the last tour at 1600, 1 hr, ₱55,
₱30 children, and the adventure tour starting
at half past every hour 0930-1530, 1½ hrs, ₱70,
₱45 children.
Map: Garden Route, A2, p220.

Tucked away in the foothills of the Swartberg
Mountains, the Cango Caves are a magnificent

Five of the best

Ostrich farms

❶ Cango Ostrich Farm
In the Shoemanshoek Valley 14 km north of Oudtshoorn,
T044-2724623, cangoostrich.co.za.
Open 0800-1700, ₨56, children ₨27, tours every
20 mins, duration 45 mins.

This is particularly convenient as it is on the way to and
from the Cango Caves. The farm attractions are also
within walking distance of each other. You can interact
directly with the birds, sit on or ride them, buy local
curios and sample Karoo wines and cheeses.

❷ Cango Wildlife Ranch
3 km north of Oudtshoorn on the R328 towards the Cango
Caves, T044-2725593, cango.co.za.
Open 0800-1700, ₨95, children ₨60, tours every
40 mins, duration 1 hr.

There are mixed opinions on this place since it is, in
effect, a zoo which stocks animals including white
lions, leopards, cheetahs and, oddly, jaguars, pumas
and two rare white Bengal tigers that produced three
cubs in 2003. There is even an albino python. However
the ranch is a leading player in conservation and
breeding, particularly with cheetah and wild dog, and
the enclosures are very spacious. After walking safely
above the animals, you have the choice of paying
a little more to pet a cheetah, or you can visit the
restaurant. A new attraction here is the Valley of the
Ancients, a well-forested string of lakes and enclosures
connected by boardwalks that are home to a number
of unusual animals. The pools are home to Nile
crocodiles, pygmy hippos, monitor lizards and otters,
while birds include flamingos and marabou storks. You
can watch the crocodiles being fed by hand and this is
probably the only place in the world that offers cage-
diving with crocodiles (₨240; children must be over 12).

❸ Highgate Ostrich Farm
10 km from Oudtshoorn off the R328 towards Mossel Bay,
T044-2727115, highgate.co.za.
Open 0800-1700, ₨40, children ₨26, tours every
15 mins, duration 1½ hrs.

This very popular show farm, named after the London
suburb of Highgate, has been owned by the Hooper
family since the 1850s. It has won prizes in the last

few years for its high standards, and is very well run
and better organized than other farms. You will learn
everything there is to know about the bird, and can then
try your hand at riding (or even racing!) them. Snacks
and drinks are served on the porch of the homestead.
As well as English, guides speak German and Dutch.

❹ Safari Ostrich Show Farm
6 km from Oudtshoorn off the R328 towards Mossel Bay,
T044-2727311, safariostrich.co.za.
Open 0730-1700, adults ₨46, children ₨24, tours depart
every 30 mins, duration 1 hr.

Has ostrich rides, educational exhibits and curio
shops, and there is also a smart homestead known
as Welgeluk. The house was built in 1910, and is a
perfectly preserved example of an ostrich palace.
There are roof tiles from Belgium, teak from Burma
and expanses of marble floors, proof of the wealth
and influence the short-lived boom brought to
Oudtshoorn families.

❺ Wilgewandel Holiday Farm
In the Shoemanshoek Valley, 2 km before the Cango
Caves, T044-2720878, wilgewandel.co.za.
Open 0800-1500, free entrance, activities from ₨5
to ₨25 per person.

Has the usual ostrich activities but also offers the
chance to ride a camel around the farm, and there
are lots of attractions for children such as farmyard
animals, a pet area, trampolines, bumper boats,
donkey cart rides and a restaurant serving anything
from tea and scones to crocodile and ostrich steaks.

network of calcite caves, recognized as among the world's finest dripstone caverns. In 1938 they were made a national monument. Despite being seriously hyped and very touristy, they are well worth a visit. The only access to the caves is on a guided tour: the most popular tour takes in six caves, while the adventure tour follows narrow corridors and involves some crawling. During the tours, each section is lit up and the guide points out interesting formations and their given names. Although one small chamber is still lit in gaudy colours, the rest are illuminated with white light to best show off the formations. These are turned off behind you as you progress further into the system as research has shown that continued exposure to light causes damage to the caves.

The caverns are not just a beautiful series of bizarre formations, but represent over a million years of slow chemical processes. The Cango cave system is known as a phreatic system, the term given to caves which have been chemically eroded by underground water. Once the caves had been exposed to air, the first deposits started to form – these now make up the incredible stalagmites, stalactites and flowstones visitors can see. The timescale of some of the formations is mind-boggling; many of the pillars took hundreds of thousands of years to form, while the oldest flowstone is over a million years old.

The standard one-hour tour is a good introduction to the caves and allows you to see the most impressive formations. It is, however, aimed at tour groups, so visitors with a special interest may find it rather simplistic. The adventure tour lasts for 1½ hours, is over 1 km long and there are over 400 steps. This can be disturbing for some people, since it involves crawling along narrow tunnels, and at the very end climbing up the Devil's Chimney, a narrow vertical shaft. It leads up for 3½ m and is only 45 cm wide in parts – definitely not for broad people. If at any stage you feel you can't go on, inform the guide who will arrange for you to be led out. Although strenuous, this tour allows you to see most of the caves, and gives a real feeling of exploration.

Tip...

Allow a morning for a round trip if based locally; if you have a car it is possible to visit the caves and Oudtshoorn on a day trip from towns along the Garden Route such as Mossel Bay, George and Wilderness. During the holidays it gets very crowded and nearly 200,000 people pass through the caves each year. Each tour has a maximum number of people, so you may have to wait an hour or more. It's a good idea to get here early in the morning to avoid queues.

There is a restaurant, a crèche, several curio shops and a small money exchange. The caves are usually around 20°C, so a T-shirt and shorts will be fine. Wear shoes with reasonable grip as after rain the floors can become a little slippery. It is a criminal offence to touch or take anything from inside the caves. Please adhere to these rules and be careful not to touch the rock formations – the acidity of the human sweat that is left from by wandering hands has already caused considerable damage. Eating, drinking and smoking are also forbidden inside.

The caverns are not just a beautiful series of bizarre formations, but represent over a million years of slow chemical processes.

Wilderness & Sedgefield

Back on the N2, Wilderness is an appealing little town with a superb swathe of sandy beach. Check locally for demarcated areas for swimming and surfing. Children should be supervised in the sea as there are strong rip currents. One of the safest spots for swimming is in the Touw River mouth. Except for the few hectic weeks at Christmas and New Year, Wilderness is generally very relaxed and has an excellent range of accommodation. The highlight, however, is Wilderness National Park, a quiet, well-managed park, with three levels of self-catering accommodation and a campsite. The next village along the N2 is Sedgefield. The village itself straddles the main road and is of little interest, but between the main road and the beach is the Swartvlei Lagoon, South Africa's largest natural inland saltwater lake, most of which lies on the inland side of the N2. The countryside around the lakes is spectacular and very peaceful.

Wilderness

Wilderness Tourism Bureau, Leila's Lane (turn left by the post office), T044-877 0045, tourismwilderness.co.za.
Mon-Fri 0800-1700, Sat 0900-1300.
Map: Garden Route, C5, p220.

The first European to settle in the district was a farmer, van der Bergh, who built himself a simple farmhouse in the 1850s. In 1928, the railway reached Wilderness on the George to Knysna line. Until recently, this 67-km line gave passengers an extraordinary view of spectacular coastal scenery and forests and it passed across the impressive curved Kaaimans River Bridge to the west of Wilderness and through the Wilderness National Park. Unfortunately, parts of this line were washed away in landslides in 2006 and it is presently closed.

The town itself doesn't have much of a centre, but stretches instead up the lush foothills of the Outeniqua Mountains and along leafy streets by the lake and river. The supermarket, restaurants, post office and tourist office are by the petrol station, where the N2 crosses the Serpentine channel.

It's a fact...

It was in 1877 that the name of Wilderness was first used, when a young man from Cape Town, George Bennet, was granted the hand of his sweetheart only on condition that he took her to live in the wilderness. He purchased some land near the lagoon in a dense patch of forest and promptly named it 'wilderness' to appease his new father-in-law.

Railway bridge over Swartvlei Lake, Western Cape.

Around the region

Wilderness National Park

4 km east of Wilderness off the N2; camp reception T044-877 1197, sanparks.org.
Office hours 0700-2000, R72, children (2-11) R36. Map: Garden Route, C5, p220.

The main attraction is the water and the birdlife in the reed beds but there are some excellent hikes and a beautiful sandy beach. The park covers 2612 ha and incorporates five rivers and four lakes – known as Island, Langvlei, Rondevlei and Swartvlei – as well as a 28-km stretch of the coastline. The series of freshwater lakes is situated between the Outeniqua foothills and the sand dunes which back on to a beautiful, long sandy beach. There are two ways in which to enjoy the beauty of the surroundings, on foot or in a canoe. You can cover more ground by walking, and there are five trails in the park. The Pied Kingfisher Trail, a 10-km circular route, can be completed in four hours. It follows the river in one direction and the beach on your return. The other walks are also forest walks, except

for the 3-km Dune Molerat Trail which takes you through dune fynbos where you may see proteas in flower in season. Canoeing is ideal for seeing birds. The main camp has canoes and pedalos for hire – these should be arranged through Eden Adventures (see page 265). One of the more interesting short routes is to continue up the Touw River past the Ebb and Flow Camps. This quickly becomes a narrow stream and you have to leave your canoe. A path continues along the bank of the stream through some beautiful riverine forest. Eden Adventures also have mountain bikes, some with child seats, to rent out for use on the trails in the park.

Sedgefield

Map: Garden Route, D5, p220.

Unless you turn off the N2, all that can be seen of Sedgefield is a collection of curio shops, supermarkets and snack bars. Between the main road and the beach is the Swartvlei Lagoon, which

Dabchick or little grebe in the wetlands around Sedgefield.

is a popular spot for watersports and birdwatching, although the two pastimes don't always go well together. On the Knysna side of Sedgefield is another lake, Groenvlei, a freshwater lake lying within the Goukamma Nature Reserve (see below).

Goukamma Nature Reserve

The turn-off is between Sedgefield and Knysna and is signposted off the N2, follow for 8 km and turn right towards the river, T044-802 5310, capenature.org.za.
Gates open 0800-1800, entry for day visitors R25, children (2-13) R12.
Map: Garden Route, D4, p220.

The reserve was established to protect 2230 ha of the hinterland between Sedgefield and Buffalo Bay. This includes Groenvlei or Lake Pleasant, a large freshwater lake, and a 13-km sandy beach with some magnificent sand dunes covered in fynbos and patches of forest containing milkwood trees. The Goukamma River estuary in the eastern part of the reserve has been cut off from the sea by the large sand dunes. The lake is now fed by natural drainage and springs, and is surrounded by reed beds which are excellent for birdwatching; more than 75 species have been identified. A 4-km hiking trail runs along the lake shore and if you are feeling energetic, there is a 14-km trail starting from the same point, which takes you across the reserve to the Goukamma River in the eastern sector, although this leaves you with the problem of return transportation. On any of the walks in the reserve, always carry plenty of drinking water and keep an eye out for snakes, especially among the sand dunes.

Tip...

Around Sedgefield's lakes and forests look out for the secretive starred robin, the blue mantle flycatcher, the difficult-to-see Victorian warbler and the rare African finfoot.

Sedgefield river mouth.

Knysna

Knysna (the 'K' is silent) is on the N2 between Cape Town (500 km) and Port Elizabeth (260 km), and is the self-proclaimed heart of the Garden Route. The name is generally believed to mean a place of wood or leaves in the language of the Hottentots. In 1804 George Rex, a timber merchant, purchased a farm on the edge of the lagoon, and the timber industry continued well into the 20th century. Unfortunately it wiped out much of the natural forest on the coast, though there are still tracts of Knysna Forest. The town is no longer the sleepy lagoon-side village it once was – far from it – but is nevertheless a pleasant spot to spend a day or two. The town itself is fully geared up for tourists, which means a lot of choice in accommodation and restaurants, as well as overcrowding and high prices. It remains quite an arty place, though, and many of the craftspeople who have gravitated to the region display their products in craft shops and galleries. Nevertheless, development is booming, with a slick waterfront complex, complete with souvenir shops and restaurants.

Noetzie Rocks in Knysna.

Knysna town

Knysna Tourism, 40 Main St, T044-382 5510,
tourismknysna.co.za.
Mon-Fri 0800-1700, Sat 0830-1300,
hours extended in high season.
Map: Garden Route, E5, p220.

Knysna Museum (Queen St, T044-302 6320, Mon-
Fri 0930-1630, Sat 0930-1230, free but donations
accepted, art gallery, tearoom and gift shop) is
housed in the Old Gaol – the first public building
erected by the colonial government in the 1870s.
Most of the collection focuses on fishing methods
used along the coast, with a variety of nets and
tackle on display. Unless you are a devoted angler
this is not going to take up too much of your time.
The highlight is in fact a fish, or to be more precise,
a coelacanth. This is a prehistoric fish that was
believed to be extinct, but a live specimen was
famously caught by a fisherman in 1938.

   Mitchell's Knysna Brewery (Arend St, Knysna
Industria, T044-382 4685, mitchellsknysnabrewery.
com, Mon-Fri 0830-1630, tours at 1000 and 1500,
Sat 0930-1230, tour at 1000, ₨50) produces a range
of homemade lagers and bitters (the latter being
very rare in South Africa), and visitors can take a tour
of the fermentation cellars, which includes tasting.
The brews are also available from many hotels and
restaurants along the Garden Route. The most
popular are the Forester's Draught pilsner-type
lager, the Bosun's Best Bitter, and the heavily spiced
Scottish-type traditional ale known as Ninety Shilling.

Featherbed Nature Reserve

Featherbed Co, Remembrance Lane, off Waterfront
Drive, T044-382 1693, knysnafeatherbed.com.
1000, 1115, 1230, ₨375, children (under 14) ₨180
(including lunch), 1430, ₨260, children (under 14)
₨100 (without lunch).
The Featherbed excursion goes from the Cruise
Cafe while the others go from the Knysna Quays.
Map: Garden Route, E5, p220.

This is a private nature reserve in the unspoilt
western side of the Knysna Heads, which can only

Knysna National Lake Area

Knysna's highlights are its natural attractions. The
Knysna National Lake Area covers over 15,000 ha,
comprising islands, seashore, forest and beach.
While the area is not effectively a national park, in
some part it is protected by South African National
Parks (SANParks), who are involved in management,
and who try to promote a healthy balance between
conservation and recreation. The main feature of the
town is the lagoon, around which much of Knysna life
revolves. The Heads, the rocky promontories that lead
from the lagoon to the open sea, are quite stunning.
More than 280 species of bird are listed in the area
and the tidal lagoon and open estuary of the Knysna
River provide an excellent place to view waders in the
summer months, and plovers, gulls, cormorants and
sandpipers are common. Large species like African fish
eagle and osprey should also be watched out for. The
area also incorporates the remaining tract of Knysna
forests on the southern slopes of the Outeniqua
Mountains, behind Knysna, which first attracted white
settlers to the region. No longer a single expanse, the
patches go under a variety of names: Diepwalle Forest,
Ysternek Reserve, Goudveld Forest, and Millwood
Nature Reserve. They are noteworthy for the variety of
birdlife and their magnificent trees. Species of special
interest include the yellowwood, assegai, stinkwood,
red alder, white alder and the Cape chestnut. A variety
of short walks has been laid out in the forests. In some
areas horse riding and mountain biking are allowed.

be reached by the Featherbed Co. ferry. The reserve
is home to South Africa's largest breeding herd of
blue duiker (*Cephalophus monticola*), an endangered
species. Also of interest is a cave once inhabited by
the Khoi, which has been declared a national
heritage site. This four-hour excursion includes
return ferry trip, 4WD vehicle ride up the western
promontory of the Knysna Heads and an optional
2-km guided nature walk through the forest, onto
the cliffs, into the caves and along the spectacular
coastline. It ends with a buffet lunch under some
milkwood trees before returning to Knysna. This is
an excellent family excursion. The Featherbed Co
also offers 1½-hour cruises around the lagoon on a
paddle cruiser at 1230 for ₨150, children ₨65 or at
1815, which includes a three-course buffet dinner,

Invisible elephants

The Knysna elephants live deep in the forest and few people have ever seen them, and little is known about their numbers or their characteristics. In 1876, several hundred elephants were recorded in the region, but under heavy pressure of ivory hunters they were reduced to 20 to 30 individuals by 1908.

In 1970 the Knysna elephant population was estimated at 11, and by 1994, only three Knysna elephants were known to survive. Then, after a study in 2007, conservation geneticists from the US University of Missouri-Columbia announced that there could be several elephants in Knysna Forest. By extracting DNA samples from dung, they established that there were five individual females and at least one bull.

Above: Knysna elephant. Opposite page: Belvedere Church, Knysna.

R350, children R180. In addition, they run the Cruise Café at the boat departure point at the Knysna Quays (see page 261).

Belvedere & Brenton-on-Sea

Turn off the N2 on the western side of the lagoon.
Map: Garden Route, E5, p220.

These villages, 12-14 km from town on the western shores of the lagoon, are in many ways really smart suburbs of Knysna. Brenton has the great attraction of having the nearest sandy beach making it very popular during the school holidays. There is a fine hotel and a limited selection of seaside cottages. Belvedere is primarily a leafy residential suburb along the banks of the river where it enters the lagoon. A large proportion of the village is made up of the relatively new Belvedere Estate, a prestigious development on 67 ha, with large houses and gardens.

The small village church, Belvedere Church, is a popular attraction in the area and is a miniature replica of a Norman church. It was built in 1855 from local stone and timber, with picturesque stained-glass windows and stinkwood fittings. The rose window on the west side was installed in 1955.

Diepwalle Forest & Elephant Trail

From Knysna, follow the N2 towards Plettenburg Bay, after 7 km turn onto the R339 and the Diepwalle forest station is about 16 km on a gravel road.
Open 0600-1800, no charge but you must sign in at the forest station where maps are on offer.
Map: Garden Route, D4/F4, p220.

Starting from the Diepwalle forest station is the 20-km Elephant Walk, an easy-going, level hike that gives a clear insight into the forest environment. The trail is marked by elephant silhouettes and takes around seven hours to complete. The hike is made up of three loops, but it is possible to shorten the walk by completing only one or two loops. The three paths are simply known as Routes I, II and III, and are 9-, 8- and 6-km long, respectively. Apart from the (very slim) possibility

of spying the rare Knysna elephant (see page 242), the main attractions are the giant forest trees, particularly the Outeniqua yellowwood. There are eight such trees along the full trail – the largest, at 46 m, is known as the King Edward VII Tree, and stands just off the R339 by the Diepwalle picnic spot at the end of Route I and the start of Route II. The end of the Outeniqua Trail meets with Route III.

Knysna Elephant Park

On the N2, 20 km from Knysna and 10 km before Plettenberg Bay, T044-532 7732, knysnaelephantpark.co.za.
Tours every 30 mins, 0830-1630, ₹160, children (3-12) ₹83, bookings not required; elephant riding 0930, 1030, 1500, 1600, ₹682, children (6-12) ₹330, children under 6 not permitted, booking essential.
Map: Garden Route, F4/F5, p220.

This small park is a refuge for orphaned elephants, and visitors are taken on tours around the forest area and are allowed to touch and play with the little elephants. Although the animals are 'free range' they are very used to human contact, making it a wonderful experience for children. Longer walks with the elephants can also be arranged and the newest option here is elephant riding, which is a two-hour excursion through the bush ending with refreshments. Sleeping with the elephants is also on offer, and six rooms have been built above the elephants' boma where they sleep at night (see page 257). This is also the only realistic chance you'll have of seeing elephants in the area – the fabled indigenous ones are far too elusive.

Apart from the (very slim) possibility of spying the rare Knysna elephant, of which there are three on record at present, the main attractions are the giant forest trees, particularly the Outeniqua yellowwood.

Plettenberg Bay

Plettenberg Bay, or 'Plett' as it is commonly known, is one of the most appealing resorts on the Garden Route. The Portuguese had a number of names for the bay, but it was only in 1778 when Governor Joachim van Plettenberg opened a timber post on the shores of the bay, and named it after himself, that a name stuck. Plettenberg remained an important timber port until the early 1800s, and for a period the bay became famous as a whaling station but all that remains is a blubber cauldron and slipway. Although it is modern and has little of historical interest, the compact centre is attractive and the main beach beautiful. Plett has now become fashionable and, during the Christmas season, the town is transformed. Wealthy families descend from Johannesburg and the pace can get quite frenetic – expect busy beaches and long queues for restaurant tables. For the rest of the year the pace is calmer and the resort becomes just another sleepy seaside town. There are three beaches that are good for swimming, and there are a number of attractions along the N2 to the east of Plett.

Plettenberg Bay

Plettenberg Bay Tourism, Melville's Corner shopping centre, Main St, T044-533 4065, plettenbergbay.co.za.
Mon-Fri 0900-1700, Sat 0900-1300, slightly longer hours during the peak summer season. Map: Garden Route, F5, p220.

While there are a few old buildings still standing which represent a little of the town's earlier history: St Andrew's Chapel, the remains of the Old Timber Store (1787), the Old Rectory (1776), the Forest Hall (1864) and the Dutch Reformed Church (1834), the main streets are just a collection of modern shopping malls and restaurants. The real attraction of this area is the sea and the outdoors. Aside from the three beaches, Robberg, Central and Lookout, there is excellent deep-sea fishing and, in season, good opportunities to spot whales and dolphins, particularly southern right whales from June to October. Plett climbs up a fairly steep hill; there are many elevated land-based vantage points as well as regular boat tours offering closer encounters with the marine life. The **Milkwood Trail** is a 3- or 5-km trail in and around the town. Follow the yellow footprints. The walk starts from the car park off Marine Drive and takes you via Piesangs River lagoon, Central beach and Lookout beach. At this point the shorter route turns back through the centre of town via some of the historic buildings, while the longer route continues via Keurbooms Lagoon and round the back of town.

Robberg Peninsula Nature Reserve

8 km south from Plett on the old airport road. T044-533 2125, capenature.org.za.
Feb-Nov 0700-1700, Dec and Jan 0700-2000, permits are available at the entrance gate, R25, children (2-13) R12. Map: Garden Route, F5, p220.

This rocky peninsula forms the western boundary of Plettenberg Bay. There are three possibilities for hiking ranging from 2-9 km; follow the 'seal' markers. Walking is easy thanks to boardwalks, and there are plenty of prominent viewpoints from which it is possible to see whales, seals and dolphins in the bay, but beware of freak waves along the coastal paths. Allow at least

Tip...

If you're trying to choose between Knysna and Plettenberg Bay as a base, Knysna offers more amenities and activities, while Plett is far more relaxed and has the better beach. Both get very busy during high season.

Point of Robberg Nature Reserve.

Around the region

four hours for the full route. If you want to go on a guided walk of Robberg, contact Robberg Guided Walks (T044-533 2632, robbergwalks. homestead.com). Eden Adventures based in Wilderness (see page 265) can also arrange 45-m abseiling in the reserve.

Keurbooms River Nature Reserve

The Cape Nature office is on the east side of the Keurbooms River Bridge on the N2, 7 km east of Plett, T044-533 2125, capenature.co.za.
Open 0800-1800, ₨25, children (2-13) ₨12, a double canoe costs ₨90 per day.
Map: Garden Route, F4, p220.

The 750-ha Keurbooms River Nature Reserve incorporates the Keurbooms River lagoon and its surrounding dunes and is a safe area for bathing, canoeing and other watersports. The headwaters of the Keurbooms River come from the Langkloof, north of the main Tsitsikamma mountain range. Its gorge is spectacular and well worth a voyage upstream to enjoy the unspoilt, unpolluted beauty. A variety of habitats are conserved, including the

Above: Fast moving windsurfer on the water at Keurbooms Lagoon.
Opposite page: Black and white ruffled lemur at Monkeyland.

relatively unspoilt riverine gorge, patches of Knysna forest along the flood banks and in protected kloofs, coastal fynbos and dune fields. The reserve is named after the Western Keurboom (*Virgilia oroboides*) or choice tree, which grows in the coastal forest edges. The environment attracts a number of birds, and look out for the Knysna lourie, malachite and giant kingfisher, Narina Trogan fish eagle, white-breasted cormorant and various sunbirds. Taking a sailing trip upstream on the Keurbooms River Ferry (see page 266 for further details) is a great way to spend a few hours. You are ferried 5 km along the river through a spectacular gorge overhung by indigenous trees and other flora. At the furthest point from the jetty there is an optional 30-minute walk through the forest with a professional guide. This is the ultimate eco-experience and a relaxing way to be introduced to the plants, sights and sounds of the forest. Make sure you are wearing sturdy footwear if you intend to join the walk.

Monkeyland & Birds of Eden

16 km east of Plett, turn off at the signpost on the N2 at the Forest Hall turning, Monkeyland and Birds of Eden are a further 2 km down the road. T044-534 8906, monkeyland.co.za, birdsofeden.co.za. Open 0830-1700, a guided tour for each attraction costs ₨125, children (3-12) ₨62.50; a combo ticket for both is ₨200, children ₨100. Map: Garden Route, F4, p220.

At the settlement known as The Crags is the well-signposted turning to Monkeyland. As the name suggests, this is a primate reserve with lemurs, apes and monkeys from several continents where the attractions are free to move about in the living indigenous forest. Most are rescued pets. Visitors are advised to join a guided walk which takes in various waterholes in the forest. Guides have a keen eye for spotting animals. One of the highlights here is the Indiana Jones-style rope bridge that spans 118 m across a canyon, offering glimpses of species that spend their entire lives in the upper reaches of the forest. The primates themselves also use this bridge (supposedly the longest of its kind in the southern

Tip…

The N2 continues east from Plettenberg Bay, but don't expect to travel too fast as there are a number of attractions and sights in rapid succession that are worth making a detour for. This is a good stretch of road, although there is a toll of around R10. The more spectacular route is via the village of Nature's Valley along the old R102, a beautifully forested road that branches off the N2 just after The Crags. Look out for ververt monkeys in the trees.

hemisphere). If you don't wish to join a tour, the day centre has a good viewpoint and the restaurant serves a tasty lunch. Great for kids.

Birds of Eden is a 2.3-ha mesh dome spanning more of the same forest with 1.2 km of walkways, 900 m of which are elevated, that go past waterfalls and dams. Along the same principal as Monkeyland, previously caged birds have been released into a natural environment and visitors, who are permitted to wander around without a guide, can get a bird's eye view of macaws, cockatoos, parrots and louries.

Nature's Valley

26 km east of Plett on the R102.
Map: Garden Route, G4, p220.

This small village has one of the most beautiful settings along the Garden Route. Since the N2 toll road was opened in 1984, most traffic bypasses this sleepy community. The village is surrounded on three sides by the western section of the Tsitsikamma National Park (see page 250). The approach by road is particularly spectacular. The R102, dropping 223 m to sea level via the narrow Kalanderkloof Gorge, twists and turns through lush green coastal forest. At the bottom is a lagoon formed by the sand dunes blocking the estuary of the Groot River. A right turn leads into the village, made up of a collection of holiday cottages and one shop that is an all-in-one restaurant, bar and tourist information bureau (T044-270 7077, natures-valley.com). Note that there are no banks in Nature's Valley. There are several *braai* spots on the sandy beach, but be warned that swimming in the sea is not safe. Canoes, rowing boats and yachts can all be used on the Groot River and lagoon, but powerboats are prohibited. As the road starts to climb out of the Groot Valley it passes the Nature's Valley Rest Camp on the right. This is the only camp at the western end of the Tsitsikamma National Park (see page 258 for booking details). Many visitors will find themselves here because it is the end of two of the Garden Route's most spectacular hiking trails, the Tsitsikamma Trail and the Otter Trail.

Bloukrans Bridge

36 km east of Plett on the N2.
Face Adrenalin, T042-281 1458, faceadrenalin.com.
0900-1700, booking not essential but recommended, bungee jump R620, which includes the Flying Fox cable slide R170 and Bridge Walk R90.
Map: Garden Route, G4, p220.

Built in 1984, 217 m above the Bloukrans River, the bridge which carries the N2 across the Bloukrans Gorge is reputedly the highest single-span arch bridge in Africa, and the view into the gorge is quite spectacular. But the main reason for stopping is the Bloukrans Bungee Jump run by Face Adrenalin. At 216 m it is the highest commercial bungee in the world. The first rebound is longer than the previous holder of the record, the 111-m bungee jump at Victoria Falls. It's a hugely exhilarating experience and the free fall once you've leapt from the bridge lasts seven seconds, travelling over 170 kph before you reach the maximum length of the bungee cord. The Flying Fox is a 200-m cable slide from a platform on land to the centre of the bridge arch. If you cannot muster the courage to do either of these, you can go on a guided bridge walk, which involves walking out to the bungee platform along the caged walkway underneath the bridge. This is not for anyone who suffers from vertigo, but if you want to support a mate who's doing a jump, it's a great way to feel some of the fear they are experiencing by standing on the lip of the bungee platform. Also at the top of the gorge is the Tsitsikamma Forest Village, a fairly new

Tsitsikamma Canopy Tour

This is a fantastic way to see the forest from a new angle, which involves climbing up into the trees and gliding between 10 different platforms on a steel rope, the longest of which is 80 m, giving extraordinary views from high above the ground. Excellent for birdwatching and the Knysna lourie may be spotted. Suitable for all ages from seven years old. Departure times are every 45 minutes (Sep-May 0700-1600, Jun-Aug 0800-1530), the excursion lasts around three hours, costs R395 and includes light refreshments. For the less active, 4WD tours of the forest are available (Storms River village, T042-281 1836, tsitsikammacanopytour.co.za).

Tip...

Stop at the Storms River Bridge, a further 5 km along the N2 from Bloukrans, where there's a viewing platform to look down into the river gorge, curio shops, restaurant, petrol station and the Tsitsikamma Information office (T042-280 3561, tsitsikamma.info, daily 0830-1630).

sustainable initiative to help local people make and sell curios to the many passing tourists. Shops are in a collection of attractive reed Khosian huts, and you can buy items such as candles or home-made paper.

Storms River village

On the N2, 8 km after the Storms River Bridge, and 4 km after the turn-off to the Tsitsikamma National Park.
Map: Garden Route, H4, p220.

Storms River Village is the first settlement in the Eastern Cape Province, and is regarded as the last town along the Garden Route. There's a good backpacker's here offering blackwater tubing (see page 258), as well as the Tsitsikamma Canopy Tour (see box). From here it's a 200-km drive along the N2 to the airport at Port Elizabeth.

Bungee jump at Bloukrans Bridge.

What the locals say

As an alternative to the N2 on returning to Cape Town from our holiday house in Plett, we follow Route 62 (route62.co.za). This leisurely drive follows the back roads through wine, wheat and olive country and pretty villages. The fertile valleys and craggy mountains are the most beautiful region of the interior of the Western Cape.

Barbara Beech, Plett holidaymaker.

Tsitsikamma National Park

This is one of the most popular national parks in the country, with a beautiful 80-km stretch of lush coastal forest and is known for its excellent birdlife. Not only is the forest protected, but the park boundaries reach out to sea for 5½ km in the eastern sector. For most of its length it is no more than 500 m wide on the landward side. At the western end, where the Otter Trail reaches the Groot River estuary, the park boundary extends 3 km inland. The main administrative office is at Storms River Rest Camp, which is almost the midpoint of the park. The park is the location for the famous 42-km Otter Hiking Trail (see box), which follows the coastline between Storms River Rest Camp and Nature's Valley Rest Camp.

The forested cliffs are the last remnant of a forest which was once found right along this coast between the ocean and the mountains. The canopy ranges between 18 m and 30 m and is closed, which makes the paths nice and shady.

The most common species of tree are milkwood, real yellowwood, stinkwood, Cape blackwood, forest elder, white pear and candlewood, plus the famous Outeniqua yellowwood, a forest giant. All are magnificent trees which combine with climbers such as wild grape, red saffron and milky rope to create an outstandingly beautiful forest.

Over 220 species of birds have been identified, including the rare Knysna lourie, and in the vicinity of the Storms River campsite and the Groot River estuary you will see a number of seabirds. Mammals include caracal, bushbuck, blue duiker, grysbok,

Essentials

The turn-off to Storms River Rest Camp off the N2 is 4 km east of the Storms River Bridge. The Nature's Valley Rest Camp is 40 km west of Storms River Mouth and can only be reached from the R102, see Nature's Valley, page 247. T042-281 1607, sanparks.org. Gates 0700-1900, office 0730-1800. Storms River Rest Camp: shop 0800-1800, stocks gift items, groceries, wine and beer; Tiger's Eye Restaurant 0730-1000, 1200-1500, 1800-1930, make reservations for evening meals by 1700, R88, children (2-11) R44. Map: Garden Route, H4, p220.

bushpig and the Cape clawless otter, but these are rarely seen in the dense undergrowth. There are a number of hiking trails of varying lengths from both rest camps. The most popular, and strongly recommended, is a 1-km walk along a raised boardwalk from the restaurant at Storms River Rest Camp to the mouth of the Storms River, where there is a suspension bridge. The path continues on the other side of the bridge and from here you can climb the hill for superb views. The other trails close to the camp are the **Lourie Trail**, 1 km through the forested slopes behind the camp; the **Blue Duiker Trail**, 3.7 km further into the forest; and the **Waterfall Trail**, a 3-km walk along the first part of the Otter Trail.

Tip...

There are two access points into the park depending on which rest camp you are staying in, although day visitors generally enter through the Storms River entrance, where there are better facilities for those on day trips.

The Otter Trail

This 42½-km five-day trail is unidirectional, and runs between Storms River Mouth and Nature's Valley rest camps. It closely follows the coast, and apart from the natural beauty and the birdlife, the trail passes some fine waterfalls, Strandloper caves and large old hardwood trees. None of the sectors are that long, but it is still fairly strenuous in parts since you have to cross 11 rivers and there are steep ascents and descents at each river crossing. The Bloukrans River crossing presents the most problems; you will at least have to wade, or even swim across. Waterproofing for your rucksack is vital. There are several escape routes to the N2 in the event hikers get into difficulty. The route is marked with painted otter footprints. At each overnight site there are two log huts, each sleeping six people in bunk beds, rainwater tanks, firewood and *braais* but hikers need to provide their own pots for cooking. Only 12 people (age 12-65) can start the trail each day, the minimum is four, and it costs R685 per person. Permits are available from SANParks (Pretoria, T012-426 5111, sanparks.org) or at the offices in Cape Town (see page 79).

View from Nature's Valley along the coast of Tsitsikamma National Park.

Sleeping

Overberg

Caledon
Caledon Hotel, Spa & Casino ℞℞℞
1 Nerina Av, T028-214 5100, cnty.com/casinos/Caledon.
1 km out of town off the N2. Modern complex based at the historic springs, with a flashy casino, 95 air-conditioined rooms and three restaurants, including an Italian one. There is a pub with log fires, extensive gardens, a number of hot and cold pools, a beauty clinic, mountain bikes for hire, full-size snooker tables, 18-hole putting golf and the excellent Victorian hot-spring baths enclosed by a pavilion.

Swellendam
Klippe Rivier Country House ℞℞℞℞-℞℞℞
T028-514 3341, klipperivier.com.
From the N2 take the R60 for 1 km, left at crossroads for 2 km. Six large double rooms in and around a restored Cape Dutch homestead (1820), declared a national monument, with brass beds, wooden floors, some with cosy fireplaces and under thatch, superb restaurant, swimming pool, a peaceful and superior location, look out for owls in the oak trees, family owned and managed, no children under eight.

Swellendam Backpackers ℞
5 Lichtenstein St, T028-514 2648, swellendambackpackers.co.za.
An excellent hostel with a small dorm in the main house, plus individual Wendy houses and safari tents (no electricity but paraffin lamps) in secluded corners around the garden, lots of camping space, internet, well-organized kitchen, home-cooked breakfasts and dinners. Can arrange hiking in the mountains and visits to the nearby Bontebok National Park. The Baz Bus calls here twice a day.

Bontebok National Park
Lang Elsie's Kraal Rest Camp ℞℞-℞
Reservations T012-428 9111, sanparks.org, for bookings under 72 hrs and campsite T028-5142735.
In a pleasant location next to the Breede River, there are 10 new fully equipped self-catering chalets sleeping four, two of which are disabled accessible. Good views of the Langeberg Mountains from the outside terraces, plus shady camping and caravan sites, some with electric points, and a new ablution block. The shop at the park entrance sells some groceries and beer but stock up on fresh food in Swellendam.

Mossel Bay & George

Mossel Bay
Diaz Strand ℞℞℞
Santos Beach, T044- 692 8400, diazbeach.co.za.
Map: Garden Route, A6, p220.
Luxury hotel in a commanding position on Santos Beach overlooking the waves, with 86 spacious rooms in a modern block, all with balconies and ocean views. Facilities include outdoor rim-flow pool, indoor heated Olympic-sized pool and wellness centre, a water theme park with tubes and a lazy river, live entertainment and the highly regarded Bahia Dos Vaqueiros restaurant (see page 259).

Protea Hotel Mossel Bay ℝℝℝ
Corner of Church and Market streets, T044-691 3738, oldposttree.co.za, proteahotels.com.
Map: Garden Route, A6, p220. This is part of the museum complex and was formerly known as the Old Post Office Tree Manor. There are 31 comfortable hotel rooms and self-catering suites in a smart manor house dating to 1846, which is the third-oldest building in Mossel Bay. Outdoor dining area with views across the bay, swimming pool, popular with tour groups, check for seasonal discounts.

1 Point Village Guest House ℝℝ
Bland St East, T044-690 7792, pointguesthouse.co.za.
Map: Garden Route, A6, p220. Good location near the Point, this neat guesthouse has six rooms, some with sea views, individually decorated in fresh colours. Heated swimming pool in courtyard, *braai* area and generous breakfasts, also rents out modern self-catering holiday cottages nearby sleeping four to eight, which are good value for families and groups.

Mossel Bay Backpackers ℝ
1 Marsh St, T044-691 3182, gardenrouteadventures.com.
Map: Garden Route, A6, p220. A comfortable house with dorms and double rooms, TV room, breakfasts and dinners available,

self-catering kitchen, pool, good location 300 m from the beach and close to bars, travel centre can organize activities such as shark cage diving, Baz Bus stop. Also 12 more upmarket guesthouse rooms (ℝℝ) in the same building.

Botlierskop Private Game Reserve Tented Suites ℝℝℝℝ
T044-696 6055, botlierskop.co.za.
Map: Garden Route, A5, p220. 19 luxury tented suites on wooden platforms, good views over river and mountains, some have private jetties for fishing, decorated in a colonial theme with four-poster beds swathed in

mosquito nets. Rates include game drives, walks and all meals. An all-round safari experience close to the Garden Route.

George
Fancourt Hotel & Country Club ℝℝℝℝ
R404, 6 km north of George Airport, T044-804 0010, fancourt.com.
Map: Garden Route, B5, p220. An upmarket resort and one of the world's leading golf destinations, set on 500 ha of land, with four 18-hole golf courses, two of which were designed by Gary Player. There are 150 rooms in the 19th-century manor house or

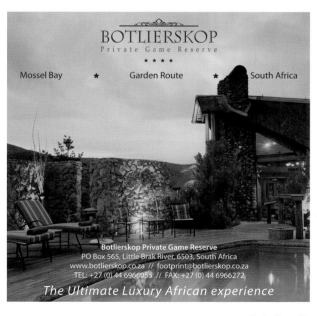

BOTLIERSKOP
Private Game Reserve
★ ★ ★ ★
Mossel Bay ★ Garden Route ★ South Africa

garden suites overlooking the golf courses, spa, gym, tennis courts, two outdoor pools, one indoor heated pool, and six restaurants. Room rates drop in low season (1 April-31 August).

Protea Hotel
King George ℝℝℝ
King George Dr, T044-874 7659, proteahotels.com.
Map: Garden Route, B5, p220.
Smart country hotel situated close to the 11th fairway of the George Golf Course, with 109 comfortable air-conditioned rooms set in a double-storey mock Victorian villa, some with balconies, good Fairway Restaurant and wood-panelled Rex Tavern pub, twin swimming pools in spacious grounds, the usual quality of service expected in a Protea, look out for specials on the website.

Outeniqua Backpackers ℝ
115 Merriman St, T082-216 7720, outeniqua-backpackers.com.
Map: Garden Route, B4, p220.
Newish hostel with 20 dorm beds and a couple of doubles, bright and airy, some with mountain views, *braai* area, breakfasts, DSTV and internet. The only backpacker option in town and a Baz Bus stop and they offer free pickups from George Airport. You can hire bikes and they'll drop you off at the top of Montagu Pass for the 15-km ride back down.

Victoria Bay
The Waves ℝℝℝ
6 Beach Rd, T044-889 0166, thewavesvictoriabay.co.za.
Map: Garden Route, C5, p220.
A superior B&B right on the beach, with three double rooms with balconies and sea views, satellite TV, fridges, separate entrances, in a 1906 historic building, breakfasts are served on the veranda, friendly, low-key place, a more pleasant location than the centre of George, and there are three separate family cottages available (B&B or self-catering).

Oudtshoorn
Rosenhof Country
House ℝℝℝℝ
264 Baron van Rheede St, T044-272 2232, rosenhof.co.za.
Map: Garden Route, A3, p220.
12 air-conditioned rooms with DSTV, swimming pool, beautiful rose garden, beauty spa, gym, jacuzzi, sauna, and there's fine food in the restaurant. Great thought and care has gone into choosing the furnishings of this restored Victorian house, and the fabrics and the ornaments create a comfortable homely atmosphere. For total privacy the two executive suites are 100 m from the main house and have their own swimming pool.

Altes Landhaus ℝℝℝ
13 km north of Oudtshoorn towards the Cango Caves, T044-272 6112, alteslandhaus.co.za.
Map: Garden Route, A2, p220.
Award-winning guesthouse in a Cape Dutch homestead on an ostrich farm, with 10 rooms, some with air conditioning and TV, and each is decorated with antiques and has its own special character. Evening meals with fine wines available on request, salt pool in pretty rose gardens with pool bar, and German is spoken.

Backpacker's Paradise ℝ
148 Baron van Rheede St, T044-272 3436, backpackersparadise.hostel.com.
Map: Garden Route, A3, p220.
Spotless lodge set over four houses, with a mix of dorms and en suite doubles, camping, volleyball court, well-stocked kitchen, pub with pool table, nightly ostrich *braais*, splash pool, internet, within walking distance of shops, free town pickup, and a daily pickup from the Baz Bus in George. Plenty of activities can be organized from here including bike hire.

Wilderness & Sedgefield

Wilderness
Moontide Guest Lodge ℝℝℝ
Southside Rd, T044-877 0361, moontide.co.za.
Map: Garden Route, C5, p220.
A well-appointed and well-run guesthouse, with seven thatched

cottages, one of them a honeymoon suite, set under milkwood trees in a beautiful garden overlooking the lagoon. Each cottage has been tastefully decorated with kilims and fine furniture. Easy access to the hiking trails in the national park, a short walk from the beach and a good spot for birdwatchers.

Fairy Knowe Hotel ℝℝ
Dumbleton Rd, T044-877 1100, fairyknowe.co.za.
Map: Garden Route, C5, p220. An old hotel with 42 rooms with slightly dated decor, but in a beautiful and peaceful forested location on the Touw River, close to Wilderness National Park, birdwatchers will enjoy regular visits by the Knysna lourie and there are a couple of resident Cape spotted eagle owls. Restaurant, bar, tennis courts and canoes and pedalos can be rented.

Fairy Knowe Backpackers ℝ
Dumbleton Rd, just off Waterside Rd, T044-877 1285, wildernessbackpackers.com.
Map: Garden Route, C5, p220. A great set-up in two farmhouses with tight staircases and creaking wooden floors, surrounded by gardens and milkwood trees, with spotless dorms and doubles, bright white bedding, camping space in the garden, bar, great breakfasts, nightly camp fires and *braais*. Also has a travel desk. A very relaxing place to rest up for a few days. The Baz Bus stops here.

Wilderness National Park Ebb & Flow Rest Camp, North and Ebb & Flow Rest Camp, South ℝℝℝ-ℝℝ
Reservations Pretoria, T012-428 9111, sanparks.org, for reservations under 72 hrs or camping contact the park reception directly, T044-877 1197.
Map: Garden Route, C5, p220. Accommodation is laid out in two camps divided by the railway and the Touw River. Both have self-catering units sleeping up to four in cottages, log cabins, or forest cabins, some with views of the river and reed beds, plus shady and grassy campsites (ℝ) next to the river with *braais* and communal ablution blocks. The nearest shop is in the village, but stock up with provisions in the supermarkets in George.

Sedgefield
Lake Pleasant ℝℝℝ
East of Sedgefield on the edge of Groenvlei, take the Buffalo Bay road off the N2, T044-349 2400, lakepleasanthotel.com.
Map: Garden Route, D5, p220. This comfortable five-star hotel has had a major overhaul and now belongs to the South African Mantis chain of luxury hotels. Set right on the lake, with 36 rooms, all with lake views, smart lounge furnished with antiques, library, cigar bar, restaurant, swimming pool, tennis court, gym, health spa.

Perfect for birdwatchers with some hides by the lake, rowing boats for hire.

Sedgefield Arms ℝℝ
Pelican Lane, off the N2 in the village centre, T044-343 1417, sedgefieldarms.co.za.
Map: Garden Route, D5, p220. A comfortable mix of self-catering cottages suitable for two to six people with patio and *braai*, or B&B. Attached restaurant and lively English theme pub, good spot for lunch on the lawn, bar with big sports screen, swimming pool, all set in leafy gardens, good value and fun atmosphere. Rates drop significantly out of season.

Goukamma Nature Reserve Goukamma Nature Reserve ℝℝ
Reservations, Cape Town, T021-659 3500, capenature.org.za.
Map: Garden Route, D5, p220. There are a number of self-catering options around the reserve including the Groenvlei & Muvubu Bushcamps on the western side, hidden away in a milkwood forest, and the Musselcracker House, on the eastern side near the river, each sleeping seven to nine, bedding is supplied but bring your own food and towels. Also on the eastern side are cheaper thatched rondavels sleeping two to five, each with its own *braai* area but with shared kitchenette and bathroom.

Knysna

Knysna town

Phantom Forest Eco-Reserve ℝℝℝℝ
Off the Phantom Pass road, 7 km west of Knysna, T044-386 0046, phantomforest.com.
Map: Garden Route, E4, p220.
This lodge offers ultra-stylish accomodation in a superb collection of 14 luxurious and eco-friendly 'tree-suites', connected by meandering boardwalks and set under the forest canopy, with elevated views over Knysna's liquid landscape. Each has a private deck and sensuous bathroom. Two great restaurants, bar, look-out points, wellness centre offering natural treats, and a and stunning pool. The perfect place to experience the Knysna forests.

Rex Hotel ℝℝℝℝ
8 Grey St, T044-302 5900, rexhotel.co.za.
Map: Garden Route, E3, p220.
Super stylish in an architectural gem of a modern building, with

> **Tip...**
>
> Recommended for families, self-catering houseboats are available for hire on the Knysna Lagoon. You do not need to have any nautical experience, they are very easy to operate and allow you to explore the lagoon at leisure. Contact Lightleys Holiday Houseboats (T044-386 0007, houseboats.co.za).

30 spacious luxury rooms, in muted browns and creams, with kitchenettes, air conditioning, satellite TV, DVD players, Wi-Fi and balconies. The Dish Restaurant is well regarded for its gourmet food, including oysters, the bar is popular with Knysna's elite and there's a gym.

Protea Hotel Knysna Quays ℝℝℝ
Waterfront Dr, T044-382 5005, proteahotels.com.
Map: Garden Route, E3, p220.
Large state-of-the-art hotel, with 123 comfortable air-conditioned rooms, most with good views over the lagoon, restaurant, cocktail bar, lounge, attractive heated swimming pool, beauty therapist and Wi-Fi. Great location next to the Knysna Quays and within walking distance of restaurants where hotel guests can sign for meals to be charged to their room account.

Knysna Belle ℝℝ
75 Bayswater Dr, Leisure Isle, T044-384 0511, knysnabelle.co.za.
Map: Garden Route, E3, p220.
Seven very stylish individually decorated rooms with a nautical feel, one with a Victorian bath tub, very good breakfasts and can provide picnics in backpacks for hiking, swimming pool, lovely balconies to relax and enjoy the views of the lagoon, mountain bikes and a rowing boat available to rent out, no children under six.

Knysna Backpackers ℝ
42 Queen St, T044-382 2554, knysnabackpackers.co.za.
Map: Garden Route, E3, p220.
Large dorms, double rooms, clean bathrooms, TV room, well-stocked kitchen, all meals on request, travel centre, set in a large rambling Victorian mansion, which is a national monument in established gardens with space for camping, and views across the lagoon from the wide veranda. An easy stroll from the town centre, a Baz Bus stop and offers free pickups from the mainline buses.

Belvedere & Brenton-on-sea

Belvedere Manor ℝℝℝ
169 Duthie Dr, Belvedere, T044-387 1055, Belvedere.co.za.
Map: Garden Route, E5, p220.
34 smart cottages arranged around a swimming pool in shady gardens, sleeping two to four people, with private verandas with views across the lagoon, kitchens, satellite TV and DVD players. All are individually furnished and have log fires. The manor house, from 1834, houses the reception and the elegant dining room. The Bell pub is housed in an old farm cottage and the highlight here is seeing the wine cellar underneath the glass floor.

Knysna Elephant Park

Elephant Lodge ℞℞℞
*T044-532 7732,
knysnaelephantpark.co.za.*
Map: Garden Route, F5, p220.
Five newly refurbished twin
rooms and one large family flat
sleeping six over the boma
where the elephants sleep,
so you can fall asleep to their
nightly sounds (and smells!), and
see them when they are out and
about. Modern and comfortable
with a spacious thatched lounge
with large picture windows for
a unique elephant-watching
experience. Restaurant is open
during the day and will cater for
dinner on request.

Hunter's Country House.

Plettenberg Bay

Plettenberg Bay

**Hog Hollow
Country Lodge** ℞℞℞℞
*Off the N2, 18 km east of
Plettenberg Bay at the Crags,
T044-534 8879, hog-hollow.com.*
Map: Garden Route, F4, p220.
One of the finest lodges along
the Garden Route set in a private
nature reserve, with 15 suites,
with ceiling fans, minibar
decorated with locally made wall
hangings and woodcarvings,
each with its own wooden
deck with hammock overlooking
the Matjies River gorge and
Tsitsikamma Mountains. Good
evening meals, swimming pool
with stunning views, library/
lounge in the main house.

Hunter's Country House ℞℞℞℞
*Off the N2, 10 km towards
Knysna, T044-532 7818,
hunterhotels.com.*
Map: Garden Route, F5, p220.
18 luxury individually decorated
thatched garden suites with
fireplace, antique furnishings and
private patio, two swimming
pools, conservatory, antique
shop, forest chapel for weddings,
child-care service and can
provide picnic baskets. One of
South Africa's top country hotels
and part of the Relais & Chateaux
group, which has won awards for
food and service, a special place
to treat yourself to.

The Plettenberg ℞℞℞℞
*40 Church St, Lookout Rocks,
T044-533 2030, plettenberg.com.*
Map: Garden Route, F3, p220.
40 air-conditioned rooms, lounge
and dining rooms furnished with
antiques, superb food and wine,

swimming pool, beauty spa,
smartest in area, another Relais &
Chateaux property, everything
you would expect in a small,
exclusive top-class, five-star hotel,
but very expensive. Request a
room with ocean views, some of
them look over the car park.
Rates double in high season.

Beacon Island ℞℞℞
*Beacon Island Cres, T044-533
1120, southernsun.com.*
Map: Garden Route, F3, p220.
Dubbed BI by holidaymakers
from Johannesburg, this
is a multi-storey building
dominating the bay, right
on the water between two
beaches, 200 rooms, three
excellent restaurants,
swimming pool, tennis, gym,
also a timeshare resort. A full
range of facilities and a superb
location but an eyesore on Plett's
sweeping beach.

Eating

Nothando Backpackers ℞
5 Wilder St, T044-533 0220,
nothando.co.za.
Map: Garden Route, F3, p220.
Camping, dorms, double rooms,
B&B, in a central location, cheap
and friendly, with extras like
hairdryers in the bathrooms, plus
offering plenty of activities with
discounts. Beds have duvets and
crisp white linen, some rooms
are en suite, small kitchen, large
TV lounge, kitchen, bar with *braai*
and pool table. Baz Bus stop.

Nature's Valley
Tranquility Lodge ℞℞℞℞
130 St Michaels Av, next to the
Nature's Valley shop and pub,
T044-531 6663,
tranquilitylodge.co.za.
Map: Garden Route, G4, p220.
Lovely reed-and-timber lodge in
pretty gardens, with seven
rooms, with double showers and
fireplaces, very nicely decorated
throughout with lots of lounging
areas. The owner is also a chef
and meals can be taken together
with other guests in the dining
room, or alone on the wooden
deck. There's a swimming pool,
outside hot pool, and each room
gets its own double kayak to
explore the lagoon.

Tsitsikamma
National Park ℞℞-℞
Reservations through Pretoria,
T012-428 9111, sanparks.org, for
cancellations and reservations
under 72 hrs contact the Storms
River Mouth camp directly,
T042-281 1607.
Map: Garden Route, H4, p220.
The Storms River Mouth rest camp
is on a strip of land between ocean
and forested hills, and is one of the
most beautiful settings of all the
national parks. There are a number
of wooden self-catering chalets
sleeping up to six, plus camping,
a shop and restaurant. There are
simpler chalets and camping at
Nature's Valley Rest Camp near the
settlement of the same name, set
among indigenous forest, 40 km
from Storms River Mouth.

Storms River Village
Tube 'n Axe ℞
Corner of Darnell and Saffron
streets, T042-281 1757,
tubenaxe.co.za.
Map: Garden Route, H4, p220.
Four-bed dorms, doubles and
some pre-erected tents on
wooden platforms, set in a
forested garden with room for
camping and vehicles. The rustic
bar has a pool table and *braai* pit,
breakfast and dinner available or
self-catering kitchen. Shuttles to
the Bloukrans Bridge Bungee,
they rent out quad bikes and
mountain bikes, and operate
blackwater tubing (see page 267)
in the Tsitsikamma National Park.
Baz Bus stop.

Overberg

Caledon
Dassiesfontein ℞℞-℞
On the N2 between Caledon
and Bot River, T028-214 1475,
dassies.co.za.
Open 0830-1730.
Country restaurant and farm stall
selling home-made bread (they
grind their own flour), cheese and
biltong, tables in the cottage are
decorated with antiques, good
chicken and game pies, buffet
lunch on Sunday, for breakfast try
the fried slice of bread with apricot
jam. A good stop for motorists.

Swellendam
Herberg Roosjie
van de Kaap ℞℞
5 Drostdy St, T028-5143001,
roosjevandekaap.com.
Tue-Sun, breakfast 0800-1000,
dinner 1900-2130.
Local word has this down as the
best place to eat in town, with a
cosy atmosphere in a candlelit
room with thick walls and a low
roof. Superb gourmet pizzas plus
hearty South African fare, like
good steaks and seafood, and
fine wines.

Koornlands ℞℞
5 Voortrek St, T028-514 3567,
koornlandsrestaurant.co.za.
Mon-Sat 1900-2200,
May-Jun closed.
A historic Cape Dutch cottage
serving local food such as
crocodile steaks, ostrich fillets,
loin of kudu, guinea fowl and

freshwater trout, washed down with local wines. Desserts include a delicious Cape brandy tart.

Cafés
Old Mill Restaurant and Tea Garden
241 Voortrek St, T028-514 2790, oldmill.co.za.
Open 0700-2100.
Good afternoon teas, syrupy waffles and cinnamon pancakes, outside tables in pretty gardens with chickens pecking around, romantic candlelit tables inside for dinner, South African dishes such as Karoo lamb or local curries.

Mossel Bay & George

Mossel Bay
Bahia Dos Vaqueiros ℞℞℞
Diaz Strand, Santos Beach, T044- 692 8400, diazbeach.co.za.
Open 0700-1030, 1900-2200.
Map: Garden Route, A6, p220.
Dominated by a giant painting on the ceiling of the Portuguese landing on the coast and sweeping ocean views, this is an upmarket spot with cigar bar, walk-in wine cellar and attentive service. The menu has interesting dishes such as pork with blue cheese or quail with apricots.

Stonehill ℞℞℞
Little Brak River, 6 km east of Mossel Bay off the N2 on the R107, T044-696 6501, stonehill.co.za.
Mon-Sat 1800-2300,
Sun 1130-1500.
Map: Garden Route, A5, p220.

Set in a 1920s farmhouse with contemporary decor, this upmarket country French restaurant makes for a romantic night out. The chef uses organic herbs and vegetables grown on the farm, and free-range meat. Try the likes of beef fillet with foie gras or lobster thermidor, and finish off with a traditional crème brûlée.

Café Gannet ℞℞
Bartholomeu Dias Museum Complex, Market St, T044-691 1885, cafegannet.co.za.
Open 0700-2300.
Map: Garden Route, A6, p220.
A well-established restaurant, popular all year round since the tour buses stop here, seafood, grills and pizza from a wood oven, enjoyable bay views from a shady outdoor terrace, with efficient and prompt service.

Tsitsikamma National Park.

George

The Conservatory at Meade House ℞℞
91 Meade St, T044-874 1938.
Mon-Fri 0800-1600,
Sat 0830-1500, Wed-Sat
1830-2200, Sun 1200-1500.
Map: Garden Route, B5, p220.
Quality restaurant set in one of
the oldest homes in George,
dine in the conservatory or in the
pretty gardens, very extensive à
la carte from cakes and muffins
to full meals of steak and grilled
fish. Also has a well-stocked shop
of gifts and books.

Kafé Serefé ℞℞
60 Courtenay St, T044-8742046.
Mon-Fri 0930-1630,
Mon-Sat 1900-late.
Map: Garden Route, B5, p220.
Elegant interiors with Persian
rugs and Arabic lamps, this
Turkish restaurant serves a range
of mezzes, some melt-in-the
mouth kebabs and aged steaks,
and for breakfast, bacon and egg
shwarmas or Turkish breakfasts of
cold meat, boiled egg, cucumber
and tzatziki. Diners are
entertained by a belly dancer on
Wednesday and Saturday nights.

La Locanda ℞℞
*124 York St, T044-874 7803,
lalocanda.co.za.*
Mon-Fri 1100-2200,
Sat 1700-2200.
Map: Garden Route, B5, p220.
Home-style Italian cooking from
genuine Italian chefs who make
their own pasta and cure their
own cold meats, and there's a
long menu of over 60 dishes, plus
weekly specials using well-
researched recipes from Italy.
Homely interior and pleasant
courtyard tables outside, South
African and Italian wine.

Oudtshoorn

Oudtshoorn Headlines ℞℞
*Baron van Rheede St,
T044-272 3434.*
Mon-Sat 0830-1500, 1745-2300,
Sun 1100-1500.
Map: Garden Route, A3, p220.
Coffee shop and restaurant
decorated in an odd mixture of
sports and railway memorabilia
specializing in ostrich dishes of
all kinds from ostrich-egg
omelettes to ostrich-liver pâté.
The Bushmen kebab is a
favourite, with ostrich, venison,
crocodile, pork/beef fillet and
chicken all on one skewer.

Kalinka ℞℞
*93 Baron van Rheede St,
T044-2792596.*
Open 1800-late.
Map: Garden Route, A3, p220.
A fine menu served in a cosy
converted sandstone town
house with a clutch of small
dining rooms. Variety of ostrich
dishes including good steaks,
plus dishes with an unusual twist
like caviar pancakes or mussels in
coconut broth.

Paljas ℞℞
*109 Baron van Rheede St,
T044-272 0982.*
Open 1700-2300.
Map: Garden Route, A3, p220.
Pan-African cuisine, with
a good selection of Cape
Malay curries, Karoo roasts,
West Coast seafood, and a few
unusual Zulu and Xhosa dishes,
this is a good place to try a
three-course meal with a
lot of different flavours in an
interesting African-style decor.

Wilderness & Sedgefield

Wilderness

The Palms ℞℞℞
*Corner of George and Owen
Grant roads, T044-877 1420,
palms-wilderness.com.*
Open daily for set four-
course dinners from 1900,
reservations essential.
Map: Garden Route, C5, p220.
Tables are in the thatched
restaurant or outside under
umbrellas, the menu changes
daily but there is a choice from
two starters and two mains
which are finished off by the likes
of petits fours and cheese, and
wine is matched to the food.

Wilderness Grille ℞℞
George Rd, T044-877 0808.
Open 0800-2200.
Map: Garden Route, C5, p220.
Seafood, steaks and pizza, good
breakfasts, light meals like
stuffed bagels, outdoor leafy
terrace, pop in throughout the

day and you'll get something substantial to eat, though service is somewhat slow.

Knysna

O'Pescador RRR
Brenton Rd, Belvedere,
T044-386 0036.
Mon-Sat 1830-late.
Map: Garden Route, E5, p220.
Long-established and popular Portuguese restaurant, traditional cosy decor, Mozambique prawns or try the spicy fish dishes, peri peri chicken or grilled sardines. There's a good range of Portuguese wines, brandy and port.

34' South RR
Knysna Quays, T044-382 7268,
34-south.com.
Open 0830-2330.
Map: Garden Route, E5, p220.
Snacks and meals daily in a deli-style seafood restaurant, try the sushi, seafood platter or paella, make up a meal from the packed fridges or buy takeaway items, including cook books, wine and home-made goodies, laid-back sunny deck overlooking the quays. Recommended.

Cruise Café RR
400 m west of the Knysna Quays,
T044-382 1693.
Mon-Sat 0800-2200,
Sun 0800-1700.
Map: Garden Route, E5, p220.
Great views of fishing boats on the lagoon, best known for seafood, plus good breakfasts and simple lunches like ploughman's platters and fish and chips; more sophisticated and pricier menu in the evening like prawn and crab risotto or roast duck, long wine and cocktail list.

Drydock Food Co RR
Knysna Quays, at the Waterfront,
T044-382 7310, drydock.co.za.
Open 1130-2200.
Map: Garden Route, E5, p220.
Modern restaurant with good views from the second floor, mostly seafood but steaks and vegetarian options too. Oysters, fish with pickles, slightly different twists on standard dishes, try west coast mussels with white wine or the kingklip *espetada*.

Knysna Oyster Co RR
Thesen's Island, T044- 382 6942,
knysnaoysters.co.za.
Open 1000-1900.
Map: Garden Route, E5, p220.
This seafood restaurant is right next to the oyster farm that has been in operation since 1949; you need to drive across the causeway to get there from town. It is perhaps the best place to try a dozen of the famous raw or cooked oysters washed down with a glass of champagne. It's one of Knysna's must-dos.

Tip...

Knysna is well known for its seafood, especially its excellent oysters which are cultivated in the lagoon. During the peak season, it is not uncommon to wait an hour or more before getting a table – be sure to book ahead at the better-known restaurants.

Paquitas RR
George Rex Dr, Knysna Heads,
T044-384 0408.
Open 1200-2200.
Map: Garden Route, E5, p220.
Relaxed family restaurant and vibey pub, burgers, pizza, pasta, seafood and steaks, but the main reason for coming here is for the stunning views of the Knysna Heads and the long beach where kids can play.

Cafés
Ile de Pain Bread & Café
The Boatshed, Thesen's Island,
T044-302 5707.
Tue-Sat 0800-1500,
Sun 0900-1330.
Map: Garden Route, E5, p220.
Superb bakery and coffee shop emitting lovely warm smells of freshly baked goodies, such as croissants and pastries. The bakers live upstairs and start baking at 0200. Good coffee, fresh fruit salad, cheeses and olives, good spot for a light brunch or lunch.

Entertainment

Plettenberg Bay

Hunter's Country House ℝℝℝ
*Off the N2, 10 km towards
Knysna, T044-532 7818,
hunterhotels.com.*
Open 0730-1030, 1230-1430,
1900-2100.
Map: Garden Route, F5, p220.
Excellent gourmet food served in
a rambling thatched house, three
dining rooms with silverware
and china, pricey but worth it,
recommended for special
occasions, booking essential. Tea
on the veranda is quite special.
The Summer House restaurant in
the garden serves simpler meals
like salads and gourmet burgers.

57 Kloof ℝℝ
*Melville Shopping Centre, corner
of Main St and Marine Dr,
T044-533 5626.*
Open 0830-late.
Map: Garden Route, F5, p220.
Modern decor and floor-to-
ceiling windows highlighting
great views, good range of meat
and fish dishes, some with an
Asian slant, large fresh salads,
unusual breakfasts such as eggs
hollandaise, and excellent
vegetarian menu.

The Lookout Deck ℝℝ
*Perched on the rocks above
Lookout Beach, T044-533 1379,
lookout.co.za.*
Open 0900-2300.
Map: Garden Route, F5, p220.
Popular family seafood
restaurant, perfect location,

excellent seafood, soups, salads
and steak, also has a busy bar,
lively, bustling atmosphere. From
the terrace you can watch surfers
share a wave with a dolphin.

The Med Seafood and Grill ℝℝ
*Village Sq, T044-533 3102,
med-seafoodbistro.co.za.*
Mon-Fri 1230-1500,
Mon-Sat 1800-late,
open daily in high season.
Map: Garden Route, F5, p220.
An established 20-year-old
European-style bistro with
al fresco dining on the leafy patio
and a nice ambience, offering
good light lunches, huge
seafood platters, excellent
duck with orange sauce and
slow-cooked lamb shanks,
plus the odd vegetarian dish.

Cafés
Thyme and Again
*On the N2 opposite the
Keurboom River turning,
T044-535 9432,
thyme-and-again.co.za.*
Open 0800-1600.
Map: Garden Route, F4, p220.
Great farm stall with tables on a
vine-covered *stoep*, serving
breakfasts and light meals like
inventive wraps and salads, plus
teas and cakes and there's a
delicious selection of still-warm
breads, pies and pastries from
the bakery. Try the home-made
ginger beer.

Mossel Bay & George

Casino
Garden Route Casino
*Pinnacle Point south of Mossel
Bay off the N2, T044-606 7777,
gardenroutecasion.co.za.*
A glitzy complex that includes
a casino with slots and gaming
tables, hotel, spa and the good
Admiral's restaurant, which
serves buffets, and there's also
the usual kiddies' supervised
entertainment centre while
parents gamble.

Theatre
Barnyard Theatre
*7 km west of Mossel Bay off
the N2, T044-698 1022,
thebarnyard.co.za.*
A rustic country theatre
showing comedy, tribute
bands and live music, and guests
sit at wooden tables around the
stage. You order food or take
your own picnic.

Knysna

Bars & clubs
Tryst
*In the industrial area,
Lower Queen St,
T044-382 0590, tryst.co.za.*
Wed-Sat 2100-late.
Dance club, with local and
visiting DJs, cocktail bar, pool
tables, big screen TVs to watch
sport, moody blue and pink
lighting and comfortable
leather sofas.

Shopping

Zanzibar's
Main Rd, T044-382 0386.
Tue-Sat 1900-0200 in season.
Set in a converted theatre, this has terraces overlooking Main Road, dance floor and pool tables, tribal decor, occasional DJs, comedy and live music, and upstairs is a quieter cocktail lounge.

Cinema
Knysna Movie House
Pledge Sq, 50 Main St, T044-382 7813, knysnamoviehouse.co.za.
Movies from 1400, closed Mon.
A pleasant restored art deco independent movie house with daily shows of new releases and half-price tickets on Tuesday.

Theatre
Knysna Playhouse
Corner Pit and Long streets, T044-382 0696, theknysnaplayhouse.co.za.
A newly restored 200-seat theatre with pleasant bar, showing local bands, plays, children's events and stand-up comedy, and also focuses on community and youth theatre.

Mossel Bay & George

Souvenirs
Model Shipyard
Ocean View Mall, Bland St, Mossel Bay, T044-691 1531, shipyard.co.za.
Mon-Fri 0900-1700,
Sat 0900-1300.
One of the few places in the world where you can buy hand-crafted model tall ships, which are exact copies of the originals and are even nautically correct, plus maritime art and antiques. There is another branch in the Clock Tower Centre at the V&A Waterfront in Cape Town.

The Goods Shed Indoor Fleamarket
68 Bland St, Mossel Bay, T044-691 2104.
Mon-Fri 0900-1700,
Sat 0900-1500, also Sun in high season 1000-1600.
This sells a variety of items including clothes, jewellery, arts and crafts, home-made food and hand-crafted furniture in interesting historical railway goods shed built in 1902.

Arts & antiques
Strydom Gallery
Marklaan Centre, 79 Market St, George, T044-874 4027, artaffair.co.za.
Mon-Sat 0900-1700.
Established in 1968, this is an art shop with interesting exhibits as well as pieces for sale from a cross section of South African artists and sculptors. They can organize delivery worldwide.

Oudtshoorn

Souvenirs
Bushmen Curios
76 Baron van Rheede St, T044-272 4497, bushmancurios.co.za.
Mon-Fri 0900-1700, Sat 1000-1300.
A shop selling every ostrich by-product imaginable, from expensive leather purses to feather dusters and tacky enamelled eggs. There are many other similar shops along Baron van Rheede Street.

Knysna

Birds of Africa
12 Waenhout St, T044-3825660, birdsofafrica.co.za.
Mon-Fri 0830-1630.
Unusual hand-carved and hand-painted wooden birds from local yellowwood and mopani trees (though only from those that have been removed after collapse) and you can watch the artists at work.

Tip...
The 125-store Garden Route Mall is out of George on the junction with the N2 (gardenroutemall. co.za, Mon-Fri 0900-1800, Sat 0900-1700, Sun 0900-1500) and has the usual South African chain stores, restaurants and a multi-screen Ster-Kinekor cinema.

Activities & tours

Bitou Craft

Woodmill Lane Centre, Main St,
T044-382 3251.
Mon-Fri 0900-1800, Sat
0900-1330, open Sun in season.
This sells local arts and crafts
including paintings, ceramics,
rugs and wooden toys and they
spin and dye their own wool to
make various woven items and
clothes. There's another branch
at Knysna Quays.

Plettenberg Bay

Art & antiques
Lookout Art Gallery
Lookout Centre, Main St,
T044-533 2210,
lookout-art-gallery.co.za.
Mon-Fri 0900-1700,
Sat 0900-1330.
Established gallery with
antiques and artwork from
local artists including paintings,
sculptures, glassware and
ceramics, and they can
arrange to ship overseas.

Souvenirs
Old Nick Village
On the N2, 3 km outside
Plettenberg Bay going east,
T044-533 1395,
oldnickvillage.co.za.
Open 0900-1700.
In a converted old trading store
dating to 1880, here are a group
of galleries, craft workshops and
studios, with a weaving museum,
shops and a restaurant. It's a good
place to pick up locally-made
souvenirs, clothes, gifts and
home decor. The original store
was forced to close in the 1960s,
when its main (black) customer
base was moved out of Plett to
new townships during Apartheid.

Tip...

There is a good African craft
market on the side of the road as
you enter Knysna on the N2 from
George, with an extensive range
of carvings, baskets, drums and
curios. There is also a cluster of
expensive curio shops and a daily
fleamarket at the Knysna Quays.

Mossel Bay & George

Diving
Electro Dive
At the harbour, T044-698 1976,
electrodive.co.za.
Can organize equipment hire
and boat charters and offers
PADI courses. The best time for
diving is between December
and the end of April. During
this period the sea is at its
calmest and conditions in the
bay are clear and safe. Close to
Santos Beach are four recognized
dive sites that can be reached
from the shore, and the
Windvogel Reef is 800 m
off Cape St Blaize.

Woodmill Lane Centre

Knysna's nicest shopping mall,
this is built around a restored
Victorian timber mill built in
1919 for Geo Parkes & Sons, a
Birmingham tool manufacturer,
who was the first exporter
of wood to England for the
making of bobbins for the
Midlands textile industry. He also
manufactured wagon parts and
a variety of tool handles. Today
it has 75 shops, fountains and
trees in the squares, and regular
performing artists and buskers.
There are several boutiques and
arts and crafts shops and a branch
of Pick 'n' Pay supermarket.
(Corner Main and Long streets,
T044-382 3045, woodmillane.
co.za, Mon-Fri 0830-1700, Sat
0830-1400, Sun 0900-1300).

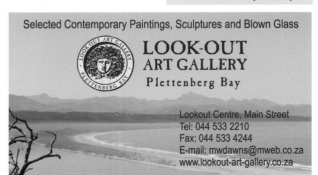

Selected Contemporary Paintings, Sculptures and Blown Glass

LOOK-OUT
ART GALLERY
Plettenberg Bay

Lookout Centre, Main Street
Tel: 044 533 2210
Fax: 044 533 4244
E-mail: mwdawns@mweb.co.za
www.lookout-art-gallery.co.za

Shark Africa
At the harbour, T044-6913796, sharkafrica.co.za.
Offers cage diving and snorkelling in pursuit of a great white shark on a 15-m catamaran aptly named *Shark Warrior*. The trip costs ₨1200, is four to five hours long and includes lunch and drinks.

Boat tours
Romonza
Vincent Jetty, at the harbour, T044-690 3101, mosselbay.co.za/romonza.
Runs daily pleasure cruises, the most popular being outings to Seal Island (see page 228). A boat carrying up to 50 people leaves on the hour 1000-1600, one hour, ₨200, children (under 12) ₨50, advanced booking is advised. The sunset cruise (Nov-Apr) lasts two hours, ₨150, children (under 12) ₨70 and there's a cash bar. Romonza also offers the only licensed boat-based whale watching in Mossel Bay (Jun-Oct), three hours, ₨550, children (under 12) ₨300.

Oudtshoorn

Cycling
Backpacker's Paradise
148 Baron van Rheede St, T044-2723436, backpackers paradise.hostel.com.
Mountain biking to the Swartberg Pass leaves daily at 0830, ₨150; you are driven to the top of the pass and enjoy the long ride downhill. On the way back to Oudtshoorn,

you can stop at the Cango Caves and all the other attractions along the R328.

Wilderness & Sedgefield

Adventure tours
Eden Adventures
T044-877 0179, eden.co.za.
A good-value adventure tour operator that organizes daily trips to the Wilderness National Park for kayaking, kloofing, mountain biking, abseiling, rock climbing and walking tours. They now offer abseiling in Plettenberg Bay's Robberg Nature Reserve (see page 245).

Windmaster Paragliding
T072-152 6093, paraglidingsa.com.
There are many thermic sites around Sedgefield and Wilderness, which are perfect for paragliding. Best conditions are October-June, though training conditions are best January-April. This company offers introductory courses, tandem flights and the full pilot's course that takes two weeks.

Knysna

Boat tours
Springtide Charters
Knysna Quays, South Jetty, T082-470 6022 (mob), springtide.co.za.
Three-hour sunset cruises on a 50-ft sailing boat including a stop for a swim. Departs

December-January 1700, February-April and October-November 1600, May-September 1500, ₨560 including sushi, seafood snacks and champagne. Can also arrange four-hour lunch excursions for ₨700 and the boat is available for charter overnight for honeymooners to stay in the lovely master cabin.

Cycling
Mountain Biking Africa
T044-382 0260, mountainbikingafrica.co.za.
Guided mountain-bike trails around the forests in the area, easy rides, lots of downhills, bikes and refreshments included, from ₨300 per person. Can also arrange multi-day rides through the Garden Route's mountain passes for experienced riders.

Diving
Hippo Dive Campus
George Rex Dr, T044-384 0831, hippodivecampus.co.za.
PADI courses from their dive centre at the Knysna Heads, equipment rental, and daily trips to reefs and to the *Paquita* wreck in the lagoon, which struck the Knysna Heads in 1903.

Tip...
For information about the boat excursion to the Knysna Heads and Featherbed Nature Reserve, as well as other boats trips offered by the Featherbed Co, see page 241.

Five of the best

Garden Route golf courses

❶ **Fancourt Hotel and Country Club** (R404, 6 km north of George Airport, T044-804 0030, fancourt.com) has four golf courses including the par 71, 5935-m, championship links course designed by Gary Player. The President's Cup tournament was played here in 2003.

❷ **George Golf Club** (Langenhoven St, T044-873 6116, georgegolfclub.co.za) has a par-72, 18-hole, 5852-m course in an attractive setting surrounded by trees.

❸ **Knysna Golf Club** (George Rex Dr, T044-384 1150, knysnagolfclub.com) is an 18-hole, par-73 course with good views of the Knysna Heads.

❹ **Goose Valley Golf Estate** (T044-533 5082, 2 km east of Plettenberg Bay, goosevalley.net) has a challenging 72 par, 6000-m, 18-hole golf course on the banks of Keurbooms Lagoon designed by Gary Player with good ocean views.

❺ **Plettenberg Bay Country Club** (Piesang Valley Rd, T044-5332132, plettgolf.co.za) has a lush 18-hole course in the middle of a private nature reserve, Piesang Valley and the Knysna lourie and woodpeckers are often seen on the course.

Hiking
Knysna Forest Tours
T044-382 6130, knysnaforesttours.co.za.
Half- and full-day guided hiking, from R350 per person in the Knysna Forest and local nature reserves, on trails of varied difficulty 3-16 km long, plus canoeing on the Goukamma River, which is great for birdwatching.

Plettenberg Bay

Blackwater tubing
Tube 'n Axe
Corner of Darnell and Saffron streets, T042-281 1757, tubenaxe.co.za.
At R495 per person, this starts with a briefing at Tube 'n' Axe, before a short drive through the Tsitsikamma forest, then a steep descent by rope ladder into the Storms River canyon followed by a float on a giant inner tube to the suspension bridge within the

Tsitsikamma National Park. The 'black water' refers to a stretch of river where you float under two overhangs of rock so close together it's like floating through a cave.

Boat tours
Keurbooms River Ferries
T044-532 7876, ferry.co.za.
Daily summer trips, 1100, 1400 and 1700, boat trip plus walk and swim lasts for 2½ hours, adults R120, children (3-12) R50, breakfast, lunch or picnic baskets can be organized in advance and there's a cash bar. The ferry departs from the jetty on the east side of the Keurbooms River Bridge on the N2, each ferry can carry up to 30 people, they are shaded and have a toilet on board, highly recommended for nature lovers. The company also rents out self-drive motor boats for R95 per hour, which carry four and you get a lesson on how to use them.

The Garden Route's golf courses attract visitors from all over the world.

Transport

Ocean Blue Adventures
Central Beach, T044-533 5083, oceanadventures.co.za.
Can organize whale-watching trips in season (Jun-Nov), about two hours, R650, children (under 12) R350, and are permitted to get within 50 m of the whales. Out of season there are cheaper (R400, children under 12 R200) trips to see seals, dolphins and marine birds. Can also organize sea-kayaking.

Ocean Safaris
Central Beach, T044-533 4963, oceansafaris.co.za.
An identical set up to the above with the same prices, and again are permitted to get within 50 m of the whales. One of the vessels is called *Fat Boy*, the local nickname for a southern right whale.

Diving
Pro-Dive
In the Beacon Isle Hotel, T044-533 1158, prodive.co.za.
Runs daily dives and rents out equipment. There are not many tropical fish but due to an abundance of planktonic matter there is a colourful reef life. For those who enjoy snorkelling, there is a popular spot in front of the Beacon Isle Hotel known as Deep Blinders; behind the reef is a sandy area where you might see stingrays.

Overberg
Long-distance buses run daily from Swellendam to Cape Town (4 hrs) and Port Elizabeth (9 hrs). Towards Cape Town, the Baz Bus arrives 1800, and towards Port Elizabeth 1200.

Mossel Bay & George
SAA have daily flights between George and Cape Town (1 hr), Durban (2½ hrs), and Johannesburg (1 hr 45 mins). Kulula and 1Time have daily flights between George and Johannesburg (1 hr 45 mins).
Long-distance buses run daily from Mossel Bay to Cape Town (6 hrs), and Port Elizabeth (8 hrs). Towards Cape Town the Baz Bus arrives 1500-1600, towards Port Elizabeth, 1330-1430.
Long-distance buses run daily from George to Cape Town (6 hrs) and Port Elizabeth (5 hrs). Towards Cape Town, the Baz Bus arrives 1500-1600, and towards Port Elizabeth 1430-1530.

Wilderness & Sedgefield

Wilderness
Long-distance buses stop in Wilderness or after George. Towards Cape Town the Baz Bus arrives 1345-1415 and from Cape Town 1500-1600.

Oudtshoorn
Long-distance buses run daily to Cape Town (8 hrs) and Knysna (2 hrs).

Knysna
Long-distance buses run daily to Cape Town (8 hrs) and Port Elizabeth (3½ hrs). Towards Cape Town the Baz Bus arrives 1230-1330, towards Port Elizabeth 1630-1730.

Plettenberg Bay
Long-distance buses run daily to Cape Town (8½ hrs) and Port Elizabeth (3½ hrs). Towards Cape Town the Baz Bus arrives 1200-1300, towards Port Elizabeth 1730-1800.

Contents

Practicalities

Getting there

Air

International flights arrive at Cape Town International Airport and Johannesburg's OR Tambo International Airport. These are linked by **British Airways** (Comair), **South African Airways** (SAA), **Kulula, Mango** and **1 Time**. SAA, **Kulula** and **1 Time** link Johannesburg and George, and **SAA** links Cape Town and George. Port Elizabeth, effectively the nearest airport to the end of the Garden Route, is linked to both Cape Town and Johannesburg with **SAA, Kulula** and **1 Time**.

From UK & Ireland
SAA and **British Airways** have daily direct flights from Heathrow to Cape Town, taking 11 hours. **Virgin** flies on a code-share agreement with SAA (Oct-Mar). These airlines also fly daily to Johannesburg (10½ hrs from London), which is linked to Cape Town (2 hrs 10 mins), George (1 hr 50 mins) and Port Elizabeth (1 hr 50 mins) by **SAA** and the domestic airlines, so weigh up fares. Flights from London are overnight and jet lag is not an issue as there is minimal time difference.

From rest of Europe
There are direct daily flights to Cape Town from Amsterdam with **KLM**, taking 11 hours. They also fly to Johannesburg via Paris and Nairobi. **Emirates** link many European cities with Johannesburg via Dubai. Indirect flights from other airlines can be economical: **Kenya Airways** flies between London, Amsterdam and Paris, and Johannesburg, via Nairobi, **Air Namibia** flies between Frankfurt and London to Cape Town and Johannesburg via Windhoek.

Tip...

For live flight information visit the Airport Company of South Africa's website acsa.co.za; phone T0867-277888; or send an SMS to T38648 with the flight number, in reply to which you'll receive up-to-date flight details.

From North America
Delta Airlines code shares with **SAA** on daily direct flights from Atlanta to Johannesburg, with connections to Cape Town. Flight time is 17 hours. **American Airlines** code shares with **British Airways**, via London Heathrow. Other hubs for North Americans include other European cities or Dubai, flying with **Emirates** from New York and then on to Johannesburg.

Airport information

South Africa's airports are modern and efficient. **Cape Town International Airport** (T021-937 1200) is 22 km east of the city centre; out of rush hour a 20-minute drive. In international arrivals is a desk for **Cape Town Tourism** (daily 0700-1700), a **Master Currency** exchange counter (open for all arriving flights) and ATMs. You can hire mobile phones at Vodacom's **Rentaphone** desk (T021-934 4951, vodacomsp.co.za), at domestic arrivals, or from MTN's **Cell Place** (T021-934 3261, mtnsp.co.za), at international departures. Both are open 0600-2300. Car hire desks in international arrivals include **Avis** (T021-934 0330), **Budget** (T021-380 3180), **Dollar Thrifty** (T021-936 2121) and **Hertz** (T021-935 2000).

Johannesburg's **OR Tambo International Airport** (T011-921 6262) is 24 km from the city centre, roughly midway between Johannesburg and Pretoria. Regardless of your eventual destination, immigration is done at Johannesburg, and you pick up luggage from international arrivals and check in again at domestic departures. The **Gauteng Tourism** office (0600-2200), **Master Currency** (open for all arriving flights), ATMs and Vodacom's **Rentaphone** desk (T011-394 8834, vodacomsp.co.za, 0600-2300) are in international arrivals. Opposite the terminal buildings is the Parkade Centre, where the car hire offices are, including **Avis** (T011-923 3730), **Budget** (T011-923 3730), **Europcar** (T011-574 1000) and **Hertz** (T011-390 2066).

Airlines

1 Time, T0861-345345 (in South Africa), T011-928 8000 (from overseas), 1time.aero

Air Namibia, T0870-774 0965 (UK), airnamibia.com.na

American Airlines, T1800-433 7300 (USA), aa.com

British Airways, T0870-850 9850 (UK), britishairways.com

British Airways (Comair), T011-441 8600 (South Africa), britishairways.com

Delta, T1800-221 1212 (USA), delta.com

Emirates, T0870-243 2222 (UK), emirates.com

Kenya Airways, T01784-888222 (UK), kenya-airways.com

KLM, T0204-747747 (Netherlands), klm.com

Kulula, T0861-585852 (in South Africa), T011-921 0111 (from overseas), kulula.com

Mango, T0861-162646 (in South Africa), T011-359 1222 (from overseas), flymango.com

South African Airways (SAA), T0870-747 1111 (in South Africa), T011-978 5313 (from overseas), flysaa.com

Virgin, T0870-574 7747 (UK), virgin-atlantic.com

Car hire websites

Aroundabout Cars aroundaboutcars.com

Avis avis.co.za

Budget budget.co.za

Dollar Thrifty thritfy.co.za

Europcar europcar.co.za

Hertz hertz.co.za

Tempest tempestcarhire.co.za

George Airport is 10 km out of town (T044-876 9310). A foreign exchange desk, Vodacom's **Rentaphone** desk (T044-876 000, vodacomsp.co.za) and ATMs are in the arrivals hall. Car hire desks include **Avis** (T044-876 9314), **Budget** (T044-876 9204), **Tempest** (T044-876 9250) and **Hertz** (T044-801 4700).

Port Elizabeth Airport is 4 km from the city centre (T041-507 7319). Vodacom's **Rentaphone** desk (T041-507 7370, vodacomsp.co.za) is in the arrivals hall as are ATMs and car hire desks including **Avis** (T041-501 7200), **Budget** (T041-581 4242), **Europcar** (T041-581 1268), and **Tempest** (T041-581 1256).

Airport transport
Shuttle services run from kiosks in the international arrivals hall at Cape Town International Airport to hotels. Alternatively, pre-book one through your hotel, or directly through **Magic Bus** (T021-505 6300, magicbus.co.za); or the **Backpacker Bus** (T021-439 7600, backpackerbus.co.za). They cost from R150 per person. Taxis running between the airport and city centre cost around R250. The **Integrated Rapid Transport** (IRT) bus plan from the airport will be operational by 2010.

In Johannesburg, **Magic Bus** (T011-394 6902, magicbus.co.za), and **Airport Link** (T011-792 2017, airportlink.co.za) provide shuttles; metered taxis can be found outside the main terminal building and there's a new station for the **Gautrain**. Taxis meet flights at George and Port Elizabeth airports.

Road

South Africa has borders with Botswana, Zimbabwe, Mozambique, Swaziland, Lesotho and Namibia. Long-distance buses ply the routes between the capital cities in these countries and are operated by **Greyhound** (greyhound.co.za), **Intercape** (intercape.co.za) and **Translux** (translux.co.za), and all bus tickets can be booked online at **Computicket** (computicket.com).

Getting around

Rail

South Africa's major cities are linked by rail, run by Shosholoza Meyl (T0860-008888 in South Africa, T011-774 4555 from overseas, shosholozameyl.co.za), but carriages are basic and the service is slow. All trains travel overnight, the Cape Town–Durban service over two nights, so they arrive at some stations at inconvenient times. Coupés sleep four or six, with wash basin, fold-away table and bunks. Refreshments are available from trolleys or dining cars, but as these are franchised to burger-type chains, the food's not brilliant. Note that all trains have a problem with security: keep your compartment locked.

Cape Town has one main railway station in the centre of town. Routes are Cape Town–Durban (Mon 1800; 38 hrs), Durban–Cape Town (Wed 1800; 38 hrs), Cape Town–Johannesburg (Mon, Wed, Fri, Sun 1030; 26 hrs), and Johannesburg–Cape Town (Mon, Wed, Fri, Sun 1230; 26 hrs). Fares start from R340 one-way to Johannesburg. Children under nine go half price.

The more upmarket service, the **Premier Classe** (T0860-008888 in South Africa, T011-774 5247 from overseas, premierclasse.co.za), between Cape Town and Johannesburg (25 hrs), departs Cape Town at 0800 on Tuesday and Saturday, and Johannesburg at 1400 on Thursday and Sunday. The Cape Town to Port Elizabeth service (25 ½ hrs) departs Cape Town at 1430 on Fridays and Port Elizabeth on Sundays at 0800. This latter service, like flights, gives the option of driving along the Garden Route in one direction and taking the train in the other direction. The carriages are a lot nicer than the regular train, with air conditioning, good food in a sit-down dining car, bar, and extras in the coupés like toiletries. Fares start from R1300 one-way to Johannesburg and include meals. Children under nine go half price.

Old-fashioned luxury trains operate much like five-star hotels on wheels. The **Blue Train** (T021-334 8459, bluetrain.co.za), is Africa's premier luxury

train, with wood-panelled coaches, luxury en suite coupés and fine dining. It runs between Pretoria and Cape Town over one day and one night. A similar luxury train experience is the **Pride of Africa**, operated by Rovos Rail (T012-315 8242, rovos.co.za), which also runs between Pretoria and Cape Town. On the Garden Route, the historic steam train, the **Outeniqua Choo-Tjoe**, runs between George and Mossel Bay (see page 231).

Road

Car
Cape Town is easily explored without a car, but car hire gives the greatest flexibility and driving isn't challenging. In the city centre, car hire can be arranged within an hour and there are numerous car hire offices around the city or at the airport. Driving is on the left. There are three highways that connect Cape Town to the rest of the country: the N2 goes along the entire South African coast via the Garden Route, Eastern Cape and KwaZulu Natal; the N1 goes to Johannesburg (the Winelands, less than 50 km from Cape Town, can be accessed from either the N2 or N1); and the N7 goes north towards Namibia. Parts of these have tolls: rates from R3 to R50 depending on the distance, which can be paid in cash or by credit card. Speed limits are 60 kph in built-up areas, 80 kph on minor roads and 120 kph on highways. Speed traps are common. Remember that if you are caught by a speed camera, the fine will go to the hire car company who have every right to deduct the amount from your credit card, even if it is some time after you have left South Africa.

Parking is easy and the sights and shopping malls have car parks. For street-side parking in the city, you pay a uniformed attendant between 0800 and 1700. Parking on average is around R5 per hour. Petrol, available 24 hours along the national highways, costs around R8 a litre; you cannot use credit cards at petrol stations and petrol is paid for in cash. An attendant fills up, washes the windscreen, and if necessary checks oil, water and tyre pressure, for which a tip of a couple of rand is the norm. In the event of an accident, call your car hire company's emergency number.

Car hire

It is worth asking at hostels or hotels for recommended local car hire companies, and be sure to shop around. Car hire companies have a range of vehicles, from basic hatchbacks and saloon cars, to camper vans and fully equipped 4WD vehicles. Rates start from around R250 per day. In general there are two types of deal on offer: a short weekend package including free mileage; or longer-term deals for a week or more. In the first case you can get very good rates for a Group A car, although you might want a larger vehicle for long journeys. The extra engine power and space of a Group B car will make for safer and more comfortable driving. In summer, air conditioning is also well worth the extra but make sure it works before you sign. Tourist offices usually recommend large international organizations such as **Avis** or **Budget**, but there are a number of reliable local companies, usually with a good fleet of cars and follow-up service. These include **Aroundabout Cars** which is a good local agent that has its own fleet in Cape Town. All of the large firms have kiosks at the airports (see page 270). Be sure to book in advance through the websites for the high season. Some of the larger companies partner with the airlines, so it's also possible to book a car online with your flight. Hirers usually need to be over 21, have a driver's licence in English and a credit card.

Bicycle

Cycling in the city centre is not advised and not really the norm. However, the Cape Peninsula is very popular for bike rides and **Cape Town Cycle Hire** (T021-434 1270, capetowncyclehire.co.za) will deliver bikes anywhere in the city and Atlantic Seaboard from R100 per day. You can also hire bikes in the Winelands and the Garden Route.

Bus/coach

Intercity buses travel along the national highways and are by operated by **Greyhound** (greyhound.co.za), **Intercape** (intercape.co.za) and **Translux** (translux.co.za), and all bus tickets can be booked online at **Computicket** (computicket.com), or at any of their kiosks in the shopping malls or any branch of Checkers supermarket. The coaches are air conditioned and have a toilet; some sell refreshments and show videos. For long journeys, the prices are reasonable (though always compare fares with the no-frills airlines), but some arrive at destinations at inconvenient times of the night. The **Baz Bus** (T021-439 2323, bazbus.com), is a hop-on, hop-off bus that is specifically designed for backpackers as it collects and drops off at backpacker hostels. The Baz Bus route is Cape Town–Durban along the coast, and Durban–Pretoria on two routes via either Swaziland or the Drakensberg. Visit the website for the full timetable.

Directory

Customs & immigration

Most nationalities including EU nationals and citizens from the USA, Canada, Australia and New Zealand don't need visas to enter South Africa. Temporary visitors' permits are valid up to 90 days. You must have a valid return ticket or voucher for onward travel and at least one completely empty page in your passport.

Disabled travellers

Facilities are generally of a high standard. The airports are fully wheelchair accessible and can provide wheelchairs for infirm travellers. Modern hotels have specially adapted rooms, but it is worth enquiring in advance at older hotels and restaurants. The Cableway to the top of Table Mountain, Cape Town's museums, the City Sightseeing bus and national park accommodation are accessible for wheelchairs. Some tourist attractions have been developed with disabled visitors in mind, such as the Braille Trail at Kirstenbosch. Most places have disabled parking right by the entrance. **Endeavour Safaris** (endeavour-safaris.com), **Flamingo Tours** (flamingotours.co.za), **Rolling SA** (rollingsa.co.za), and **Titch Tours** (titchtours.co.za) all organize tours for travellers with special needs.

Etiquette

There is no special advice regarding etiquette in South Africa though politeness is always rewarded. Cape Town has a large Muslim community so the usual signs of respect concerning modest dress in Islamic areas (Bo-Kaap, for example) are appreciated.

Families

Cape Town and the Garden Route are popular family holiday destinations and there is plenty to do; in December and January the region is packed with South African families during the school holidays. In the supermarkets, you will find plentiful supplies of all you need to feed and look after your little ones, and many restaurants have kids' menus. Hygiene throughout the country is of a good standard; stomach upsets are rare and the tap water everywhere is safe to drink. Most accommodation has family rooms or adjoining rooms suitable for families, and there are plenty of family chalets or bungalows. Children get significant discounts on accommodation and entry fees.

Health

There are plenty of private hospitals in the region, which also have 24-hour pharmacies, run by **Medi-Clinic** (mediclinic.co.za) or **Netcare** (netcare. co.za). It is essential to have travel insurance as hospital bills need to be paid at the time of admittance, so keep all paperwork to make a claim. There are no abnormal health hazards.

Insurance

It is vital to take out full travel insurance and, at the very least, the policy should cover personal effects and medical expenses, including repatriation to your own country in the event of a medical emergency. Make sure that it also covers all activities that you want to undertake. There is no substitute for suitable precautions against petty crime, but if you do have something stolen whilst in South Africa, report the incident to the nearest police station and ensure you get a police report and case number. You will need these to make any claim from your insurance company.

Money

The South African currency is the rand. To change cash or traveller's cheques, all banks (Mon-Fri 0830-1530, Sat 0830-1130) have foreign exchange facilities, while bureaux de change in the airports and shopping malls are open longer hours, seven days a week. ATMs are everywhere, and most shops, restaurants and sightseeing places accept debit or credit cards. The only thing you need to pay for in cash is petrol.

Police

For emergencies phone 10111, or from a cell phone 112. There are many police stations in Cape Town and the other towns and the police are recognized by their blue fatigues. In Cape Town there is an additional Metro Police force, in black uniforms, which can often be seen on mountain bike, horseback or on Segways (two-wheeled electrical vehicles).

Post

Both internal and international mail is generally reliable. If you are sending home souvenirs, surface mail to Europe is the cheapest but will take at least six weeks. Letters to Europe and the US should take no more than a few days. There is a 'speed service', but this costs significantly more. It's best to use registered mail for more valuable items so that you can track their progress, or a courier service. There is a store locator on the post office website (sapo.co.za). **Postnet** (postnet.co.za), usually found in the shopping malls, also offers mail, courier and business services.

Safety

South Africa has had more than its fair share of well-publicized crime problems, but despite the statistics, much of the serious, violent crime is gang-based and occurs in areas that tourists are unlikely to visit, such as the Cape Flats. Dangers facing tourists are on the whole limited to traditional mugging or, on occasion, carjacking. The simplest points to remember are to avoid altogether what are considered to be dangerous areas, not to walk around any urban centres at night and to avoid driving after dark. Normal sensible precautions apply; don't flash your wealth, keep valuables hidden, and don't leave anything on display in a car. If driving always carry a mobile phone.

Telephone

South Africa's country code is +27; international direct dialling code 00; directory enquires T1023; international operator T0009; international enquires T1025. You must dial the full three-digit regional code for every number in South Africa, even when you are calling from within that region.

Time difference

South Africa is GMT +2 (+1 during UK summertime).

Tipping

In restaurants, 10-15% is the norm for good service, though service is added to the bill for groups of six or more. It is common practice to tip petrol pump attendants and, if parking on the street, car guards (identified by a work vest), both R2-5. Rounding up prices for taxis is usual, and tip tour guides if you've enjoyed a tour.

Tourist information

There are dozens of tourist offices in the region which are listed in the relevant chapters. Cape Town Tourism (tourismcapetown.co.za) covers the whole of the Western Cape.

Voltage

South Africa functions on 220/230 volts AC at 50 Hz. Most plugs and appliances are three-point round-pin (one 10 mm and two 8 mm prongs). Hotels usually have two-pin sockets for razors and chargers.

Glossary

Babbelas Hangover.

Bakkie A pickup car.

Bergie From the Afrikaans berg, mountain, this originally referred to vagrants who slept on Table Mountain when they were not allowed to stay overnight in the white areas of Green Point and Sea Point during Apartheid. It is now a mainstream word for anyone who is down at heel.

Biltong Dried meat to chew on as a snack, similar to beef jerky, often spiced.

Boerwors Spicy beef or game sausage popular for braaiing.

Braai Outside barbeque, usually a metal grill where you light your own fire underneath with wood or coals.

Dassie or rock hyrax A small herbivore that lives in mountainous habitats and is reputed to be the species mostly closely related to the elephant. The name comes from the Afrikaans 'das', meaning badger. They are commonly seen around the top Table Mountain Aerial Cableway station.

Dorp Literally meaning 'town', although usually refers to a small urban centre with just a collection of houses and a few farmers wandering around.

Howzit? A common greeting and a corruption of 'how is it?', but is used simply to say 'hello.

Indaba From the isiZulu word for 'matter of discussion', this means meeting or conference. It can also mean problem, as in 'that's your/my indaba'.

Jol A slang word derived from the Cape dialect which can refer to anything from a nice picnic to an all-night rave.

Just now Meaning an event or task will happen in a little while: 'I'll go to the shop just now'.

Kopjie A hill or outcrop of rocks, which are usually balanced on top of each other and a common feature on wide open plains.

Kraal Traditional African hut for living in, usually thatched with mud or stone walls.

Kwaito The music of South Africa's urban black youth. A mixture of South African disco, hip hop, R&B, and with a heavy dose of house beats.

Lapa Thatched shelter, usually without walls, for entertaining, especially when braaiing.

Lekker Common expression for good, but also means great time, enjoyable and tasty.

Mossie The common name of the Cape sparrow, but is also used to refer to any small undistinguished wild bird.

Muti Derived from the isiZulu word 'umuthi', this means medicine and typically refers to traditional African medicine.

Now now Something will happen immediately; 'get in the car now now'.

Platteland Afrikaans for 'flat land' and means farmland or countryside, or any rural area in which agriculture takes place including the Cape Winelands.

Potjiekos Three-legged cast-iron pots used for cooking over coals.

Robot South African term for traffic lights.

Rooibos tea A South African herbal tea made in the Cape from the *Cyclopia genistoides* bush. In Afrikaans the word means 'red bush'.

Shebeen Township pub.

Snoek Popular and tasty fish, caught off the Cape coast and often eaten smoked.

Tread Your Own Path
Footprint Handbooks
New design and compact format

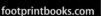

Index

Index

Index

Footprint story

1921

Ireland had just been partitioned, the British miners were striking for more pay and the federation of British industry had an idea. Exports were booming in South America – how about a handbook for businessmen trading in that faraway continent? The Anglo-South American Handbook was born that year, written by W Koebel, the most prolific writer on Latin America of his day.

1924

Two editions later the book was 'privatized' and, in 1924, in the hands of Royal Mail, the steamship company for South America, it became The South American Handbook, subtitled 'South America in a nutshell'. This annual publication became the 'bible' for generations of travellers to South America and remains so to this day. In the early days travel was by sea and the Handbook gave all the details needed for the long journey from Europe. What to wear for dinner; how to arrange a cricket match with the Cable & Wireless staff on the Cape Verde Islands; and a full account of the journey from Liverpool up the Amazon to Manaus: 5898 miles without changing cabin!

1939

As the continent opened up, The South American Handbook reported the new Pan Am flying boat services, and the fortnightly airship service from Rio to Europe on the Graf Zeppelin. For reasons still unclear but with extraordinary determination, the annual editions continued through the Second World War.

1970s

Many more people discovered South America and the backpacking trail started to develop. All the while the Handbook was gathering fans, including literary vagabonds such as Paul Theroux and Graham Greene (who once sent some updates addressed to "The publishers of the best travel guide in the world, Bath, England").

1990s

During the 1990s the company set about developing a new travel guide series using this legendary title as the flagship. By 1997 there were over a dozen guides in the series and the Footprint imprint was launched.

2000s

The series grew quickly and there were soon Footprint travel guides covering more than 150 countries. In 2004, Footprint launched its first thematic guide: Surfing Europe, packed with colour photographs, maps and charts. This was followed by further guides such as Diving the World, Snowboarding the World, Body and Soul escapes, Travel with Kids and European City Breaks.

2010

Today we continue the traditions of the last 89 years that have served legions of travellers so well. We believe that these help to make Footprint guides different. Our policy is to use authors who are genuine experts and who write for independent travellers; people possessing a spirit of adventure, looking to get off the beaten track.

Tread your

Footprint Lifestyle guides

Books to inspire and plan some of the world's most compelling travel experiences. Written by experts and presented to appeal to popular travel themes and pursuits.

66 99

A great book to have on your shelves when planning your next European escapade
Sunday Telegraph

Footprint Activity guides

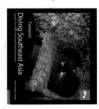

These acclaimed guides have broken new ground, bringing together adventure sports and activities with relevant travel content, stunningly presented to help enthusiasts get the most from their pastimes.

66 99

This guide is as vital as a mask and fins.
David Espinosa, Editor of Scuba Diver Australasia

own path

Footprint Travel guides

For travellers seeking out off-the-beaten-track adventures. Rich with places and sights and packed with expertly researched travel information, activities and cultural insight.

66 99

Footprint can be depended on for accurate travel information and for imparting a deep sense of respect for the lands and people they cover
World News

Available from all good bookshops or online footprintbooks.com

Footprint credits

Project editor: Felicity Laughton
Picture editors: Kassia Gawronski,
Angus Dawson
Layout & production: Angus Dawson
Maps: Kevin Feeney
Series design: Mytton Williams
Proofreader: Carol Maxwell

Managing Director: Andy Riddle
Commercial Director: Patrick Dawson
Publisher: Alan Murphy
Publishing managers:
Felicity Laughton, Jo Williams
Digital Editor: Alice Jell
Design: Rob Lunn
Picture research: Kassia Gawronski
Marketing: Liz Harper,
Hannah Bonnell
Sales: Jeremy Parr
Advertising: Renu Sibal
Finance & administration:
Elizabeth Taylor

Print

Manufactured in Italy by EuroGrafica
Pulp from sustainable forests

Footprint Feedback

We try as hard as we can to make each
Footprint guide as up to date as possible
but, of course, things always change.
If you want to let us know about your
experiences – good, bad or ugly – then
don't delay, go to footprintbooks.com
and send in your comments.

Every effort has been made to ensure
that the facts in this guidebook are
accurate. However, travellers should still
obtain advice from consulates, airlines etc
about travel and visa requirements before
travelling. The authors and publishers
cannot accept responsibility for any loss,
injury or inconvenience however caused.

Publishing information

FootprintAfrica
Cape Town, Winelands & Garden Route
1st edition
© Footprint Handbooks Ltd
January 2010

ISBN 978-1-906098-86-5
CIP DATA: A catalogue record for this
book is available from the British Library

® Footprint Handbooks and the Footprint
mark are a registered trademark of
Footprint Handbooks Ltd

Published by Footprint
6 Riverside Court
Lower Bristol Road
Bath BA2 3DZ, UK
T +44 (0)1225 469141
F +44 (0)1225 469461
www.footprintbooks.com

Distributed in North America by
Globe Pequot Press